OCR Cambridge Nationals in ICT

Units R001 & R002

R001: Understanding Computer Systems
R002: Using ICT to Create Business Solutions

Microsoft® Office 2010 & Windows® 7

Created and published by:

CiA Training Ltd
Business & Innovation Centre
Sunderland Enterprise Park
Sunderland
SR5 2TA
United Kingdom

Tel: +44 (0) 191 549 5002
Fax: +44 (0) 191 549 9005
E-mail: info@ciatraining.co.uk
Web: www.ciatraining.co.uk

ISBN: 978-1-86005-983-4
Release: OCN01v1

Copyright Notice

Acknowledgements

Microsoft® is a registered trademark and Windows® is a trademark of the Microsoft Corporation. Screen images reproduced with permission. Any other trademarks that appear in this book are acknowledged as the property of their respective owners.

Websites

Websites are constantly changing. At the time of writing all addresses and links are correct, but this may change. If a named website is unavailable you will need to search for an alternative. To help, a list of *Useful Links* to other websites is provided online at www.bigplanetsupport.co.uk.

Contents

About this book

Hello and welcome to *Big Planet Theme Park* – the world's first *ICT* amusement park. From high-speed rollercoasters to haunted castle rides, there really is something for everyone.

This book is split up into 8 separate sections. In each section you will visit a different area of the theme park and meet one of the people who work there. Each person will tell you a little bit about themselves and their job, and then show you how to use ICT to complete a number of simple, everyday tasks.

The practical skills that you learn in each section can then be used to solve ICT problems in your own life – at home, in education and at work.

Enjoy your visit to *Big Planet Theme Park* and have fun!

Monty Spangles

Park Director

Introduction

OCR Cambridge Nationals in ICT

You live in a world where **Information and Communication Technology (ICT)** is used in almost every aspect of modern life, from business, education, media and banking to social networking, gaming and shopping. Technologies such as personal computers, digital cameras, MP3 players, mobile telephones and Internet websites have all completely changed how we study, work and spend our free time. They make communication easier, allow us to work with large amounts of data quickly and easily, and give us access to a vast worldwide network of information and services. Due to this, people and businesses are now more connected and reliant upon technology than ever before.

To get the most out of your own education and employment opportunities, you need to be able to use ICT confidently, effectively and independently. The *Cambridge Nationals in ICT* qualification seeks to give you that ability, providing the knowledge and skills needed to successfully use computing technology in all aspects of your daily life – at home, in education and at work.

Learning objectives

The aim of this book is to provide the knowledge and skills necessary to achieve the *Cambridge Nationals in ICT* qualification. A range of step-by-step exercises guide you through the most useful features of *Windows 7* and *Office 2010*, and help you to build confidence in their use. Additional problem solving activities specific to your level are also included to reinforce learning.

Remember that achieving a *Cambridge Nationals in ICT* qualification is not just about knowing how to use computing technology, but realising how to apply that practical knowledge to solve unfamiliar problems in every aspect of your life. Each of the 8 sections in this book are therefore based on authentic work-related scenarios drawn from real life, each of which teaches a relevant set of skills that are highly valued in further education and employment.

After completing this book you will be able to:

* Select and use the best ICT tools and techniques to complete a given task

* Find, select and manage information and analyse its fitness for purpose

* Apply knowledge and skills to plan, develop and evaluate suitable solutions

* Solve industry-relevant problems using a range of software features

* Present, share and communicate information and engage with others

* Stay safe and secure, and respect all applicable laws and regulations.

Software and data files

This book was designed to be used with *Microsoft Office 2010* running on *Windows 7*. If you are using a different version of *Office* or *Windows*, some features may look or function slightly differently to that described.

 Data files accompanying this book enable you to practice new skills without the need for lots of data entry. These files must be downloaded from our website. To do this, go to **www.ciatraining.co.uk/data** and follow the simple on-screen instructions.

Your *FastCode* for this book's data is: **OCN01**

The data files will be installed in the following location on your computer:

Documents \ DATA FILES \ OCR Cambridge Nationals

If you prefer, the data files can also be supplied on CD at an additional cost. Contact our sales team at **info@ciatraining.co.uk**.

Notation used

Key presses are included within angled brackets. For example, <**Enter**> means press the **Enter** key on your computer's keyboard once. Also, unless otherwise specified, clicking the mouse means click the *left* mouse button *once*.

Recommendations

Each section in this book is split up into lots of individual exercises. Most exercises consist of a written explanation of a specific software feature or technique followed by a practical, stepped activity. As each activity builds upon and extends the last, it is important that you work through all of the exercises in sequence. If you do not, you may encounter data file problems.

Also try to read the whole of each exercise before starting to work through it. This aids the learning process and helps to prevent unnecessary mistakes.

Planning and evaluating

Tasks specific to your level are available at the end of each section. To help you plan and organise your solutions to these activities, a **Planning Checklist** is provided at the end of this book.

A **Review Checklist** is also provided to help you evaluate how well your solutions work in practice, how they can be improved, and how you might approach problems differently next time.

1 | Basics of ICT

Hi, my name's Hassan...

I'm a member of the customer services team at *Big Planet Theme Park*. Located at the park entrance, it's my job to welcome visitors and organise ticket sales. I also help out at the gift shop which sells a wide variety of books and souvenirs.

To do my job, I need to be able to work well in a team and deal with customers in a helpful and professional manner. I also need to use a wide variety of ICT systems to register sales, print tickets, manage stocks and keep in touch with visitors. Although there's a lot to learn, it's exciting work and I really enjoy using all the latest computers, mobile gadgets and software programs.

In fact, before I started working at the park, I'd only ever used a computer at home to surf the Internet, play games and talk with friends online. I had no idea how much more you can do with modern technology – it's used everywhere and already affects my life in ways I'd never imagined. I was also surprised to find out about all of the important laws and guidelines that apply to me as an ICT user. Luckily, it turns out these simple rules are very easy to understand and really do make a whole lot of sense.

What you will learn:

In this section you will explore the basics of ICT and learn how to safely and legally use the various computing technologies available to you. You will also find out about the most popular software applications on the market and how and why they are useful.

Knowledge, skills and understanding:

* Appreciate the uses of ICT in business, education and at home

* Spot important health and safety issues when using ICT

* Understand the laws and regulations that affect you

* Select and use information correctly and responsibly

* Recognise the problems that viruses can cause and learn how to avoid them

* Find out how to keep personal details and sensitive information safe

* Select the right software application(s) to complete a task

* Work accurately, safely and securely

1.1 What Exactly is ICT?

The term **ICT** stands for **Information and Communication Technology**. Pretty much any device or computer program that creates, stores or uses digital information can be considered an ICT system, including:

* Hardware such as desktop computers, laptops, netbooks, tablets and games consoles

* Software applications such as web browsers, word processors, spreadsheets, databases, e-mail systems, graphics programs and games

* Internet technologies such as *Google*, *Twitter*, *Facebook* and *Flickr*

* Mobile devices such as smart phones, GPS systems, digital cameras, iPads and iPods

* Peripheral items such as printers, scanners, keyboards and mice

As ICT devices continue to get smaller and cheaper to make, it is becoming more and more common for manufacturers to combine multiple technologies in one device. For example, many modern mobile phones now include a digital camera, voice recorder, multimedia player, games platform and Internet browser. This is a trend that is likely to continue and expand into other areas of everyday life.

> **Note:** ICT systems are used in more places than you may realise: car engines, vending machines, home heating systems. Even some "smart" refrigerators have built-in Internet connections to automatically reorder groceries, and as you are reading this scientists are working hard to make "wearable computers" a reality!

1.2 Why is ICT Important?

Computing and mobile technologies have completely transformed how people live their lives – at home, in education and at work. It has changed how people communicate with each other, how they store and access information, how they work, and how they spend their spare time. In fact, ICT systems allow people to better explore ideas, handle lots of information, find answers to questions, solve problems, and become more productive in their personal and professional lives.

So, if you want to be an active member of your own society and succeed in education and a future career, your ability to fully understand and use ICT technology safely and effectively will be an essential skill to have.

1.3 Health and Safety

Before you start working with equipment of any kind, you first need to know how to use it safely and responsibly. ICT devices are no different, and whether you use them at home, in education, or as part of your job, you are required <u>by law</u> to take reasonable care of your own safety and the safety of others.

> **Note:** In both education and work, the people in charge of you are legally required to make sure you are well-protected and well-trained. For ICT users, this means providing you with equipment that is safe, secure and comfortable to use.

Modern ICT systems present a number of health and safety hazards that you <u>must</u> be aware of. Whenever you use an electronic device of any sort, no matter where it is, you should always watch out for the following hazards:

* Electrical injuries and fires from damaged wires or incorrect connections

* Electrical injuries and fires from overloaded power sockets (too many plugs connected to one outlet)

* Injuries and fires caused by badly stored materials (paper and other items piled up and around equipment)

* Breakdowns and breathing problems due to poor ventilation (many ICT devices need to be kept cool and some types of printer can produce unhealthy fumes)

* Trips and slips due to trailing cables or problems accessing your work area

> **Note:** Never eat or drink when using an ICT device. Food and liquids can easily be dropped or spilled which can damage equipment or cause electrical injuries.

When you are on the move you need to be even more alert for dangers. For example, watch out for any hazards that could trip you up or cause a serious fall, and never use a mobile device (such as a telephone or tablet computer) when driving or operating dangerous machinery.

> **Note:** Never misuse ICT equipment or attempt to repair a broken device yourself. If you have any problems always contact a qualified technician.

Depending on your age, level of ability and where you study or work, there may also be other health and safety hazards to be aware of. For example, you may need to wear protective clothing and keep out of areas where dangerous materials or machinery are stored. Watch for warning signs and follow any health and safety information given to you.

> **Note:** Always tell someone in charge about any health and safety concerns you have. If you do hurt yourself or damage a piece of equipment, you <u>must</u> report it.

Activity:

1. Look around you. Check that there are no cables lying across the floor that you or somebody else could trip over.

2. Check that there are no cables hanging down behind your desk that could tangle with your feet as you work. This includes power cables and Internet connection wires.

> **Note:** Take care when adjusting cables. Always make sure your computer equipment is turned off and unplugged from the wall before you start.

3. Look out for and immediately replace worn or frayed cables. <u>Never</u> examine a suspect wire or device until it has been turned off and unplugged.

4. Check for sockets or power extensions that have too many plugs in them. Overloaded electrical sockets can easily cause fires or injury.

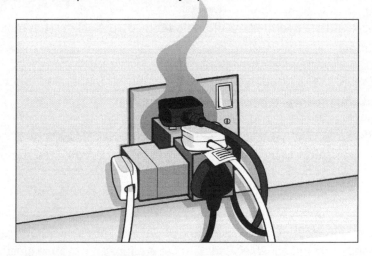

5. Remove any unnecessary clutter from your work environment and avoid storing items where they could fall and cause injury or damage.

6. Finally, check your surroundings for any other potential dangers: obstructions, trip hazards (e.g. wires, boxes, bins and bags), fire hazards, and so on.

> **Note:** In every building in which you study or work, you should always know where the emergency exits and fire extinguishers are located.

1.4 Your Work Space

If you sit at a computer or use ICT equipment for long periods of time, it can start to get uncomfortable and – in severe cases – cause injury. To stay safe and well you need to learn how to avoid these problems *before* they start. Remember: prevention is *always* better than cure!

> **Note:** The most common complaints reported by ICT users are eye strain, aches and pains in the arms, neck and back, and headaches. If you start to experience these problems regularly you need to act fast to prevent them getting worse.

When using ICT equipment always remember the following simple precautions:

* Take regular breaks away from all of your ICT devices (one or two minutes every hour).

* Look away from screens regularly (and remember to blink often).

* Vary your work activities so that you do not perform the same task for too long.

* Don't sit with a poor posture or hold heavy ICT devices for long periods of time.

* Use simple stretching exercises to relax your muscles and stay active.

If you use a desktop or laptop computer for any length of time, it is also important that you set up your work space correctly. The following advice will help:

* Position your computer monitor directly in front of you with the top of the screen at roughly the same height as your eyes.

* Adjust the screen to reduce glare and reflections from lights or windows.

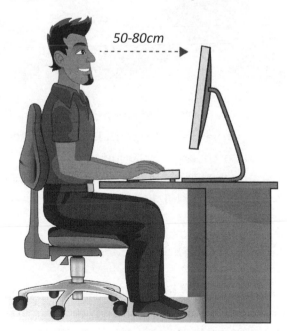

* Adjust the position of your chair so that you can sit upright at your desk about one arm's length away from your screen (50 to 80 centimetres is recommended).

✱ Set up your chair so that it fully supports your back and make sure your feet rest firmly on the floor. Foot and wrist rests can be used to help.

✱ Place your keyboard and mouse directly in front of you and do not stretch to reach them. Your forearms and hands should always remain parallel with the floor.

Activity:

1. Adjust your chair so that your back is straight and your hands are placed comfortably over the mouse and keyboard. Your feet should lie flat on the ground.

2. Check that the computer screen you are using is positioned at a comfortable height and angle so that you can see it without straining. Make sure there is no glare or reflection.

3. Adjust the position of the screen, keyboard and mouse so that you are comfortable operating the computer.

1.5 Hardware

ICT devices come in a variety of forms: digital cameras, smart phones, MP3 players, and of course desktop, laptop and tablet computers. All of these devices are known as **hardware**, which is a term that refers to any piece of physical technology that you can touch.

Desktop PC (inc. monitor, keyboard and mouse)

Laptop

Mobile Phone

Tablet

Two of the most popular types of ICT computing device are the **desktop** computer and the **laptop** computer. Smaller, cheaper versions of laptops known as **netbooks** are also quite common, but these simply allow users to connect to the Internet and are often slow to use. Also gaining in popularity are **tablet** computers, which are smaller again and usually feature a large touch screen. Of course, one of the most popular ICT devices in the world today is the **mobile phone**.

1.6 Input and Output Devices

Any piece of hardware that is used to enter information into an ICT system is known as an **input device**. There are many different kinds of input device, some of which you will be familiar with:

✱ Common computer peripherals such as keyboards, mice and trackballs (which you use to tell the computer what to do)

* Built-in control devices such as laptop touch pads or mobile phone touch screens

* Gadgets for recording audio and video such as microphones and webcams

* Image capture devices such as scanners, photocopiers and digital cameras

* Barcode scanners and card readers (discussed in more detail later)

* Remote control devices such as wireless games controllers and TV remotes

* Sensors that can detect and react to changes in the environment such as light, sound, temperature and movement (*Xbox Kinect* and *PlayStation Move* are good examples)

Any piece of hardware that is used to send information <u>out</u> of an ICT system is known as an **output device**. Again, there are many different kinds of output device, including:

* Computer monitors and laptop, tablet, TV and mobile phone screens

* Projectors and large video displays

* Speakers and headphones

* Computer-controlled motors, manufacturing tools and industrial robots

* Printers and plotters (a plotter is a special high-quality printer that produces precise, large scale drawings such as building plans and engineering designs)

> **Note:** The two most common types of printer are **inkjet** and **laser**. Inkjets are cheap to buy and are great for personal home use. Laser printers are usually more expensive but produce faster, higher quality prints which are ideal for use in business.

> **Note:** Did you know that it is now possible to print solid objects? 3D printers allow you to recreate a computer-aided design (**CAD**) by "printing" the object layer-by-layer!

1.7 Data Storage

All of the information that you enter or use on an ICT device is known as **data**. It is usually held in a permanent storage area on your device and is moved into memory when required.

> **Note:** Data held in memory will be lost when a computing device is switched off. To keep this data you must save it as a **file** on an available storage device.

Data can be stored on your ICT device in many different ways, depending on the type of technology you are using. For example, on a desktop or laptop computer, data can be saved to the **hard disk drive** (HDD) or **solid state drive** (SSD) inside the device. On a mobile phone, MP3 player, digital camera or tablet computer, it can be stored on a "flash" **memory card**.

Note:	Always follow the manufacturer's instructions when connecting a new peripheral.

Secondly, you can use **Wi-Fi** or **Bluetooth** to connect the peripheral and ICT device together using radio waves (known as a **wireless** connection). One device transmits data and the other receives, similar to how TV and radio works. These are slightly more complicated to set up but allow you to place and use peripherals wherever you want without the need for connecting wires.

Note:	Wireless connections are also ideal for connecting two ICT devices together and exchanging files between them.

1.10 Networks

A **network** is the name given to two or more ICT devices that are connected to each other. Once connected, devices on the network can share data (such as files) and resources (such as printers).

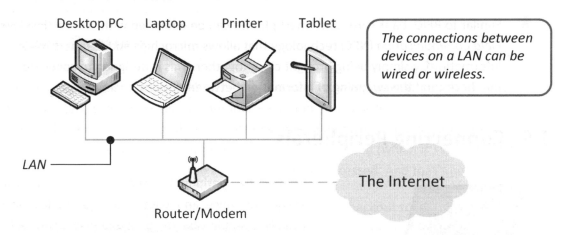

Desktop PC   Laptop   Printer   Tablet

The connections between devices on a LAN can be wired or wireless.

LAN

Router/Modem

The Internet

Note:	A small network that covers only one room, building or site is called a **LAN** (Local Area Network). Larger networks are called a **WAN** (Wide Area Network).

Setting up a typical home or small office network is usually very simple. All that is needed is a **router** to control the flow of data between devices and a **modem** to access the Internet. ICT devices connect to the network via the router using cables or wireless Wi-Fi connections.

Note:	These days, most routers have a built-in modem and wireless functionality.

For larger networks, a **server** is sometimes used. This is a dedicated computer which automatically looks after the security of the network, manages shared services (such as Internet access and e-mail), and stores shared files. Depending on the size of the network, more than one router (or **switch**) may be used.

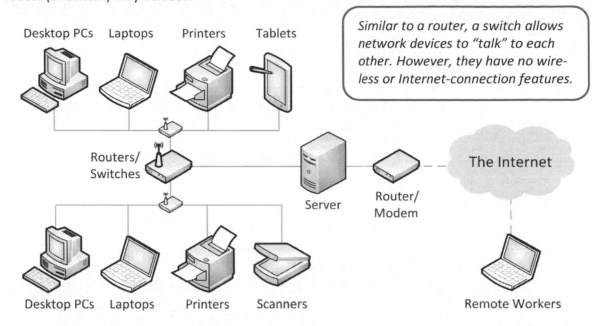

Desktop PCs   Laptops   Printers   Tablets

Similar to a router, a switch allows network devices to "talk" to each other. However, they have no wireless or Internet-connection features.

Routers/
Switches

Server

Router/
Modem

The Internet

Desktop PCs   Laptops   Printers   Scanners

Remote Workers

> **Note:** Want to work from home? Networks make this possible by allowing you to connect an ICT device to your work's server across the Internet. Once connected, you can access files and use shared resources as though you were "on site". This is known as working **remotely** and is becoming increasingly popular.

> **Note:** Although a network can be expensive to set up in terms of time and hardware costs, the benefits they offer often save money in the long run. For example, you can share costly resources such as printers and Internet connections.

1.11 Software

The term **software** is used to describe the instructions that tell an ICT device what to do, how to do it, and when. Software does not exist in the real world and can't be touched, but it can be used to perform a specific task when "run" on a device. Without software, most modern computing hardware wouldn't be much use at all.

> **Note:** Specific pieces of software that you use to perform a task are also known as **programs** or **applications** ("**apps**" on mobile devices).

In the course of your life, you will often find problems that can be solved using ICT. However, you need to be able to choose the best software application(s) for the task you have been given. To help you do this, the following notes will help you to understand the differences between the most popular types of software applications available.

> **Note:**   Each of the software applications described in the table below will be looked at in more detail in the following sections of this book.

1

Software Type	Description
Operating System	An operating system allows you to organise all of your files into folders, start programs and manage your computer's settings. Software of this sort is often referred to as **system software**. As you will learn more about in Section 2, system software usually comes with a lot of **utility programs** that let you perform simple computer maintenance tasks.
Word Processing	Word processing software lets you create professional documents such as letters, essays, reports and books.
Spreadsheets	Spreadsheet software allows you to work with lots of numbers and calculate a variety of different types of sums. It is often used to do accounts and budgets.
Presentations	Presentation software can be used to create slideshows to go with a spoken lecture or talk. It can also be used to create handouts for students, or automatic presentations that run in a loop.
Publications	Desktop publishing software can be used to create high quality printed materials with lots of graphics. This includes flyers, posters, banners, brochures, magazines, greeting cards and advertisements.
Databases	Databases can be used to store and manage large quantities of information (e.g. customer or product details). You can also query a database to find out information quickly.
Web Browsing	Web browsing software allows you to access the vast amounts of information and file downloads available on the Internet.
E-mail	E-mail software allows you to send messages and file attachments to other ICT users anywhere in the world. You can also use this software to organise your time and create personal "to-do" lists and calendars.

There are also many other more specialised software applications available that can be used to help with a wide variety of tasks. Popular examples include:

* Photo and image editing software (e.g. *Adobe Photoshop*)

* Animation and multimedia software (e.g. *Adobe Flash*)

* 3D and computer-aided design (CAD) software (e.g. *Google Sketchup*)

* Audio and music editing software (e.g. *Audacity, Adobe Soundbooth*)

* Video editing software (e.g. *Windows Movie Maker, Adobe Premiere*)

* Web page creation software (e.g. *Microsoft Expression Web, Adobe Dreamweaver*)

* Video games and entertainment software (e.g. *Xbox Dashboard, BBC iPlayer*)

1.12 Tracking and Monitoring

As you will find out later, there are a lot of laws and rules that tell you what you can and cannot do when using ICT technologies – break these and you can get into a lot of trouble! In education and at work, it is even more important that you behave correctly and legally. To make sure you do that, the people in charge of your safety can track or monitor your use of ICT.

For example:

* Internet and e-mail monitoring systems can log all of the data that comes into and out of an ICT device. It is also possible to record and playback a person's on-screen actions.

* Key loggers record all of the data typed into an ICT system. They are often used to monitor the performance of staff, especially where a lot of data entry is required.

* Telephone calls can be monitored and the exact number, duration and content of each call recorded. Time spend idle between calls can also be checked to spot time-wasting. This form of tracking is very popular in call centres.

* Tracking devices can be added to vehicles and equipment to accurately monitor and report their location. This information can be used to check that resources are used effectively and that remote employees are where they should be.

> **Note:** Tracking devices use the Global Positioning System (**GPS**) to find out where they are in the world. They do this by locating at least 3 of the 24 GPS satellites orbiting the Earth. Using that information and a little simple maths, the devices can work out their own position anywhere on the planet's surface or in the air.

Of course, it is not only your place of study or work that can track your actions and activities when using ICT. Information is now big business – especially online – and a lot of companies will try to gather personal information about you as you use the Internet (often without your permission). This includes data on your location, what you search for and buy, and how you like to spend your free time. This allows them to build up a **personal profile** of you and your interests (which is valuable information to businesses looking to advertise their products).

> **Note:** You will find out more about Internet tracking and monitoring in Section 8.

1.13 Leaving a Trace

As you use ICT in your everyday life, you nearly always leave a footprint behind of where you have been, what you did, how you did it, and when. Despite what you might think, you are never completely anonymous when using ICT and most of your actions can be tracked back to you. Even when you try your best to hide your own identity, you can nearly always be found and held responsible for your actions – so be careful!

For example, did you know that information about your telephone calls – who called who, when and for how long – is nearly always recorded by your network provider? They are also able to track your location by following your mobile phone signal (a process known as **triangulation**). And that's not all: when you visit a web page, your ICT device's unique network identifier (known as an **IP address**) can be recorded. And if you use a credit or debit card, your bank stores information about what you bought, where and when you bought it, and how much it cost.

> **Note:** Most companies are required by law to keep your personal information private and confidential. However, if you do anything illegal, authorities can gain access to that data in order to track you down.

> **Note:** Uploading and downloading illegal music and video files and posting intentionally hurtful and malicious comments online can often get you into a lot of trouble. People who do this can easily be traced and prosecuted by the police.

1.14 Laws and Regulations

Computers and electronic communications now form an important part of many people's lives, so it is not surprising that a large number of laws and regulations exist to control it. These include:

Law/Regulation	Description
User Licences	When you buy a piece of software you get a **licence** to use it, so giving away copies for others to use (or downloading pirate software) is illegal. Organisations often purchase multiple licences so that many users can work with the software at the same time.
Copyright, Designs and Patents Act	This law protects any original work (text, images, music, videos, etc.) from being copied or used by other people. To obtain a licence to use them you must first get the permission of the owner (and perhaps pay a small fee). In practice, this law prevents you from stealing text and images from the Internet and passing it off as your own work.
Data Protection Act	This law protects all personal data that a business or organisation stores about people. In particular, it requires that only information that is needed for a "specific purpose" can be stored (and only when the owner has given their permission). The law also requires that information is kept safe and secure at all times and isn't given away to other people.
Computer Misuse Act	This act makes it illegal to try to gain unauthorised access to – or in any way damage – another person's ICT system.
Health and Safety	The *Health and Safety at Work* laws protect you from physical harm. All employers and places of education must take reasonable efforts to look after the wellbeing of their staff or students.

Most ICT providers also provide an **acceptable usage policy** which tells you what you can and can't do with their device, product or service. This document is designed to prevent damaging, illegal, inappropriate or unacceptable use of ICT technology.

1.15 References

Whenever you use information created by somebody else in your own work (whether using ICT or not), you are required to acknowledge copyright and **reference** it correctly. To do this, you simply need to mention where you got the information from (known as its **source**). This gives credit to the original creator and protects you from being accused of copyright infringement or **plagiarism**.

> **Note:**   Plagiarism means copying somebody else's work and passing it off as your own.

So, when you reference material in your own work, you must mention all of the following:

* The full name of the person or company that created the material

* The name of the publication that contains the material (if relevant)

* Where you found the material, such as a book's page number or an Internet address

* The year that the material was created, updated or published

It is common practice to simply include the author's surname (or company name) and publication date in brackets after you reference their material, and then include full details in a list of sources at the end of your work (known as a **bibliography**).

> It is well known that "computing and mobile technologies have completely transformed how people live their lives – at home, in education and at work" (Khan, 2012).

> **Note:**   If you copy text word-for-word, use "speech marks" to show it is a direct quote.

> Bibliography
> Khan, Hassan (2012), OCR Cambridge Nationals in ICT, CiA Training Ltd, page 12.

> **Note:**   If you want to reference a web page, include its address, title and date of access.

1.16 Evaluating Information

Don't always believe everything that you read in a magazine or hear on TV. Although the information has usually been approved and checked for accuracy, this is not always the case. You need to stop and consider how trustworthy the information is before you believe it or use it in your own work, especially if it is found online where very little quality control exists. This is not always easy to do, but the following tips will help:

* Consider the source of the material that you are reading. Who has written it and why, and do they have any evidence to support their claims?

* Consider the publisher's authority in their area. Are they well known for producing reliable and accurate information?

* What is the intention of the publisher? Is the information they are providing aimed at informing you of facts, presenting a viewpoint, persuading you of a belief, or trying to sell you something?

* Forums or "blog" posts will most likely be based on biased (one-sided) opinion. You should take care when using information of this type.

* The articles stored on editable web pages or "wiki" sites (e.g. *Wikipedia*) are created by the general public (who are usually not experts) and should not be fully trusted.

* Well known and legitimate business websites are fairly trustworthy, but they are also likely to be biased towards promoting their own products and company goals.

* Materials obtained from well-known government or scientific sources (e.g. the *National Geographic* website) are usually a good source of reliable and accurate information.

* Consider the age of the information you find. It could be out of date or no longer relevant.

* Finally, if you decide to use a piece of information, try to confirm specific details by reading around the subject. Do other authors agree?

Remember, if you are basing your work on other people's research, you need to be confident that the facts and figures you use are totally reliable, accurate and fit for purpose. The quality and relevance of your work depends on it, and you may be asked to justify and defend your choices.

1.17 Accessibility

Some people have mental and physical disabilities that can restrict how they use ICT. However, manufacturers and developers are required by law to make sure that their products are open to everyone, regardless of ability. For ICT devices, special **assistive technologies** such as larger keyboards, bigger buttons and different types of pointing device (e.g. eye trackers and joysticks) can be used to help people with restricted movement. Software utilities can also be used to help those with limited hearing, vision or speech. For example:

* Voice recognition software turns spoken words into on-screen text or computer commands. This type of software is useful for people with limited mobility who have difficulty using a mouse or keyboard.

* Screen reader software reads out any text shown on an ICT device. This type of software is helpful for visually impaired people.

* Screen magnifiers enlarge parts of the screen and aid people with low vision.

> **Note:** Simple software accessibility settings will be looked at again in Section 2.

1.18 Basic ICT Security

Computers and mobile ICT devices have totally changed the way we work and communicate with each other. However, this widespread use and reliance on technology has also created a number of important privacy and security issues which you – as an ICT user – need to be aware of and fully understand.

Firstly, your personal photos, videos, music and documents are all very important and it can be a disaster if you lose them. At work, however, business documents, customer data, credit card details and passwords are even more valuable. Consider what would happen if this data was lost due to hardware failure, equipment loss or accidental deletion.

Secondly, personal and business information is very valuable to criminals. If "hackers" are able to gain access to an ICT device and get hold of sensitive and confidential data, they can and probably will use it to commit a crime. This will cause a lot of trouble and embarrassment for everyone involved and may end up costing a great deal of money!

> **Note:** **Hacking** is the term used to describe unauthorised access into an ICT system.

To keep yourself and others safe, you must take steps to protect all ICT devices and the data they contain from being lost or stolen. There are a number of ways to do this, including:

* Using strong passwords to stop people from accessing your computer without permission

* Storing and using data safely and responsibly (and backing it up regularly)

✱   Using antivirus programs to prevent software damage or theft of data

✱   Taking care to make sure hardware devices are not stolen

You will find out more about these important issues in the following exercises.

1.19 Passwords

To prevent other people from gaining access to your ICT devices, you need to protect them with a **password** or **PIN** (Personal Identification Number). If a device is stolen or left unattended for a time, passwords and PINs will act as your own personal entry codes and stop unauthorised use.

> **Note:**   As well as a password, most computer systems require the use of a user ID (a **username** or **log-in name**) which uniquely identifies you on a computer or network. It is a name that is given to you and *only you*, and together with your password proves your identity and right to access information and resources.

A good password should be made up from a combination of numbers and both **uppercase** (big) and **lowercase** (small) letters. It should also be *at least* 8 **characters** long.

PASSWORD: `Nat10nAL5`

> **Note:**   In IT, a character is a single letter, number or symbol. A good tip to help create a strong yet memorable password is use numbers in place of letters, as shown above.

It is a good idea to use a password that you can easily remember, but not one that is easy for others to guess. For example, don't use your name or the word **password**. The same rule applies to PINs: don't use any easy-to-guess combinations such as **1234** or your date of birth.

> **Note:**   PIN numbers are usually 4 digits long and only contain the numbers 0 to 9. They are most often used to secure mobile devices or bank cards.

> **Note:**   Did you know that the small microchip on a bank card stores the owner's PIN number? When they use the card to pay for something in a shop or restaurant, for example, the number on the chip is checked to make sure that it matches the PIN entered on the card reader (known as **chip and PIN**). This prevents people from stealing and using the card illegally.

Always keep your passwords and PIN numbers safe and try to avoid writing them down. It is also good practice to change your passwords and PINs often. Remember: never give your security information to other people and try to avoid using the same details for different purposes.

> **Note:**   If you use a computing device that is connected to the Internet, there is a very small chance that a hacker could access it from another computer elsewhere. However, if you use a good password or PIN, they will not be able to do this.

1.20 Information Security

As most people and businesses now rely on ICT technology, it is important that the information those devices contain is kept safe. In the workplace, the impact of losing information can be disastrous. At the very least, customers will lose confidence and stop doing business with you and your company. However, if the information fell into the wrong hands and was used to commit a crime (e.g. identity theft or credit card fraud), you and your employer could end up in court. This will not only cost a lot of money, but you will probably also lose your job!

The following simple guidelines will help you keep information safe:

*   Always respect and value information – especially if that information belongs to someone else – and treat it with the care it deserves.

*   Never disclose private or sensitive information to anyone you do not fully trust and who does not have permission to use it.

*   Protect your ICT devices from unauthorised access by using a strong password or PIN.

*   Protect your computing devices from viruses using antivirus software (which you will learn more about in later exercises).

*   Further protect your ICT devices from hackers by using a **firewall**.

> **Note:**   **Firewalls** are used to stop unauthorised users from accessing ICT devices remotely across the Internet. Don't worry: as you will learn more about in Section 2, modern ICT devices usually have built-in firewalls that automatically protect you.

*   Keep your operating system and software up-to-date by checking for updates (which you will learn more about in Section 2).

*   Password protect sensitive documents that you send by e-mail or place on a mobile device (you will see an example of how to do this in Section 3).

*   Backup your own data regularly in case it is lost or accidentally deleted (in a business this may be done for you by the person in charge of your network).

> **Note:**   An easy way to backup your own personal data is to use a portable storage device such as a USB memory stick or external hard drive. Simply plug it into your computer's USB port and copy files straight from your computer to the device. That's all there is to it – you can then keep your backup in a safe and secure place.

1.21 Hardware Security

Although ICT devices are very expensive, the information they contain is sometimes even more valuable. You need to protect and take care of your equipment and make sure it does not fall into the wrong hands. The following simple guidelines will help you do this:

* Handle ICT hardware with care – it is easy to damage computer equipment.

* Don't expose devices to heat, cold or water.

* Store ICT devices in a secure place with locked doors and windows.

* Never leave your ICT devices unattended where other people can see them.

* Special cables can be used if required to tie ICT devices to desks.

Mobile storage devices and removable media such as memory sticks, CDs and DVDs are an excellent way to transport files. However, these are also very easy to lose. Take extra care with these and try to avoid using them to transport sensitive, confidential or valuable information.

1.22 Viruses and Malware

The most well known and feared threat in modern computing is the **virus** – a small piece of "malicious software" (or **malware**) designed to "infect" and cause harm to a computer. All viruses are man-made and get their name from the way they automatically copy themselves onto other ICT devices.

The effects of a virus can vary enormously. Some simply change a web browser's home page, others decrease the performance of a computer, and a small few cause real damage to file systems by destroying data and preventing operating systems and programs from working correctly. Even more seriously, some malware can identify private and sensitive information within files and then transmit that data to another person via the Internet.

Some other common forms of computer malware you may hear about are:

* **Spyware**. This type of software hides on your computer and interferes with your use of the system. Spyware can also record secure and personal information and send it to another person via the Internet.

✱ **Adware**. This type of software "pops up" annoying advertisements from the Internet.

✱ **Worms**. This type of software can damage files on your computer, and like viruses are able to copy themselves to other devices (often via e-mail).

✱ **Trojans**. These are files that look harmless (for example pictures, documents and spreadsheets) but contain any number of the threats shown above.

> **Note:**   A virus is not the same thing as a **bug**. A bug is simply an error or fault in a piece of software that stops it working correctly. Software updates are released to fix bugs.

Always remember that computer viruses can <u>only</u> be introduced to a system from outside (they do not suddenly appear out of nowhere). Common sources of viruses are e-mail attachments, Internet downloads, pirated CDs or DVDs, and even external USB storage devices (if they have been attached to another infected computer).

1.23 Antivirus Software

One way to defend against viruses is to install **antivirus software**. This is a small utility program that runs in the background on your computer and scans all files and incoming data – including e-mail attachments and Internet downloads – for <u>known</u> malware.

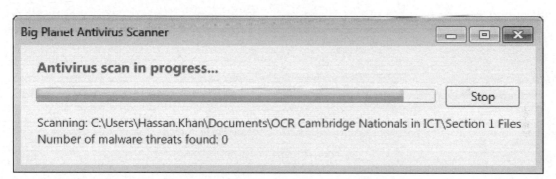

Unfortunately, new viruses appear every day. To make sure your antivirus program learns about these new threats it needs to be kept up-to-date. This involves downloading the latest **updates**, which your antivirus program will usually do automatically.

> **Note:**   Antivirus software can also be used to scan files "on-demand", including your entire computer, which is useful for checking downloaded files and e-mail attachments <u>before</u> you open them.

At the time of writing, some common antivirus programs include *Norton Internet Security*, *McAfee VirusScan*, *NOD32*, *Trend Micro Internet Security* and *AVG*. Once installed, these programs will watch for and immediately delete any *known* malware that enters your system.

> **Note:**   You will learn more about malware and staying safe online in section 8.

1.24 ICT Considerations

Many problems that need to be solved at home, in education and at work can benefit from the significant speed and accuracy advantages that ICT systems offer. However, the types of hardware and software you choose may be limited by a number of significant factors, such as:

Consideration	Description
Availability	Do you have the correct ICT hardware and software available to you to solve a problem? Remember that the latest software often requires the latest hardware in order to run properly. You also need to make sure you have access to any information needed, that it is correct and fit-for-purpose, that you are legally allowed to use it, and it is in a format you are able to work with.
Cost	A lot of software and modern ICT devices are very expensive. Can you afford to purchase them? Can you justify their need and show that they will help improve your productivity? If not, you may need to make do with the resources that are available.
User Needs	Do the ICT systems available to you have all of the features that are needed to help solve your problem? Are they easy to use and do you have the skills required? If not, you may need training or support. If you have any physical or mental disabilities, you should also choose the ICT resources that best suit your needs. Also think about the needs of your audience and the best format to present your work to them.
Data Security	Depending on how you plan to use ICT, you should make sure that the hardware and software selected is appropriate for the task. For example, if you are working with confidential, sensitive or private information, you will need to use ICT that is safe and secure in order to prevent loss of data or unauthorised access.

If you are planning to use ICT to help somebody else solve a problem (for example, by creating a spreadsheet or database for them to use), you will need to consider all of the above points from their point of view.

> **Note:**   Useful planning and review checklists are provided at the back of the book to help you consider a number of important issues when creating your own ICT solutions.

1.25 Next Steps

Well done! You have now completed all of the exercises in this section. If you feel you are ready to test your knowledge and understanding of the topics covered, move on to the following **Develop Your Skills** activities. If there are any subjects covered in this section that you are unsure about, you should revisit the appropriate exercises and try them again before moving on.

Develop Your Skills...

At the end of every section you get the chance to complete two activities. These will help you to develop your skills and prepare for your exam. Don't forget to use the planning and review checklists at the back of the book to help organise and review your work.

> **Note:** Answers to these activities are provided in this section's **Sample Solutions** folder.

Develop Your Skills: Safety & Security

In this activity, *Hassan* is facing a number of safety and security concerns. Can you help him?

Activity 1

To keep customers informed about new promotions and offers at *Big Planet Theme Park*, my manager has asked me to record the contact information of visitors. To do this, I've been given a brand new desktop computer. However, before I use it, there are a few safety and security concerns that I must first consider...

Q Are there any laws that apply when recording customer information?

Q How can I prevent unauthorised access to my computer?

Q Which of the following passwords do you think is best to use and why?

   A: `bigplanet`   **B:** `password`   **C:** `HassanKhan`   **D:** `HKhan3487`   **E:** `3487`

Q How can I protect the data stored on my computer from loss or damage?

Q I'm thinking of plugging my new computer into a socket on the other side of the office. I think the wires will *just about* stretch. Do you have any concerns about this?

Notes:

Develop Your Skills: Software Decisions

In this activity *Hassan* needs help to choose the best software applications for a number of different tasks. You will need to use the ICT skills that you have learned in this section to recommend and present a suitable solution.

Activity 2

Next Wednesday the park is running a special "Buy 1 Get 1 Free" offer on all tickets. To advertise and promote the event, I've been asked to use my new computer to do a number of different tasks.

However, I just can't decide which software application to use for each job. Can you help? Each task that I must complete is shown below on the left and all of the applications I can use are shown on the right. Can you suggest the *best* application to use for each task?

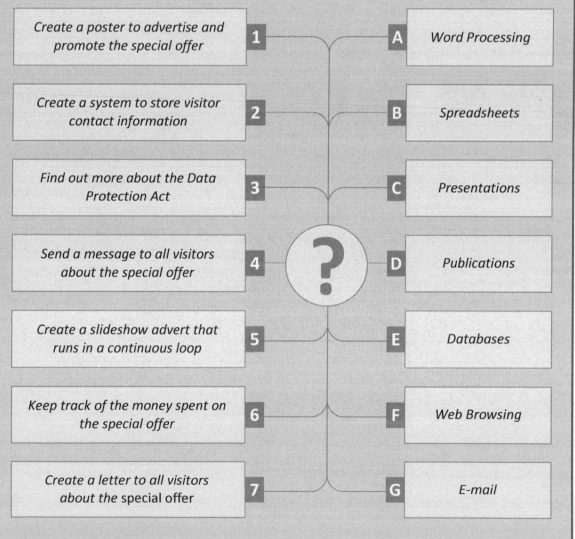

Tasks		Applications
Create a poster to advertise and promote the special offer	**1** — **A**	Word Processing
Create a system to store visitor contact information	**2** — **B**	Spreadsheets
Find out more about the Data Protection Act	**3** — **C**	Presentations
Send a message to all visitors about the special offer	**4** — **D**	Publications
Create a slideshow advert that runs in a continuous loop	**5** — **E**	Databases
Keep track of the money spent on the special offer	**6** — **F**	Web Browsing
Create a letter to all visitors about the special offer	**7** — **G**	E-mail

Hint: in this exercise each task is best performed using <u>one</u> of the applications shown (and every application is used once).

SECTION 12 | Microsoft Windows

2 | Microsoft Windows

I'm a member of the *Big Planet Theme Park's* reception desk team. We deal with all incoming and outgoing park communications and receive lots of customer enquiries by telephone, e-mail and post. It's a rewarding job and working with the general public is really good fun.

My main role at the reception desk is to welcome park visitors and quickly answer any questions that they have. Of course, to do this well, I need to be able to find and access information *fast*. That's why I use *Microsoft Windows* – it allows me to organise all of my important data into files and folders that are easy to create and search through.

I also use *Windows* to manage my computer's settings and start software programs and utilities. With a little practice you'll quickly discover how to do this yourself and how to customise *Windows* to work best for you. And although *Windows* isn't the only operating system available, it's definitely the most widely used at home, in education and at work.

What you will learn:

In this section you will use the operating system *Microsoft Windows 7* to help *Fiona* complete a number of everyday tasks at *Big Planet Theme Park*. You will see how to log on and off, change computer settings, respond to common problems, start programs, and perform a variety of simple file management tasks.

Knowledge, skills and understanding:

* Perform simple file management tasks and create efficient file storage systems

* Use *Windows* effectively, start programs, and change computer settings

* Work accurately, safely and securely

Data files

The files needed to complete the activities in this section are provided in the **Section 2** data folder (see note on page **vii** to download these files). Any files or folders that you create or edit in this section can be saved in the same folder.

2.1 About Microsoft Windows

Microsoft Windows is an **operating system (OS)** that allows you to interact with and use a computer. It is a very powerful piece of **system software** that controls all of the hardware connected to a computer such as the monitor, the keyboard, the mouse, and so on. It also lets you find, access and run **programs** that can be used to perform a number of specific tasks.

> **Note:** There are many types of operating system software available, depending on the type of ICT device you are using. For example, **OSX** is an operating system for *Apple* desktop computers, and **Android**, **iOS** and **Windows Phone** are popular operating systems for mobile smart phones. The *Windows* skills you learn in this section will help you to understand and use most other operating systems.

2.2 Logging On

Windows allows more than one person to "sign in" and use a computer. Each person has their own settings and private storage spaces in which to keep their files.

To access your own files and start using the computer, you first need to **log on** to *Windows*. This involves entering a **username** and a **password** that is known only by you.

> **Note:** If you are using *Windows* at home and you do not share your computer with others, you may not need to log-on.

At home you may only need to select a user name and, if required, enter a password. If your computer is connected to a network, however, you will first be prompted to log-on by pressing the key combination <**Ctrl Alt Del**>.

> **Note:** You will need to press and hold the <**Ctrl**>, <**Alt**> and <**Delete**> keys down together.

> **Note:** If there is a light on your computer but nothing on the screen, the computer is in stand-by mode. Move the mouse or press a key on the keyboard to wake it up.

2.3 The Windows Desktop

When you have successfully logged on, the *Windows* **Desktop** will be displayed. This is the starting point for all tasks performed in *Windows*. From here it is possible to start all the programs installed on the computer and access all of the utilities and features of *Windows*.

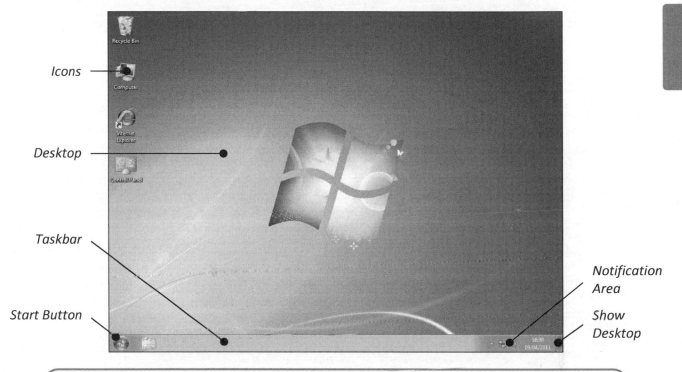

Icons

Desktop

Taskbar

Start Button

Notification Area

Show Desktop

> **Note:** The *Windows* **Desktop** is an example of a **Graphical User Interface**, or **GUI**. A GUI allows you to interact with your computer using pictures, symbols and icons rather than complicated and hard-to-remember text commands.

> **Note:** As you will see later, *Windows* can be customised according to your own preferences and that of the organisation which owns and runs the computer. Nearly every aspect of its appearance can be changed. For this reason, the screens shown in this book may not quite match that of your computer. The basic layout and functionality, however, should be exactly the same.

The **Icons** that appear on the **Desktop** represent the programs, folders and files stored on the computer. They are small pictures that you usually **double click** to start or open.

Computer   Recycle Bin   Internet

> Note: To change the position of an icon on the **Desktop** you can simply drag and drop it to another location. Alternatively, to quickly arrange your icons, right-click on an empty area of your **Desktop** and select a layout option within **Sort by**.

Along the bottom of the **Desktop** is an area known as the **Taskbar**. This is used to access and manage running programs and usually remains on screen at all times.

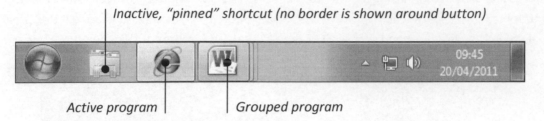

Inactive, "pinned" shortcut (no border is shown around button)

Active program | *Grouped program*

The **Start** button on the left of the **Taskbar** is used to start nearly all programs and *Windows* features. More than one program can be run at the same time (this is known as **multi-tasking**), and as each program is started, it becomes **active** and an icon for it appears on the **Taskbar**. If the same program is opened many times, *Windows* may group icons together to save space.

> Note: You can **Pin** your favourite programs to the **Taskbar** to make them easier to access. To do this, right click a program's icon and select **Pin to Taskbar**. Pinned items appear on the **Taskbar** but are not active until you click them.

The **Notification Area** on the right of the **Taskbar** displays the date and time. On occasion, short status messages and alerts from *Windows* may also appear here. These are usually important and you should pay attention to them.

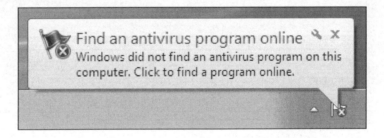

Some programs also install small icons in the **Notification Area** to provide status updates and allow you to quickly access settings (which you can do by double-clicking them).

> Note: The **Show Desktop** button found to the far right of the **Taskbar** can be used to "minimise" (or hide) all windows and display the **Desktop**.

2.4 The Start Menu

At the left of the **Taskbar** is the **Start** button. Clicking the **Start** button opens the **Start Menu** which can be used to "run" any program installed on the computer. The **Start Menu** can also be used to search for information, access private files and folders, find help and support, and control the computer's settings.

Activity:

1. From the *Windows* **Desktop**, click the **Start** button. The **Start Menu** appears.

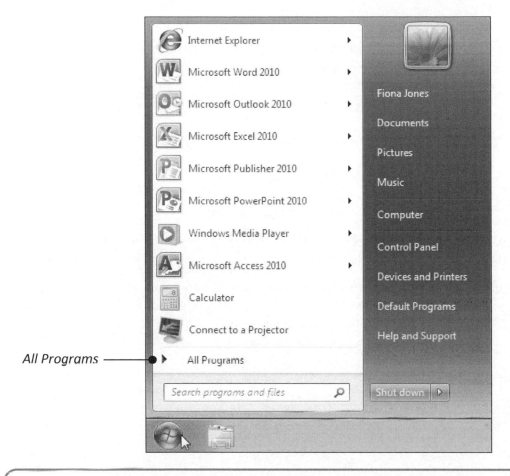

All Programs

> **Note:** The shortcuts that appear on the left of the **Start Menu** change depending on the programs you have used most recently. The small arrows to the right of some of the shortcuts, ▸, provide access to most recently used files for those programs.

2. Notice the buttons on the right of the **Start Menu**. These provide fast access to your private files and folders and allow you to access computer settings and find additional help and support.

> **Note:** The **Shut down** button can be used to turn off or restart your computer. If there are any updates for your computer, these can be installed before shutting down.

3. Click **All Programs** towards the bottom of the left area of the **Start Menu**. A list containing all of the programs that are installed on your computer is shown.

4. Click the **Start** button again to close the **Start Menu**. Alternatively, simply click away from the **Start Menu** to close it.

2.5 Working with Windows

Windows are rectangular boxes that appear on the **Desktop** and can be dragged around to any position and size you like. Inside a window, you can interact with programs, adjust computer settings and manage files and folders. Many windows can be open at the same time and each can perform a variety of different, simultaneous tasks.

Once opened, a window can be **maximized** (filling the whole screen), **minimized** (appearing only as an active button on the **Taskbar**), or **restored** (to any size in-between).

Activity:

1. Click the **Start** button and then click **Computer** from the right of the **Start Menu**.

2. The **Computer** view is opened in a window. This view shows any and all storage devices that are currently connected to your computer (you may see a different set of icons).

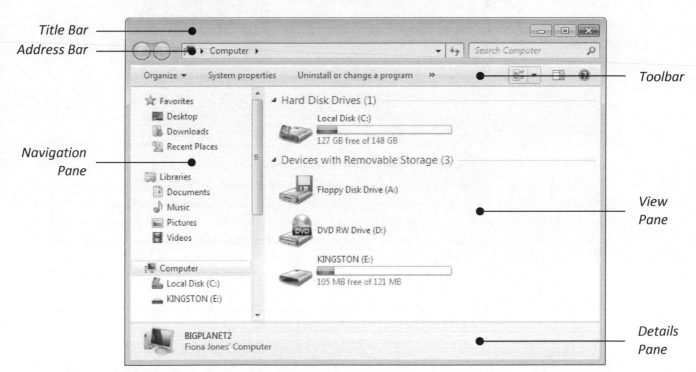

> **Note:** This type of window is known as a **Windows Explorer** window. It allows you to navigate through the folders on your computer. The **Address Bar** shows the current folder name that is on view in the window.

> **Note:** If your window does not appear with the **Navigation Pane** and **Details Pane** as shown above, click the **Organize** button on the **Toolbar** and select **Layout**. Make sure **Details Pane** and **Navigation Pane** are selected (shown with a tick).

> **Note:** Below the **Address Bar** is the **Toolbar**. This is a row of buttons that allows you to perform simple tasks such as creating new folders or changing the current view. You will learn more about these in a later exercise.

3. Notice the three **Window Control Buttons** at the top right of the window. These are **Minimize**, [▭], **Maximize**, [▭], and **Close**, [✕].

4. The **Maximize** button increases the size of the window to the maximum size available. If the **Computer** window is not maximized already, click the **Maximize** button now.

> **Note:** If the window is maximized, the **Maximize** button is replaced by the **Restore Down** button, [▭]. This restores the window to its last (non-maximized) size.

5. Notice that the window now fills the screen. Click the **Restore Down** button, [▭], to reduce the size of the window.

6. The **Minimize** button hides a window completely, leaving only its active button on the **Taskbar**. Click the **Minimize** button, [▭], on the **Computer** window now.

7. When a window is minimized, the program or task inside the window continues to run. The **Computer** window can be restored by clicking its **Taskbar** button. Do that now.

8. Move the mouse pointer over the **Title Bar** of the **Computer** window. Click and drag the window to a new location anywhere else on the screen.

> **Note:** You can drag a window to the far left or right side of the **Desktop** to have it automatically resized to fill that half of the screen.

9. The size of the window can also be changed. Move the mouse pointer over the right edge of the window until the pointer changes to a double headed arrow.

10. Click and drag to increase or decrease the width of the window. The same technique can be used to increase or decrease the size of the window in all four directions.

11. The size of a window can be changed in two directions at once. Place the mouse pointer over the bottom right corner of the window so that it changes to a two headed diagonal arrow.

12. Click and drag to increase or decrease the size of the window.

> Note: If more than one window is open at a time, they will overlap. The active window will always appear on top.

13. Click the **Start** button and then click **Documents** from the right of the **Start Menu**. A second window is opened which shows your personal documents. Drag the **Documents** window so that it appears on top of the **Computer** window (if it is not already).

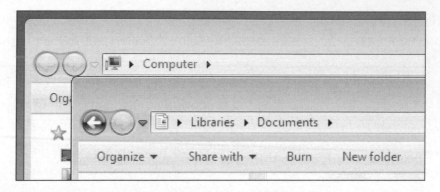

14. Notice that the **Taskbar** has automatically grouped the two **Windows Explorer** windows. Click the **Taskbar** button and a pop-up appears above allowing you to select which window you would like to activate.

15. Select **Computer** to activate that window and bring it to the front. Click anywhere on the **Documents** window behind to bring that window to the top again.

> Note: You can also move between active windows by holding down the <**Alt**> key and pressing <**Tab**>.

16. Click the **Close** button, [X], to close the **Documents** window. Then close the **Computer** window.

2.6 Logging Off

If you use a computer in a public place or you share your computer with others, you must <u>always</u> log off when you finish your work. This does not shut the computer down completely but simply ends your session and allows other people to log on afterwards. Logging off closes any open windows or running programs. Importantly, anyone who tries to use the computer after you will not be able to gain access to your private files.

Activity:

1. Click the **Start** button and then click the arrow button on the **Shut down** button (be careful not to click the **Shut down** button itself as this will immediately turn off your computer).

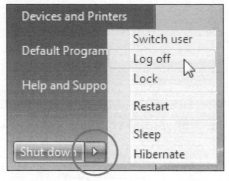

2. From the options that appear, click **Log off**.

> **Note:** Selecting **Switch user** allows you to log-on as another user without first logging out. **Sleep** and **Hibernate** will put your computer into a low-power standby mode.

3. You are logged out of *Windows* and returned to the log-on screen. Log back in again.

> **Note:** If you are only leaving your computer for a few minutes you can simply lock it rather than log off. To do this hold down <⊞> and press <L>. The computer will be locked and you will need to enter your password again to gain access.

2.7 Files, Folders and Libraries

Files are small packages of information such as documents, pictures or MP3 songs. In *Windows*, all of your files are kept in **folders**. By using sensible and meaningful names, you can use folders to sort and organise your files into logical groups that are easy to find later. Also, as folders can contain other folders (called **subfolders**), you can create groups within groups.

> **Note:** At home, in education and at work, it is always important to be well organised. If you don't keep a tidy desk and filing system you can never find anything when you need it. The same applies to the files that you store on your computer.

In *Windows*, you may notice that your documents, music, pictures and videos appear in their own separate **Libraries**. These are simply the merged contents of one or more folders, and are designed to bring together files of similar types into one simple view.

Activity:

1. From the **Start Menu**, open **Documents**. The **Documents** library view opens in a **Windows Explorer** window.

2. The data files for this book can be found in your **Documents** library. The folder **DATA FILES** will appear in the list.

Documents library
Includes: 2 locations

Arrange by: Folder ▼

Name	Type	Date modified
DATA FILES	File folder	19/04/2011 08:54

3. Double click the **DATA FILES** folder icon to open that folder and view its contents. Notice that the **path** in the **Address Bar** changes to show that you are now within the **DATA FILES** folder.

▸ Libraries ▸ Documents ▸ DATA FILES ▸

> **Note:** A **path** is the name given to the unique location of a file in a computer system. It describes the route you must take through the folders to find a file. Each folder in the path is generally separated by a ▸ or \ symbol.

4. Double click the **OCR Cambridge Nationals** folder to view the subfolders within. Finally, double click **Section 2** to view the data files for this section. 18 items are displayed.

5. On the **Toolbar**, click the drop-down arrow on the **Change your view** button, (labelled **More options**) and select **Details**. This is one of 8 views that you can select, and by default shows the files in alphabetic order with file type, date and size information.

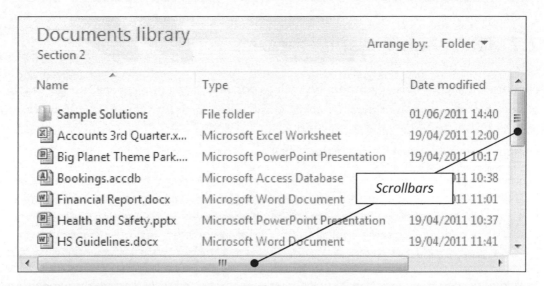

Documents library
Section 2

Arrange by: Folder ▼

Name	Type	Date modified
Sample Solutions	File folder	01/06/2011 14:40
Accounts 3rd Quarter.x...	Microsoft Excel Worksheet	19/04/2011 12:00
Big Planet Theme Park....	Microsoft PowerPoint Presentation	19/04/2011 10:17
Bookings.accdb	Microsoft Access Database	011 10:38
Financial Report.docx	Microsoft Word Document	011 11:01
Health and Safety.pptx	Microsoft PowerPoint Presentation	19/04/2011 10:37
HS Guidelines.docx	Microsoft Word Document	19/04/2011 11:41

Scrollbars

> **Note:** If **scrollbars** appear on the right and bottom of the window then there is too much data to show in the space available. Click and drag these up/down or left/right to view more of the window's contents.

6. Click the **Change your view** button (*not* the **More options** drop-down arrow) to select the next view available (**Tiles**). The files are displayed in a grid with large icons.

7.　Continue to click the **Change your view** button until you return to **Details** view (or use the **More options** drop-down to go directly to it).

8.　On the **Toolbar**, click the **New folder** button,  , to create a new folder in the current location. A new folder appears and you are prompted to enter a name.

Name	Type
New folder	File folder
Sample Solutions	File folder

9.　Type in the name **Reports** and press <**Enter**>.

> **Note:**　It is important that you give folders sensible, meaningful names so that you (or others) can identify their contents at a glance. It also makes searching for files and folders a great deal easier.

10.　Using the same technique, create 4 more new folders called **Publications**, **Presentations**, **Image Library** and **Databases**.

11.　Double click on the **Presentations** folder to open it, and then create two new folders (or subfolders) called **Training** and **Marketing**.

> **Note:**　Files that are related to one another, or belong in the same logical group as each other, should be stored together in the same folder.

12.　To return to the previous folder, click the **Back** button located to the left of the **Address Bar**. This can be used to move back to the previous folders viewed one step at a time.

Back/Forward Buttons

> **Note:**　Similarly, the **Forward** button can be used to return to the last subfolder visited.

> **Note:**　Each individual folder shown in the **Address Bar** path can be clicked to quickly jump back to that specific folder. These are known as **parent** folders. The first folder in the folder structure is called the **root** folder.

13.　Leave the **Documents** data files window open for the next exercise.

2.8 Copying Files

There are many reasons why you might want to create a **copy** of a file. For example, you may want to create a copy of your data for backup purposes (to place on an external storage device so that you can take it elsewhere) or to use as a starting point for a new file.

Activity:

1. With the **Documents** window open and the contents of the **Section 2** data files folder on view, click <u>once</u> on the file **Financial Report**.

2. From the **Toolbar**, click the **Organize** button and select **Copy**. The file is copied and the copy placed in memory.

3. Click the **Organize** button again and select **Paste**. The copied file is pasted into the current folder.

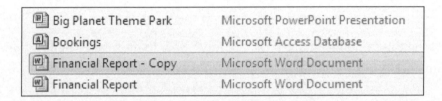

> Note: When a file is copied and pasted to the same folder, **Copy** is automatically added to the file name. It is not possible to have two files with exactly the same name in the same *Windows* folder.

> Note: Any changes made to the copied file will not affect the original.

4. **Maximise** the window (if it is not already) and create a new folder called **Copies**.

5. Using the **Organize** button, copy the file **Bookings**.

6. Open the **Copies** folder and, using the **Organize** button again, **Paste** the copied file. Notice that the file retains the same file name.

7. Click the **Back** button once to return to the **Section 2** folder.

8. Select the file **Logo** by clicking it once. Holding down the <**Ctrl**> key, drag the file over the **Copies** folder. Notice that the mouse pointer changes to the **Copy to** cursor.

9. Release the mouse button to drop a copy of the file into the **Copies** folder, and then release the <**Ctrl**> key. Open the **Copies** folder to find the copied file.

10. Click the **Back** button once to return to the **Section 2** folder.

> **Note:** Using this technique, files and folders can be copied between different windows on your computer or to and from removable media devices such as memory sticks or writable CDs and DVDs. If your computer is networked to other computers it is also easy to copy objects between them. However, be aware that all devices have a limited size and can only hold a finite amount of data.

11. Notice the **Navigation Pane** on the left of the window. This can be used to explore the folder structure of your computer. Move the mouse pointer over the pane and small **Expand/Collapse** buttons appear to the left of the folder names.

Expand/Collapse Button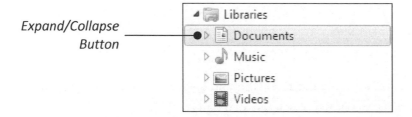

> **Note:** The **Navigation Pane** also allows you to access and explore the folder structure of other computers on your network.

12. Click the **Expand/Collapse** button to the left of **Documents** to display the contents of that library.

13. Next, expand **My Documents** to see the contents of that folder.

14. Expand folders in the following order: **DATA FILES**, **OCR Cambridge Nationals**, **Section 2**.

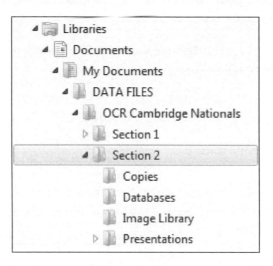

15. Make sure **Section 2** is selected in the **Navigation Pane**. The contents of that folder appear in the main view panel.

16. Click once on the file **Health and Safety**. Holding down <**Ctrl**>, drag the file to the **Copies** folder on the **Navigation Pane** to copy it. Release the mouse then the <**Ctrl**> key.

17. On the **Navigation Pane** select the **Copies** folder (within the **Section 2** folder). The contents of that folder now appear in the main **View Pane**.

18. Select the **Section 2** folder in the **Navigation Pane** and leave the window open.

2.9 Moving Files

It is good practice at home, in education and at work to keep your electronic files well organised. This usually involves grouping related files into appropriately named folders so that you can quickly find information when you need it.

Activity:

1. With the **Section 2** data files window open from the previous exercise, click <u>once</u> on the document file **Financial Report** (<u>not</u> the copy that you created earlier).

2. From the **Toolbar**, click the **Organize** button and select **Cut**. The file is cut and placed in memory (notice that the cut file now appears faded).

3. Open the folder **Reports** and select **Paste** from the **Organize** button. The file is moved from the original folder to this one.

4. Return to the **Section 2** folder to confirm that **Financial Report** is no longer present.

5. Use the same technique to move the **Accounts 3rd Quarter** file to the **Reports** folder.

> Note: If you move a file to a location where a file with the same name already exists, you will be given the option to **replace** the existing file in the destination folder or **rename** the copied file. You will see this in practice in the next exercise.

6. Drag and then drop the **Bookings** database file onto the **Databases** folder to move it. Notice that the **Move to** cursor appears.

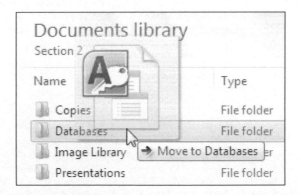

> Note: To select more than one file (or folder) at a time, hold down <**Ctrl**> and click each item. To select a range of files (or folders), hold down <**Shift**> and click the first and last item. To select all items in a folder, press <**Ctrl A**>.

7. Hold down the **<Ctrl>** key on your keyboard as you select the image files **Logo** and **Park View** together. Release **<Ctrl>** and drag either file to the **Image Library** folder.

8. Both selected files are moved. Next, expand the **Presentations** folder on the **Navigation Pane** to show the 2 subfolders **Marketing** and **Training**.

9. Drag the files **Big Planet Theme Park** and **Rumbling Rails** to the **Marketing** folder.

10. Next, drag the files **Health and Safety** and **New Staff Induction** to the **Training** folder. Check that all files have been moved correctly.

11. Move the following files to the **Publications** folder: **Park News**, **HS Guidelines** and **Theme Park Monthly**. Move the **Personnel** file to the **Databases** folder.

12. Create a new folder called **Media Files** and move the following files from the **Section 2** folder into it: **Theme Tune** and **Pirate's Cove**.

13. Great! All files are now well organised and will be much easier to find later. You will deal with any remaining files later in this section.

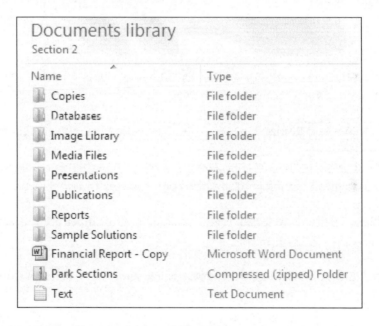

14. Leave the **Section 2** data files window open for the next exercise.

2.10 Organising Folders

You can organise folders using all of the same techniques used to organise files. However, when you copy or move a folder, it is important to understand that <u>all</u> of its contents – including subfolders – are copied or moved as well.

Activity:

1. With the **Section 2** data files window open from the previous exercise, click <u>once</u> on the folder **Databases** to select it.

2.   From the **Toolbar**, click the **Organize** button and select **Copy**. The folder is copied and placed in memory.

3.   Open the **Copies** folder and select **Paste** from the **Organize** button. The copied folder appears containing a duplicate of the original folder's contents.

> **Note:**   You can copy files and folders in *Windows* by pressing <**Ctrl+C**>, cut files and folders by pressing <**Ctrl+X**>, and paste files and folders by pressing <**Ctrl+V**>.

4.   Open the **Databases** folder to check the contents of the copied folder. The databases **Bookings** and **Personnel** appear. Return to the **Copies** folder.

5.   Try to drag and drop the database file **Bookings** into the folder **Databases**. As the folder already contains a file with that name, the following dialog box appears.

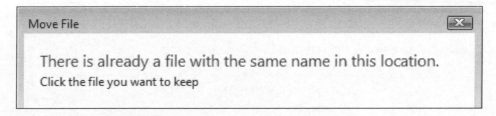

6.   Examine the three options available and read their descriptions: **Move and Replace**; **Don't move**; **Move, but keep both files**.

7.   Select **Move and Replace** to overwrite the existing file with the copied file.

8.   Create a new folder (in the current folder) and name it **Backup**. Move the folder **Databases** into it, along with the files **Logo** and **Health and Safety**.

9.   The files and the **Databases** folder (including all of its contents) are moved. Explore the **Backup** folder to confirm this.

10.   Select the **Section 2** folder in the **Navigation Pane** and leave the window open.

2.11 Renaming Files and Folders

From time to time you may need to change file and folder names as their contents change. It is always good practice to give your files and folders sensible and meaningful names. If a file or folder is well labelled, you should not need to open it to find out what it contains.

> **Note:**   If a folder contains too many files, consider organising them into subfolders.

Activity:

1.   With the **Section 2** data files window open from the previous exercise, click <u>once</u> on the document file **Financial Report - Copy**.

2.   From the **Organize** menu, click **Rename**. Notice that the file's name appears highlighted in a text box, ready for editing.

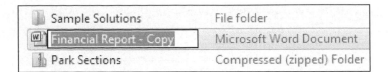

Sample Solutions	File folder
Financial Report - Copy	Microsoft Word Document
Park Sections	Compressed (zipped) Folder

3.   Enter **Budget Report** as the new file name and press <**Enter**>. The file's name has been changed. Move the file to the **Reports** folder.

4.   Right click on the **Media Files** folder to display a drop-down menu.

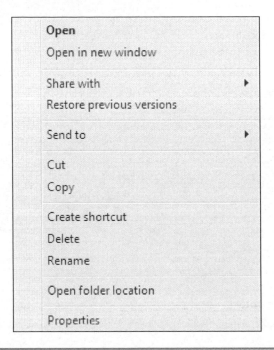

> **Note:**   Right-clicking an object in *Windows* usually displays a **context-sensitive menu** that can be used to perform the most common actions for that item. The menu is called context-sensitive as the items on it change depending on the object clicked.

5.   Examine the options shown (more may appear on your menu). There are a number of powerful file management shortcuts available here.

> **Note:**   **Open in a new window** lets you open the selected folder in a new window. This is sometimes useful when moving files from folder to folder. **Create shortcut** lets you create a link to this folder that can be placed elsewhere.

6.   For now, click **Rename** and then change the folder name to **Sound and Video**.

> **Note:**   A very slow double click on a file or folder's name also lets you rename it.

7.   Leave the **Section 2** data files window open for the next exercise.

2.12 Deleting Files and Folders

Files and folders can be **deleted** when they are no longer needed. This removes them from your computer and frees up space for other files and programs to use.

> **Note:**   Deleting items from your computer moves them to the **Recycle Bin** on the **Desktop**. If you delete an item accidentally it can always be found there.

Activity:

1.   With the **Section 2** data files window open from the previous exercise, click <u>once</u> on the document file **Text**.

2.   Press the <**Delete**> key on your keyboard. A prompt appears asking you to confirm that you want to delete this file.

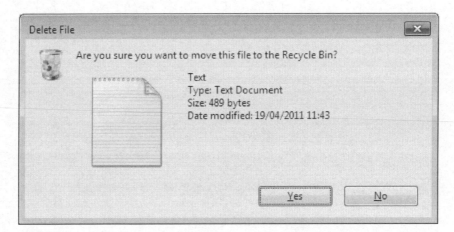

3.   Click **Yes**. The file is moved to the **Recycle Bin** (you will find out more about this later).

4.   Display the **Organize** menu and click **Undo**. Your last action is undone and the **Text** file reappears in the folder.

5.   Right click once on the **Text** file and then select **Delete** from the shortcut menu. At the prompt, select **Yes** to move the file to the **Recycle Bin** again.

6.   Next, select the **Copies** folder. Then, click the **Organize** button and select **Delete**. At the prompt, select **Yes** to move this folder to the **Recycle Bin**.

> **Note:**   Be careful: if you delete a folder, <u>all</u> of its contents will be deleted too.

7.   Use the **Organize** button to **Undo** the deletion.

8.   Select the **Copies** folder again by clicking it once. Then press <**Delete**> and select **Yes** to move the folder to the **Recycle Bin** again.

9.   Leave the **Section 2** data files window open for the next exercise.

2.13 The Recycle Bin

When files or folders are deleted they are not instantly removed from your computer. Instead, they are placed in a special folder on the **Desktop** called the **Recycle Bin**. Until the **Recycle Bin** is emptied the contents can always be restored to their original locations.

> **Note:** Once the **Recycle Bin** is emptied, the contents are permanently deleted and can no longer be recovered.

Activity:

1. **Minimize** the **Section 2** data files window to return to the **Desktop** (or click the **Show** [...] he **Taskbar**). Locate the **Recycle Bin** icon.

Recycle Bin

> [...] exercise that the icon for the **Recycle Bin** changes depending on [...] ontains deleted items.

> [...] e **Bin** icon. The contents of the **Recycle Bin** are displayed in a new [...]

> [...] of your **Recycle Bin** will depend on the files and folders you [...]

> [...] le **Text** that you deleted in the previous exercise. From the [...] **this item** button.

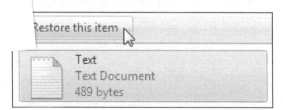

4. The file is removed from the **Recycle Bin** and restored to (i.e. put back in) its original location. Display the **Section 2** data files window again to find the **Text** file.

5. Delete the **Text** file again and it is moved back into the **Recycle Bin**.

> **Note:** Only files deleted from your own computer are placed in the **Recycle Bin**. Files deleted from external storage devices are deleted immediately, so be careful!

6. On the **Recycle Bin** window, click **Empty the Recycle Bin** on the **Toolbar**. A prompt appears asking you to confirm the permanent deletion of all items in the folder.

7. If you are absolutely sure that you do not need any files currently contained in the **Recycle Bin** folder, select **Yes**. Otherwise select **No**.

8. Close the **Recycle Bin** window and minimise the **Section 2** data files window. If you deleted the contents of the **Recycle Bin** the **Desktop** icon will now appear empty.

Recycle Bin

> **Note:** You can also empty the contents of the **Recycle Bin** by right-clicking its icon on the **Desktop** and selecting **Empty Recycle Bin**.

9. Maximise the **Section 2** data files window and leave it open for the next exercise.

2.14 Zipped Folders

Files occupy space on your computer, which only has a limited amount of storage room available. To save space you can archive older files that you no longer use by moving them into one or more **compressed** folders. This process is known as **zipping**.

As you will see in *Section 8*, it is possible to share files via the Internet or by e-mail. As zipping allows you to package multiple files into one smaller file, this technique makes it much easier and quicker to send and receive files.

Activity:

1. With the **Section 2** data files window open from the previous exercise, click <u>once</u> on the document file **Park Sections**. Notice the compressed (zipped) icon in the **Details Pane**.

Park Sections
Compressed (zipped) Folder

> **Note:** You can double click to open and view the contents of a zipped folder as you would any other folder in *Windows*. However, you cannot save any changes to the files contained within (unless you save them to a different location).

2. To work with the contents of this zipped folder, right click on it to display a shortcut menu. From the options displayed, select **Extract All**.

> **Note:** You can also drag files and folders to and from a zipped folder.

3. The **Extract Compressed (Zipped) Folders** dialog box appears. The folder path shown matches the location of the zipped file.

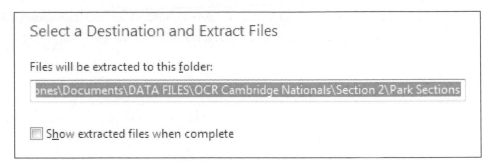

Select a Destination and Extract Files

Files will be extracted to this folder:

    ones\Documents\DATA FILES\OCR Cambridge Nationals\Section 2\Park Sections

☐ Show extracted files when complete

4. Make sure **Show extracted files when complete** is <u>not</u> selected and then click **Extract**.

5. After a moment the zipped files will be extracted and the dialog box will close automatically. Notice that a new folder, **Park Sections**, has now appeared.

6. Open the new **Park Sections** folder to reveal 9 files. You can now edit and work with these files as you would any other. Return to the **Section 2** folder.

7. Right-click the **Park Sections** <u>folder</u> and select **Properties**. The **Park Sections Properties** dialog box appears which provides information about the selected file or folder. Notice the **Size** of the folder (and all of its files) is **411 KB**.

> Note: File sizes are commonly measured in **Bytes (B)**, **KiloBytes (KB)**, **MegaBytes (MB)**, **GigaBytes (GB)**, and **TeraBytes (TB)**. There are 1024 Bytes in a KiloByte, 1024 KiloByes in a MegaByte, 1024 MegaBytes in a GigaByte, and so on.

8. Click **OK** to close the dialog box. Next, right-click the **Park Sections** <u>zip file</u> and select **Properties**. Notice the **Size** of the zip (and all of its files) is **309 KB**, smaller than the original folder. Click **OK** to close the dialog box.

9. The **Image Library** folder currently contains two files. To "zip" this folder and its contents, right click on the folder icon and select **Send to | Compressed (zipped) folder**.

| Send to | ▶ | 📁 | Compressed (zipped) folder |
| Cut | | 🖥 | Desktop (create shortcut) |

10. After a moment, the zipped folder **Image Library** appears. Press <**Enter**> to confirm the file name. The zipped folder can now be easily sent by e-mail to other people.

> Note: A zipped folder is actually a file like any other. That is why a zipped folder and a normal folder can share the same name.

11. Delete the **Image Library** and **Park Sections** folders, leaving the zipped files.

12. Close the **Section 2** data files window.

2.15 Storage Media

Information can be stored on your computer using a variety of ICT devices and "optical" media. These include internal and external hard drives, USB memory sticks, CDs and DVDs.

> **Note:** Optical media is the name given to discs such as CDs and DVDs. ICT devices use lasers to "read" or "write" data on them. CDs and DVDs are a form of read-only memory (**ROM**), but special rewritable discs can be used to store your own data.

Activity:

1. From the **Start Menu**, open **Computer**. The **Computer** view opens which shows a list of all the ICT storage devices currently connected to your computer.

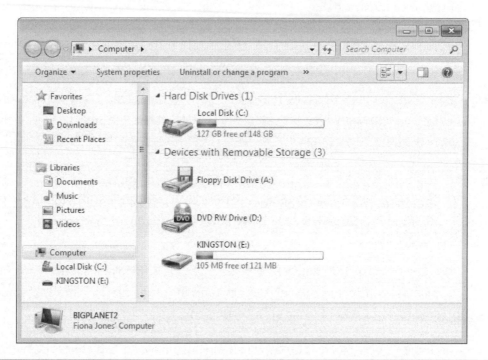

> **Note:** As external devices such as digital cameras and MP3 players have storage space to hold pictures and music, these will appear here also.

2. All devices that are connected to your computer are given a **drive letter** to identify them. Your computer's hard disk is usually given the letter **C**, your first CD or DVD reader given the letter **D**, and so on. What labels do your storage devices have?

> **Note:** To explore the contents of a device and view the files and folders contained on it, simply double click its icon. All devices connected to your computer, or available across a network, use the same folder structure as *Windows*.

3. Double click the icon for drive **C**, and then spend a moment exploring the files and folders shown. All of the files that *Windows* and your programs need to work are stored on **C**.

> **Note:** If your computer is connected to a network, you can access the storage devices of other available computers by expanding **Network** on the **Navigation Pane**.

4.   When you are finished exploring your computer's storage devices, close the **Computer** window.

2.16 Starting and Closing Programs

All programs available in *Windows* can be started using the **Start** button on the **Taskbar**. Clicking this displays the **Start Menu** that contains a list of all programs available to you. Some simple utility programs such as a **Calculator** and **Notepad** are provided with *Windows*. However, more complex and powerful software such as *Microsoft Office* needs to be obtained on CD or via a web download and **installed** manually.

> **Note:** When you **install** a program, all of the files needed to run it are automatically copied to the correct folders on your computer and the program is "registered" with *Windows*. Nearly all programs that you obtain on CD or via a web download have to be installed before they can be used.

Activity:

1.   Click the **Start** button once and then select **All Programs** to display the list of all programs that are currently installed on your computer.

2.   Click the **Accessories** folder once to open it, and then click once on **Calculator** to start the **Calculator** program. The **Start Menu** closes automatically.

3.   The **Calculator** program starts in its own window. This useful tool is ideal for performing simple calculations – try it yourself.

4. Click the **Minimize** button, . The program is minimised and appears as a button on the **Taskbar**. Although not visible, the program is still running in the background.

5. Use the **Start Menu** to start a second instance of the **Calculator** program. There are now two **Calculators** running (which can be used completely independently). Notice that *Windows* automatically groups the **Taskbar** buttons.

6. From the **Accessories** folder in the **Start Menu**, start the **Notepad** program. This useful tool allows you to create basic text files – give it a try.

> **Note:** Some programs such as antivirus utilities will start automatically when you turn your computer on. Others can be started as and when needed.

7. When you are finished, click the **Notepad** program's **Close** button, ☒. If you are prompted to save any changes that you have made, select **Don't Save**. The program is closed and is no longer running.

8. Close both instances of the **Calculator** program.

9. Next, explore some of the other programs installed on your computer by yourself. Don't be afraid to experiment and start programs that are available on the **Start Menu** – this is perfectly safe and will never cause any unwanted damage to your computer.

> **Note:** Why not try the fun **Paint** and **WordPad** programs found in **Accessories**, or the useful **Windows Media Player** that can be used to create and view your own music and video libraries?

10. When you are finished, close any open programs and return to your **Desktop**.

2.17 Introducing Microsoft Office

Microsoft Office is a collection of very powerful computer programs that are used by businesses and individuals around the world. Installed on most *Windows* computers, the package contains a number of well known programs such as *Word*, *Excel*, *PowerPoint*, *Publisher*, *Access* and *Outlook*.

Activity:

1. Click the **Start** button, and then select **All Programs** to display a list of all the programs that are currently installed on your computer.

2.   Click the **Microsoft Office** folder once to open it (this folder may be labelled slightly differently depending on how *Office* was installed). A list of programs appears, including:

Application	Description
Word	A word processing program for creating documents.
Excel	A program for creating spreadsheets.
Access	A program for creating databases.
PowerPoint	A program for creating and giving presentations.
Publisher	A desktop publishing program for creating publications.
Outlook	An e-mail, calendar and task management program.

3.   Locate and click once on **Microsoft Word 2010** to start the program. After a moment, the program's **user interface** will appear.

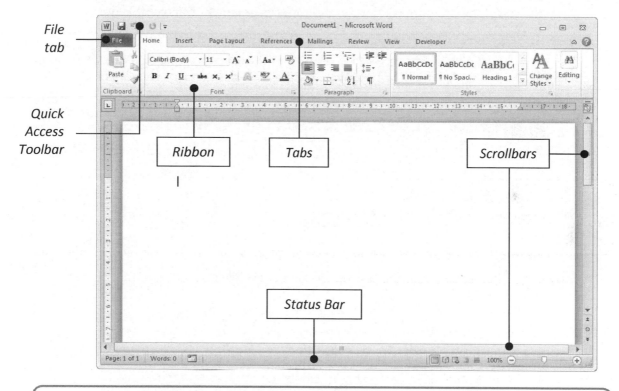

File tab

Quick Access Toolbar

Ribbon

Tabs

Scrollbars

Status Bar

Note: If any **dialog boxes** "pop up" (short messages that require user input), always read the message text provided and consider your actions before responding.

4.   Familiarise yourself with the various parts of the *Microsoft Word* window. All programs in the *Microsoft Office* collection use the same basic screen layout:

Quick Access Toolbar	Commands which you use most often are placed here, such as **Save**, **Undo** and **Redo**,

Ribbon	The **Ribbon** is a collection of program commands that appears across the top of all *Office* programs. Commands are placed into related groups so that they are easier to find.
Tabs	Each tab, when clicked, shows a different set of program commands on the **Ribbon**. Depending on what you are doing, other tabs may also temporarily appear here.
File Tab	The **File** tab shows a number of commands to control file opening, saving and closing. Printing and help features are also available here.
Scrollbars	Scrollbars allow you to move around a page of information that is too big to fit on your screen.
Status Bar	Useful program information and notifications appear here.

Note: Notice that the name of the program and the file you are working on are shown at the top of the program window; in this case **Document 1 - Microsoft Word**.

5. Examine the **Ribbon**. The **Home** tab is currently selected and a number of program commands are shown.

Home tab

Font group

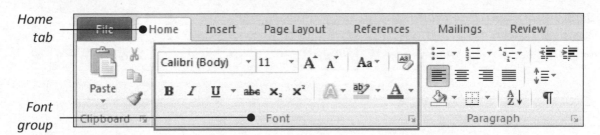

6. Locate the **Font** group and, without clicking, place your mouse pointer over the **Bold** button, **B**. After a moment, a **ToolTip** will appear explaining the use of that button.

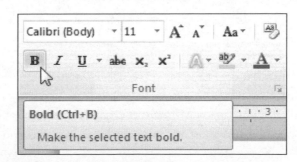

Note: **ToolTips** are really useful for finding out the purpose of a program command. Most buttons that appear on the **Ribbon** will feature a **ToolTip** that describe their use.

7. Click the **Insert** tab on the **Ribbon**. A number of program commands for inserting items into the on-screen document appears, again arranged into related groups.

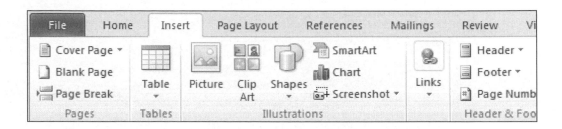

> **Note:** You will find that many *Microsoft Office* programs share the same **Ribbon** tabs. The **Ribbon** will stay on screen at all times, but can be minimized by clicking the **Minimize the Ribbon** button, ⌃, located to the right of the tab titles.

8. Click the special **File** tab to reveal a number of program features for saving, opening, printing, protecting and creating new files. You will learn more about these in later sections. For now, click the **Home** tab again to return without making any changes.

9. To close *Microsoft Word*, click once on the program's **Close** button, ⌧.

10. If you are prompted to save any changes, select **Don't Save**. The program is closed and is no longer running.

11. Use the **Start Menu** to start each of the other *Microsoft Office* applications: *Excel*, *PowerPoint*, *Publisher*, *Access*, and *Outlook*. Familiarise yourself with the screen layout of each application and notice the similarities between them.

12. When you are finished, close any open programs and return to your **Desktop**.

2.18 Opening and Closing Files

Saved files can be opened in one of two ways: you can start a compatible program and use its **Open** command to locate a file, or you can simply double click a file in **Windows Explorer** to open it in its default program. In general, files should only be opened in the program that created them.

Activity:

1. Use the **Start Menu** to start *Microsoft Word*. When the program window appears, display the **File** tab and select **Open**.

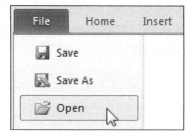

2. The **Open** dialog box appears which shows a **Windows Explorer** view of your **Documents** library. Locate the data files for this section.

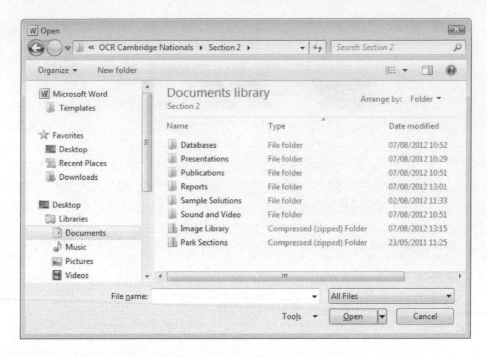

3.   Open the **Publications** folder and click once to select **Park News**.

> Note: Notice the drop-down button labelled **All Files**. This can be used to show only certain types of files (e.g. *Word* documents, *Excel* worksheets, and so on).

4.   Click the **Open** button. The **Park News** document is opened and displayed on-screen, ready for editing. It is a short newsletter describing a new ride at the theme park.

5.   Display the **File** tab and select **Close**. The document is now closed again.

> Note: The technique described here can be used to open and close files in nearly all *Windows* programs. Files can also be opened by double clicking them in **Windows Explorer**, as you will see later.

6.   Leave *Word* open for the next exercise.

2.19 Creating and Saving Files

To create a new file in *Windows* (e.g. a document, spreadsheet, presentation, publication or database), you must first choose the program best suited to create that type of file (e.g. *Word*, *Excel*, *PowerPoint*, *Publisher* or *Access*).

In this exercise you will create and save a *Word* document. The technique described can be used to create and save files of different types in nearly all other *Windows* programs.

Activity:

1.   Using *Microsoft Word*, display the **File** tab and select **New**.

2.   A list of possible document types appears. With **Blank document** selected under **Available Templates**, click the **Create** button found towards the right side of the window.

3.   A new *Microsoft Word* document is created. At the moment this file only exists in your computer's memory and will be lost when your computer is turned off. To save the document as a file so that you can use it later, display the **File** tab and select **Save**.

4.   As this document has not yet been saved, the **Save As** dialog box appears which shows a **Windows Explorer** view of your **Documents** library. Locate the data files for this section.

5.   Find the text in the **File name** box. Change this to **empty document**.

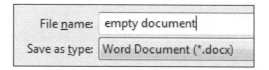

> **Note:**   Notice the **Save as type** drop-down box. This can be used to save a file in a different format so that it can be opened in other programs.

6.   Click **Save**. The **Save As** dialog box is closed and the document is saved (the file name has now appeared on the **Title Bar**).

> **Note:**   Saving the document again will overwrite the contents of the last saved file. You will not be prompted to enter another file name. If you wish to save the file with a different name, use **Save As** instead.

7.   Display the **File** tab and **Info** is automatically selected. Notice the file properties shown on the right side of the screen which describe the currently open file.

8.   Close *Microsoft Word* and the open file is closed automatically.

9.   Open the **Documents** library and locate your new saved file in the **Section 2** folder.

> **Note:**   Files and folders that you create in your **Desktop** or library folders can only be accessed by <u>you</u> (after logging in). This is because your private folders have **access rights** (called **permissions**) which prevent other people from opening them. If you want, you can **share** folders with others connected to your network using the **Share with** button on the **Windows Explorer Toolbar**.

10.   Leave the **Documents** window open for the next exercise.

2.20 Finding Information

Over time you will create and save a lot of files. However, trying to find a specific piece of information amongst all of these files and folders can sometimes be like trying to find a needle in a haystack. Luckily, the *Windows* search features are on hand to help.

Activity:

1. With the **Section 2** data files window open from the previous exercise, click <u>once</u> in the **Search** box at the top right and enter the keywords **theme park**.

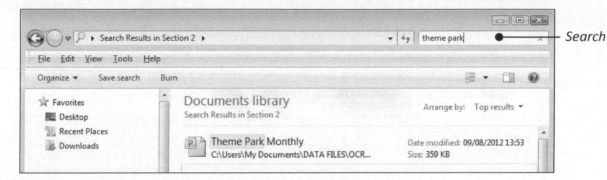

2. As you type, *Windows* automatically searches for files matching the search criteria and displays the results. The keyword text can appear in file or folder names or in the actual contents of a file itself.

> **Note:**   The *Windows* search feature is not a replacement for a good, well-designed and meaningfully labelled folder structure.

3. Double click the entry in the search results list titled **Theme Park Monthly**. *Windows* recognises that this file is a **publication** and starts the program *Microsoft Publisher*.

4. This file contains a short monthly newsletter for staff at the theme park. Close *Publisher*.

5. To clear the search results click the **Clear** button, ☒, in the **Search** box once (<u>not</u> the window's **Close** button). The contents of the **Section 2** data files folder reappear.

> **Note:**   The small text box located at the bottom of the *Windows* **Start Menu** can also be used to search for files or programs.

6. Close the **Section 2** data files window.

> **Note:**   You can also use this search technique when exploring the contents of any data storage media, such as CDs and DVDs, USB memory sticks and external hard drives, and even local internal networks. Of course, a lot of information can also be found on the Internet nowadays, which you will learn more about in Section 8.

2.21 Control Panel

The *Windows* **Control Panel** contains tools that control how the *Windows* environment looks and performs. For example, the sound volume, screen resolution, date, time and background picture can all be changed from here.

Any changes made on the **Control Panel** are saved until changed again, and any changes made will still be in effect after closing and restarting *Windows*.

Activity:

1.   Click the **Start** button and, from the list on the right, select **Control Panel**.

2.   The **Control Panel** window opens. Notice that the various settings are grouped under related headings.

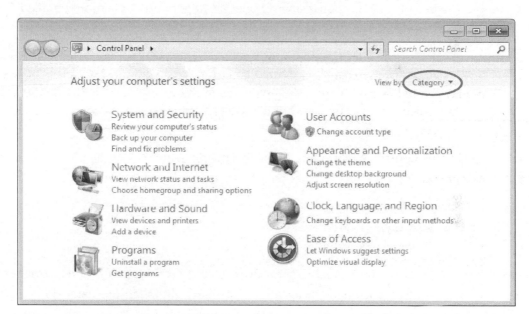

> **Note:**   If the **Control Panel** does not appear as shown above, make sure that **Category** is selected in the **View by** drop-down list.

3.   Examine the various options available on this screen. These allow you to do the following:

Category	Description
System and Security	Adjust your computer's security settings, back-up files, change power options and update your software.
Network and Internet	Share files and change how your computer connects to a local network or the Internet.

Hardware and Sound	Add, remove and configure the hardware attached to your computer including mice, printers and internal display and sound devices.
Programs	Manage the programs that are installed on your computer, or remove them altogether.
User Accounts	Add or remove computer users and change account details, security levels and passwords.
Appearance and Personalisation	Change the way *Windows* looks, from desktop backgrounds to text colours and sizes.
Clock, Language and Region	Change your computer's date and time, and alter regional settings such as language and currency.
Ease of Access	Useful settings to allow you to more easily access your computer if you are vision, hearing or mobility impaired.

Note: You can place your mouse pointer over a category title for a more detailed **ToolTip**.

Note: Depending on your **User Account** type (accessible via **User Accounts**), you may be restricted from making significant changes to your computer. As a rule, if you are connected to a network, only the person in charge of that network (known as the **Administrator**) will be allowed to make changes that affect other users.

4.   Leave the **Control Panel** open. In the following exercises you will explore some of the categories described in more detail.

2.22 File Extensions

Nearly every file in *Windows* has a **file extension**; a short combination of letters that identifies a file's **type** (e.g. a *Word* document or *Excel* spreadsheet). Although file extensions are normally hidden in **Windows Explorer**, it is still important that you learn how to recognise them.

Activity:

1.   With the **Control Panel** open, click once on **Appearance and Personalization**.

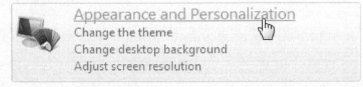

2.   A second list of system settings is displayed. Select **Folder Options** to display the **Folder Options** dialog box. From here you can adjust a number of settings which control how files and folders are displayed in *Windows*.

3. Click the **View** tab at the top of the dialog box and uncheck **Hide extensions for known file types** (if it is not unchecked already).

4. Click **OK** to apply the change and close the dialog box.

> **Note:** Any changes you make in the **Control Panel** will only affect you. The settings for other users will not be affected.

5. Minimise the **Control Panel**, open your **Documents** library and navigate to the **Section 2** data files. Notice that the two zipped files created earlier now have **zip** file extensions.

📄 Image Library.zip   📄 Park Sections.zip

> **Note:** File extensions appear after a full stop in the file name. As such, if you change a file's name, make sure you do not accidentally change the file extension also.

6. Open the **Reports** folder. There is one *Microsoft Excel* spreadsheet present with an **xlsx** file extension and two *Microsoft Word* documents with **docx** extensions.

7. Examine the table below and familiarise yourself with some of the most popular file extensions used today. The **Section 2** data files folder contains many of these file types.

> **Note:** Compressed video, audio and image files can be **lossy** or **lossless**. If they are lossy, a *little* quality is usually lost when the file is compressed.

Extension	File Type
docx/doc	*Microsoft Word* document
xlsx/xls	*Microsoft Excel* spreadsheet
pptx/ppt	*Microsoft PowerPoint* presentation
accdb/mdb	*Microsoft Access* database
pub	*Microsoft Publisher* publication
pdf	*Adobe's* portable document format
fla/swf	*Adobe's Flash* animation format
wma/mp3/aac	Compressed, lossy audio files
wav/aiff	Uncompressed, lossless audio files
mov/avi/mp4	Compressed, lossy movie files

jpg/gif	Compressed, lossy graphics or photo files
png/tiff/bmp	Uncompressed, lossless graphics or photo files
txt	A plain text file
rtf	A text file with rich text formatting
csv	A text file containing comma separated values
htm/html	General web page format
zip	A zipped file or folder
exe	A program that will run when double clicked

> **Note:** File formats are either **proprietary** or **open**. Proprietary formats are developed by software companies such as *Microsoft* and only their software will be able to read the data correctly. Open file formats can be read by many types of software.

8. Close the **Section 2** data files window and use the **Control Panel** to **Hide extensions for known file types** again.

9. Return to the **Control Panel's** main starting screen by clicking **Control Panel Home** (located on the window's **Navigation Pane**) and leave it open for the next exercise.

2.23 Display Settings

The display quality of the information that you see on your computer screen – words, pictures, videos – is directly affected by **screen resolution**. The higher your resolution the more crisp and clear your display becomes but the smaller everything appears. *Windows* will usually choose the best screen resolution for you automatically, but if you find this uncomfortable to work with you can manually choose a more appropriate setting.

If you continue to find it difficult to read text in *Windows* you can also adjust your computer's font sizes. A range of more advanced **accessibility** features is also available to help those with low vision interact with and use a computer more effectively.

Activity:

1. With the **Control Panel** open, click once on **Appearance and Personalization** again.

2. Examine the various options that appear to see what changes are possible.

> **Note:** Notice the various settings available to change your desktop background picture, theme colours (i.e. default text and window colour), and **Taskbar** and **Start Menu** options.

3. Click once on **Display**. Read the description of this setting and click on each of the three size options in turn to see a small preview. Selecting **Medium** or **Larger** would increase *Windows'* font and icon sizes.

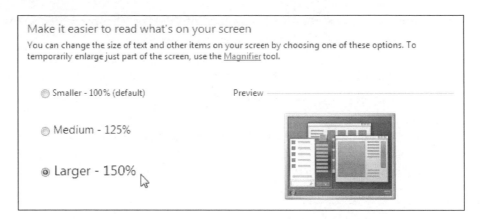

4. From the **Navigation Pane** on the left, select **Adjust resolution**. From here it is possible to change the screen resolution.

5. Drop down the **Resolution** box and examine the various screen resolutions available.

> **Note:**   At *Big Planet Theme Park* the computers use a resolution of 1024x768. This means that there are 1024 pixels (or single coloured dots) displayed in a grid across the screen and 768 down the screen.

6. Click **Cancel** to return to the **Display** settings without making any changes.

7. Click once on **Appearance and Personalization** on the **Address Bar** to return directly to that screen.

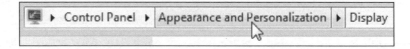

8. Select **Ease of Access Center** to view a number of settings for users with low vision. The **High Contrast** setting and **Magnifier** are particularly useful.

9. Return to the **Control Panel's** main starting screen by clicking **Control Panel Home**.

2.24 Sound Settings

Sound settings in *Windows* are grouped into two main categories: **Playback** and **Recording**. **Playback** controls how sounds are made by your computer; **Recording** controls how sounds are captured by your computer.

Activity:

1. With the **Control Panel** open, click once on **Hardware and Sound**. Examine the various options that appear to see what changes are possible, and then select **Sound**.

2. The **Sound** dialog box opens. Display each of the tabs (**Playback**, **Recording**, **Sounds** and **Communications**) and explore the various options available.

3. Return to the **Playback** tab. The default device inside your computer used for playing sound is displayed with a tick symbol, ✅.

4. Select this default device and click the **Properties** button, Properties .

5. On the **Speakers Properties** dialog box display the **Levels** tab. You can adjust your computer's playback volume here.

> Note: An icon to adjust sound volume may also be available in the **Notification Area** on the **Taskbar**, 🔊. Click this icon once to quickly adjust audio playback levels.

6. Click **Cancel** to return to the **Sound** dialog box without making changes. Next, display the **Recording** tab and view the **Properties** of your default recording device.

7. Explore the settings available, and then click **Cancel** to return to the **Sound** dialog box without making changes.

8. Click **Cancel** again to close the **Sound** dialog box. Then, return to the **Control Panel's** main starting screen by clicking **Control Panel Home**.

2.25 Windows Firewall

Windows Firewall is used to help keep a network-connected computer safe and prevent other people from remotely gaining access. It is simply a piece of utility software that automatically monitors incoming and outgoing data and stops any unauthorised access to system files.

Activity:

1. With the **Control Panel** open, click once on **System and Security**. Examine the various options that appear to see what changes are possible, and then select **Windows Firewall**.

2. Familiarise yourself with the options available on this screen.

> Note: Three **network locations** are shown: **Domain networks**, **Home or work (private) networks**, and **Public networks**. You will probably be connected to one of these.

Home or work (private) networks   Connected

> **Note:** When you connect an ICT device to a new network for the <u>first</u> time, *Windows* will prompt you to choose a network location type for it. Depending on your choice, *Windows* will automatically set up, save and apply the best security settings.

3.   Click the expand button, , to the right of each network location to view the settings for that connection type. Read the short description that appears for each location:

Network Location	Description	Security
Domain networks	Networks at a workplace that are attached to a domain (a domain is the name given to a company network).	Lowest
Home or work (private) networks	Networks at home or work where you know and trust the people and devices on the network.	Medium
Public networks	Networks in public places such as airports or coffee shops.	Highest

> **Note:** So, when you connect your *Windows* device to a public network (e.g. a Wi-Fi hotspot at a café) choose **Public networks**. This prevents other people from accessing your computer. At home, where you may want to exchange files and share resources between devices, select **Home or work (private) networks**.

4.   Click the **Back** button once to return to the **System and Security** screen.

2.26 Software Updates

As bugs and security problems are found in *Windows* and other *Microsoft* programs, the creators release updates to fix the errors. It is therefore important that you download these updates to keep your computer running well. Luckily, **Windows Update** will do this automatically for you.

Activity:

1.   With the **System and Security** screen open, click once on **Windows Update**. If your computer has all of the latest updates installed, this message will appear.

Windows is up to date
There are no updates available for your computer.

> **Note:**   Keeping your computer up-to-date protects it from malware and hackers.

2. Windows will usually check for updates automatically and install them when you shut down your computer (which you should always let it do). To check for and install updates manually, click **Check for updates** on the **Navigation Pane**. Do that now.

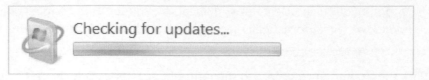

3. Checking for updates will take a little time to complete. While *Windows* is searching, click **Change settings** on the **Navigation Pane**. Examine the settings available on this screen.

> Note: If you are using a public or shared computer, it is possible that only the network **Administrator** will be able to make changes here.

4. Click the **Back** button to return to the **Windows Update** screen. If the check has finished, there may be updates available to download and install. <u>Do not</u> do this now.

> Note: It can sometimes take a long time to download and install updates, and you may need to restart your computer a number of times during the process. Consider returning to this screen at the end of this section and completing the update.

5. Click the **Back** button once to return to the **System and Security** screen. Don't worry if *Windows* is still searching for updates – it will continue to do so in the background until it is finished (a pop-up in the **Notification Area** will appear if updates are found).

> Note: Different types of software have other ways of searching for and downloading updates. If a program that you trust informs you that an update is available, it is always a good idea to download and install it.

2.27 Backing Up

Regular **backing up** is essential if you have important data stored on your computer that you cannot lose. In business, this is often done daily. At home, you may decide to backup your personal files less frequently (perhaps only once a month or so). Of course, the more regularly you backup, the less chance you have of losing recent changes and new files.

> Note: For security reasons, storage capacity and ease of use, it is recommended that you backup to a removable hard drive rather than a CD, DVD or USB memory stick.

If your computer suffers a hardware failure (which unfortunately happens more often than you might think), you can then use the backup to **restore** your data. This copies the files and folders stored in the backup back onto your (fixed) computer.

Windows has a built-in **Backup and Restore** feature which makes backing up and restoring files easy. However, as this process requires a backup device, we will only take a brief look at the settings available.

Activity:

1. With the **System and Security** screen open, click once on **Backup and Restore**. Examine the options that appear.

> Note: There are two main types of backup in *Windows*. You can either backup all of your personal files and folders, or you can backup the entire computer (**Create a system image**). The first option is recommended as it is the fastest and easiest.

2. If you have never created a backup before – and would like to do so – click **Set up backup**.

3. After a moment, the **Set up backup** dialog box appears. You are first prompted to select a location to store your backup (from the list of ICT storage devices currently connected to your computer).

> Note: Note that you can also **Save on a network**. However, for smaller LANs, it is better to save your backup to an external storage device and then take it off-site.

4. If you have a backup device connected to your computer, select it from the **Backup Destination** list and click **Next**. If not, just read steps **5** and **6** and then click **Cancel**.

5. It is best to let *Windows* find and backup all of your files and folders automatically. To do this, make sure **Let Windows choose** is selected and then click **Next**.

> Note: By default, *Windows* will now schedule a backup to occur automatically at the same time each week (7pm on a Sunday night). For the backup to occur, your computer must be switched on and your backup storage device connected. If you prefer, you can run the backup manually instead at any time you like.

6. If you would like to perform the backup now, click **Save settings and run backup**. If not, click **Cancel**. As it can take a long time to run the backup, it may be best to do this later!

> Note: To restore data, simply make sure the backup device is connected and select the option to **Restore my files** on the **Backup and Restore** screen.

7.   Return to the **Control Panel's** main starting screen by clicking **Control Panel Home**.

> **Note:**   As each backup you make often overwrites the last one, businesses will from time to time make a second copy of a backup on separate ICT storage media. This is never deleted and provides a "snapshot" of data that can be returned to at a later date (if needed). These special types of backup are called **archives**.

2.28 Printers

Printers are a great way to produce hard copies of information stored on your computer. Using *Windows* it is easy to find, manage and use peripheral printer devices that are connected to both your own computer and to computers elsewhere on your network.

> **Note:**   Think before you print! Unnecessary printing is a waste of resources and money.

Activity:

1.   With the **Control Panel** open, locate the **Hardware and Sound** group and click once on **View devices and printers**.

2.   The **Devices and Printers** view appears showing all external connected devices and available printers.

> **Note:**   A direct link to the **Devices and Printers** view is available on the **Start Menu**.

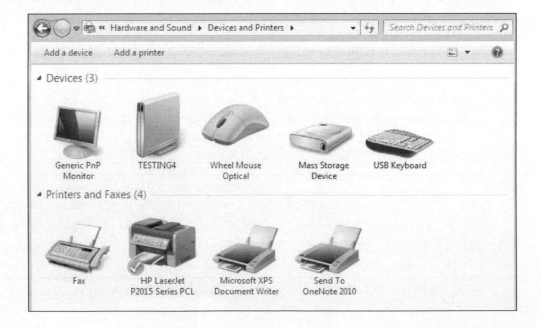

> **Note:** Your view will show a different set of device and printer icons. Your default printer, if you have one, is shown with a tick symbol, ✅.

> **Note:** It is also possible to add a new printer to the selection available. Clicking **Add a printer** starts the **Add Printer** wizard which guides you through the process.

3. If a printer is available, click once to select its icon. Notice that a number of additional options specific to that printer now appear on the **Toolbar**.

| See what's printing | Print server properties | Remove device |

> **Note:** The default printer is the printer used when printing from a program. To choose a different printer as the default, right-click an icon and select **Set as default printer**.

4. Click **See what's printing**. A window appears which lists all items that are currently waiting to be printed (this is likely to be empty). This is known as a **print queue**.

> **Note:** Items in a printer's queue can be **Paused**, **Restarted** or **Cancelled** using the **Document** menu. If a paper jam occurs on the printer, these settings can be used to restart the print after you have resolved the problem.

5. Close the printer queue window by clicking the **Close** button, ❌.

6. To adjust the default settings for a printer, right click on the printer icon and select **Printing preferences** from the shortcut menu.

7. Click each of the tabs at the top of the dialog box that appears to see which aspects of the printer's operation can be changed.

8. When you are finished, click **Cancel** to close the dialog box without making any changes.

> **Note:** All external devices such as printers, mice, keyboards and storage devices need **driver software** in order to work. Drivers are small pieces of software that instruct *Windows* how to use a device and are usually found and installed automatically when you connect new hardware to your computer. If they are not, you can often find the software on a disc or website that accompanies the device.

9. Close the **Control Panel** window to return to the **Desktop**.

2.29 Program Crashes

> **Note:** Saving your work regularly will help avoid data loss as a result of program crashes.

Every once in a while a program will stop working when you are using it, often with little or no warning. In this case the program is said to have **crashed**. Fortunately, this does not happen very often, but when it does it is very easy to close and then restart the program.

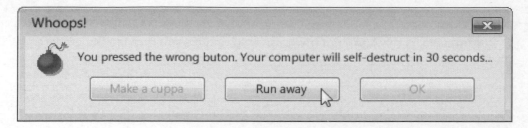

Activity:

1. Using the **Start Menu**, start the **Calculator** program.

2. Assume this program has crashed and stopped working. When this happens the program will no longer respond to mouse clicks and key presses – it is said to be **frozen**. In many cases you will not be able to use the **Close** button to end the program.

> Note: *Windows* will often automatically detect a program that has stopped working and offer to close or restart it for you. In this case it is always worthwhile waiting a few minutes to see if the program starts working again on its own.

3. To force the program to close, press the key combination <**Ctrl Alt Del**>.

4. From the options that appear, select **Start Task Manager**. The **Windows Task Manager** dialog box appears.

5. Display the **Applications** tab to find the **Calculator** program running (other programs may appear here also).

6. Select **Calculator** from the list and click **End Task**. The **Calculator** program is closed immediately.

7. Close the **Task Manager** to return to the **Desktop**.

> Note: Many problems with your computer or external devices can be solved by simply turning them off and back on again. It's amazing how often this works!

2.30 Next Steps

Well done! You have now completed all of the exercises in this section. If you feel you are ready to test your knowledge and understanding of the topics covered, move on to the following **Develop Your Skills** activities. If there are any features of *Microsoft Windows* covered in this section that you are unsure about, you should revisit the appropriate exercises and try them again before moving on.

At the end of every section you get the chance to complete two activities. These will help you to develop your skills and prepare for your exam. Don't forget to use the planning and review checklists at the back of the book to help organise and review your work.

> **Note:** Answers to these activities are provided in this section's **Sample Solutions** folder.

Develop Your Skills: Creating a Folder Structure

In this activity you will be asked to create a simple *Windows* folder structure for *Fiona*. You will need to use all of the ICT skills that you have learned in this section to plan, develop and present an appropriate solution.

Activity 1

Starting soon, the reception desk team will handle all customer enquiries about the theme park's latest ride: *Rumbling Rails*. To allow us to respond to questions and requests for information quickly and efficiently, we first need to prepare a folder structure to store all of the information about the new ride.

The files won't arrive until next week, but we need to prepare by creating the folder structure as soon as possible. If I describe the types of files that are coming, would you create the folders for me?

Firstly, we need a new folder called **Rumbling Rails**. Inside that folder create a structure of subfolders to accommodate files of the following types:

* *Promotional materials*, containing separate *leaflets*, *flyers* and *brochures*

* *Videos* of the new ride, separated into *small*, *medium* and *large* files

* *Pictures* of the ride, separated into *small*, *medium* and *large* files

* A range of documents containing information on ride *statistics*

Create this structure in the **Section 2** data files folder. Remember: the folder names need to be meaningful so that the relevant files can be found easily later on.

Develop Your Skills: File Management Theory

In this activity, *Fiona* has received three different enquiries from theme park staff. You will need to use the ICT skills that you have learned in this section to help her provide a suitable answer to each of the questions asked.

Activity 2

Zahra from *Pirate's Cove* has just called in to the reception desk. She is preparing a training course for new employees and would like to get hold of the park's **Health and Safety PowerPoint** presentation. This file is currently stored on *Fiona's* computer; what's the best way to give *Zahra* a copy? You'll have to be quick as she's waiting for it!

Notes:

Hassan from customer services has called into reception looking for advice. He is using a brand new computer to record visitor contact details and has accumulated a lot of data. However, he's worried about his computer breaking down and all of that valuable information being lost. What advice can you give *Hassan* to prevent this from happening?

Notes:

One of my colleagues is having problems with her printer, so *John* from the *IT Centre* has installed a lovely new one – it scans and copies too! However, whenever she tries to print, the old one still appears as the default printer. Can you explain how she can change her computer's settings so that the new printer is selected by default?

Notes:

© CiA Training Ltd 2012

SECTION 13 | Microsoft Word

3 | Microsoft Word

Hi, my name's Priti...

I'm a member of the ride construction team here at *Big Planet Theme Park*. We've just finished building a brand new roller coaster called *Rumbling Rails* – a thrilling high speed train ride through rocky canyons and icy mountain passes!

My role in the park's construction team is to evaluate building plans and make sure environmental regulations are followed. Most of the time this involves using a computer to collect and analyse data on-site. However, it's also my job to communicate my findings to others in a variety of different ways. To do this, I use the word processing application *Microsoft Word* to create professional reports and documents quickly and easily.

You have probably used *Microsoft Word* many times in your life already. If you've ever used a computer to write a letter, essay or short story then you will already know how to use basic word processing features. However, did you know that word processors are just as popular and useful in business? In fact, people working in a variety of different professions use them all of the time to create a wide range of reports, memos, mailings and newsletters.

What you will learn:

In this section you will use the program *Microsoft Word* to help *Priti* complete a number of everyday tasks at *Big Planet Theme Park*. You will see how to use simple word processing techniques to design, create and edit professional documents for a variety of purposes.

Knowledge, skills and understanding:

* Use *Microsoft Word* to create and edit professional word-processed documents

* Learn how to use the best tools and features to solve a range of everyday problems

* Apply professional editing, formatting and layout techniques

Data files

The files needed to complete the activities in this section are provided in the **Section 3** data folder (see note on page **vii** to download these files). Documents that you create or edit can be saved to the same folder.

3.1 Using Microsoft Word

One of the most common types of computer program in use today – at home, in education and at work – is the word processing application. This popular type of software enables you to produce professional, well-styled documents for many different purposes. Typical word processed documents you can create include:

* Letters and marketing "mail shots"

* Brochures, newsletters, books and documentation

* Reports, essays and memos

Microsoft Word is a word processing application that is an appropriate choice for any task that requires a largely text based solution, particularly if printed output is required. The entry and formatting of text is easily handled by such a program, as is the ability to include different types of object such as images and charts. Perhaps more important is the application's ability to present text professionally using a variety of alignment tools and tables.

> Note: Many of the simple text editing and formatting techniques taught in this section also apply to most other *Microsoft Office* programs.

Another important advantage of *Microsoft Word* is its widespread use. Most people will have this program installed on their computer and will know how to use it. This makes it easy to send documents to others by e-mail, and if your solution needs to be changed by others (perhaps if you are working on a project together) then it is highly likely they will be able to do so.

3.2 Inserting and Deleting Text

In a word processing application, any key pressed on an ICT device's keyboard appears in the document at the **insertion point** (where the **cursor** flashes). Each letter, number or symbol typed in is called a **character**.

Entering text into a document is easy | ● —— *Insertion point or cursor*

The cursor can be moved to any place where text *already* exists by pointing and clicking (or by using the arrow keys on the keyboard). New text that you type is inserted at the cursor position, and text that is already there can be deleted using the <**Delete**> or <**Backspace**> keys.

> Note: Recall from Section 1 that the keyboard and mouse are known as **input devices**, as they allow you to enter information into a computer or other ICT device. Monitors and printers are known as **output devices**.

> **Note:** The <**Delete**> key removes characters one at a time to the right of the cursor. The <**Backspace**> key removes characters one at a time to the left.

Backspace —

Enter —

Shift —

— *Delete*

— *Arrows*

> **Note:** The layout of your keyboard may appear differently to that shown above.

When a line of text reaches the right edge of the area you in which you can type, it will automatically move onto the next line (this is called **word wrap**). You only need to press <**Enter**> if you want to move onto a new line before you reach the end of the current one. This is called a **paragraph break** as it is used to break the current line of text and start a new paragraph.

> **Note:** A paragraph is a block of text that is made up from one or more related sentences that are grouped together. New paragraphs always start on a new line.

Activity:

1. Start *Microsoft Word* and open the document **Progress Report** from the data files folder. *Priti* wants to send this simple document to the rest of her team, but it contains a number of small errors that must be corrected first.

2. Display the **View** tab on the **Ribbon** and locate the **Document Views** group. Make sure **Print Layout** view is selected.

> **Note:** There are 5 main ways to view a document in *Word*. The default **Print Layout** view shows your document as it will look when printed and is generally the best view to use. In this section it will be assumed that you are using **Print Layout** view.

3. To allow you to see more detail in a document, you can **zoom** in. On the **Status Bar** at the bottom right of the screen, click the **Zoom In** button to increase the zoom level to **110%**.

4. Click the **Zoom In** button four more times to increase the zoom level to **150%**.

5.   This does not change the size of the document, just your view of it. From the **Zoom** group on the **View** tab, click the **100%** button to reset the zoom level to normal.

100% button —————————

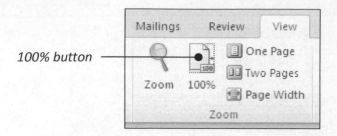

> **Note:**   If you find it easier on your eyes, or if you simply want to see more detail, you can increase the zoom level for your documents at any time during this section.

6.   Click once in the middle of the word **unpacked** on the first numbered line.

> – in the process of being unpacked.

7.   Characters to the left of the cursor are deleted by pressing the <**Backspace**> key, and characters to the right of the cursor are deleted using the <**Delete**> key. Delete the word **unpacked** using these key presses.

8.   In its place type the word **tested**.

> **Note:**   To type a capital letter or one of the symbols printed on the top of a key, e.g. **%**, **£**, **@**, **?**, hold down the <**Shift**> key first.

9.   There is an error in the report's title. Change **Rambling Rails** to **Rumbling Rails**.

10. Change the date to today's date.

11. On the second numbered line, remove the word **almost**.

> **Note:**   You can use the <**Caps Lock**> key if you are typing a lot of capitalised text. Pressing the <**Caps Lock**> key turns the feature on; pressing it again turns it off.

12. On the third numbered line, change the *Dollar* symbol (**$**) to a *Pound* symbol (**£**).

13. In the last paragraph of text, change the day of the meeting from **Thursday** to **Friday**.

14. From the **Quick Access Toolbar** at the top left of the screen, click **Undo**, [↶]. The last edit is undone and **Thursday** is replaced.

> **Note:**   The **Undo** button is a really useful feature in *Office*. It allows you to undo changes and correct mistakes by stepping back through each action one step at a time.

15. From the **Quick Access Toolbar**, click **Redo**, 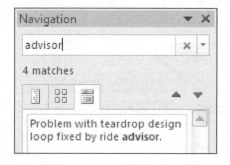. This repeats the last edit again and **Friday** reappears.

> Note: You can also use <**Ctrl Z**> to **Undo** actions and <**Ctrl Y**> to **Redo** actions.

16. Place the cursor at the end of the last paragraph (after the word **present.**). Create a space and enter the following sentence: **If you would like to attend please let me know.**

> Note: When typing text, it is good practice to leave a single space after punctuation marks such as full stops, commas, exclamation and question marks.

17. Press <**Enter**> to start a new paragraph. Press <**Enter**> again to leave a blank line and start another paragraph.

> Note: Holding <**Shift**> and pressing <**Enter**> creates a **line break**. Unlike a paragraph break which creates a new paragraph, the new line is still part of the same paragraph. This is sometimes useful when formatting documents.

18. Type your own name at the bottom of the report.

19. Use the **File** tab to save the document with the file name **latest progress report**, and leave the document open for the next exercise.

3.3 Finding and Replacing Text

The **Find** and **Replace** features in *Word* allow you to quickly search for and easily change specific pieces of text in your documents.

Activity:

1. With the document **latest progress report** open, click the **Find** button, [🔍 Find], in the **Editing** group on the **Home** tab. The **Navigation** task pane appears and the cursor is shown flashing in the **Search** box.

2. Type the word **advisor**. As you type, *Word* will automatically search for and highlight words that match your search criteria. Four matches will eventually be found.

3. Notice that a small extract from each paragraph where the word is found is displayed in the **Navigation** pane. Click each extract in turn to select that match in the main text.

4. Close the **Navigation** task pane (by clicking the small ☒ at the top right of the panel) and then place the cursor at the start of the document (in front of the main title text).

> Note: The keyboard shortcut <**Ctrl Home**> will take you to the start of a document.

5. From the **Editing** group, click **Replace**, ᵃᵇ Replace . The **Find and Replace** dialog box appears.

6. The search text **advisor** should appear automatically in the **Find what** box (as it was the last search performed). If it does not, enter it now.

7. In the **Replace with** box, enter the word **expert** and then click the **Replace All** button. Each instance of the word **advisor** is replaced with the word **expert**. A dialog box appears informing you that **4 replacements** have been made.

> Note: The **Replace** button can be used to replace each occurrence of the search text one instance at a time. If you do not want to replace a specific match, you can use the **Find Next** button to skip to the next occurrence.

8. Click **OK** and then **Close** to dismiss the **Find and Replace** dialog box.

9. Save the document using the same file name and close it.

3.4 Basic Text Formatting

There are many text formatting tools available in *Microsoft Word* that you should already be familiar with. For example, you can make text **bold**, *italic* or **underlined**, you can adjust the **font type** and **size**, and you can apply a variety of **colours** to draw the reader's eye to certain important pieces of information. There is also specialised formatting that can be applied such as **superscript**, **subscript** and **double underline**.

All text formatting options are available in the **Font** group on the **Home** tab.

Activity:

1. Open the file **Memo**. This practice document contains 18 plain lines of text, each of which needs to be correctly formatted.

> Note: To format a specific piece of text you must first **select** it. To do this, use your mouse to click and drag from the start of the required text to the end.

2. Complete the document by formatting each line so that it matches its own description. At your level you should be able to apply the required formatting without any help.

> This line is underlined.
>
> ***This line is bold, italic and underlined.***
>
> This line is double underlined.

> Note: Used properly, different text styles can help emphasise information and make it easier to read. It can also give your documents a more professional appearance. However, too many text styles and colours can have the reverse effect.

3. Save the document as **memo complete** and close it.

3.5 Cut, Copy and Paste

The **cut**, **copy** and **paste** commands allow text to be moved around a document from one place to another quickly and easily. When you cut text, it is removed from its original location; when you copy it, the original is left untouched.

When items are cut or copied in *Office* applications, they are placed in a temporary storage area known as the **Clipboard**. Up to 24 cut or copied items can be held on the **Clipboard** at a time.

Activity:

1. Open the document **Issues** which contains a list of outstanding tasks for the new *Rumbling Rails* ride.

2. Show the **Clipboard** by clicking the **Clipboard** dialog box launcher at the bottom of the **Clipboard** group.

3. As the **Clipboard** is shared between all *Microsoft Office* applications, there may already be some items stored on it. If so, click the **Clear All** button, .

4. Click and drag to highlight the first sentence: **Name for ride to be decided**. Then, click the **Cut** button on the **Ribbon**, ✂ .

5. An entry for the cut text appears on the **Clipboard**.

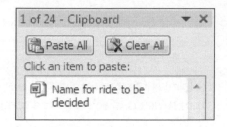

6. Move the cursor to the end of the document and start a new paragraph. Then, click the **Paste** button on the **Ribbon** to insert the cut text into the document at the cursor position (click the **Paste** button's icon, not the drop-down arrow).

7. Next, select all of the sentence: **Test computer software**.

8. Click the **Copy** button, 📋. The copied text is placed on the **Clipboard** above the first item. Filling the **Clipboard** in this way is known as **Collect and Paste**.

9. Create a new paragraph at the end of the document and then click the first item on the **Clipboard** to paste that text. Notice how the original text is left untouched.

10. Use the **Clear All** button, 🔲 Clear All , to clear the **Clipboard**.

> **Note:** You can use **<Ctrl X>** to **Cut**, **<Ctrl C>** to **Copy** and **<Ctrl V>** to **Paste**. It is also easy to copy and paste text and objects between documents and other *Office* programs.

11. Next, copy the first three items in the list one at a time.

12. Position the cursor at the end of the document on an empty line (create a new paragraph if needed), and then click **Paste All**, 🔲 Paste All , on the **Clipboard** task pane.

13. The three copied items are now pasted back into the document in the order they were added to the **Clipboard**.

> **Note:** Once you have selected a piece of text, you can also **drag and drop** it elsewhere in a document.

14. Close the **Clipboard** and then close the document <u>without</u> saving.

3.6 Bullets and Numbering

Lines and paragraphs of text can automatically be **numbered** or **bulleted**. *Word* will automatically add space around the numbers and bullets to make points in a document clearer and improve the professional appearance of the text.

• Bullet 1	1.	Number 1
• Bullet 2	2.	Number 2
• Bullet 3	3.	Number 3

If an item is added to or removed from a numbered list, then the remaining items are automatically renumbered.

Activity:

1. Open the document **Issues** and select all of the text in the document.

> **Note:** To quickly select all of the text in a document in one go, simply press **<Ctrl A>** on your keyboard.

2. With the **Home** tab displayed, number the text by clicking the **Numbering** button, in the **Paragraph** group (click the **Numbering** button's icon, not the drop-down arrow).

3. This is a useful technique for creating lists of items. Select and then delete line number **5**, which refers to the loop the loop.

4. Place the cursor at the end of the numbered list and press **<Enter>** to start a new line. Type **Test that track is safe**.

5. Select all of the text in the document again, and then click the **Numbering** button, . The automatic numbering is removed.

6. Click on the **Bullets** button, , to bullet the paragraphs instead. This is useful for creating a list of points where the sequence is not important.

7. Save the document as **issues bulleted** and close it.

3.7 Tab Stops

Tab stops are a really useful tool for precisely aligning text horizontally (i.e. across the page) in a document. Tabs are displayed on the ruler with small markers (by default every **1.27 cm**). When you press the <**Tab**> key on your keyboard, the cursor moves to the tab marker's position.

> Note: It is good practice to use tabs to align text in your documents. You should <u>never</u> use lots of spaces as these are inconsistent and look very unprofessional.

Activity:

1.   Start a new, blank document. On the **Home** tab, click the **Paragraph** group's dialog box launcher and click the **Tabs** button (at the bottom) to display the **Tabs** dialog box.

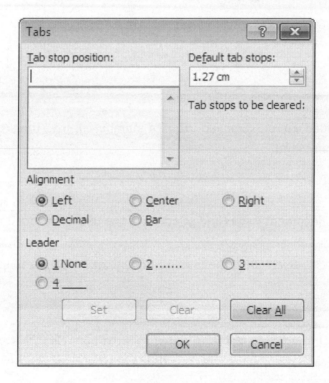

2.   Enter **1 cm** in the **Tab stop position** box. Check the **Alignment** is **Left** (you will see other alignment types in the next exercise), and then click **Set** to set the first tab.

3.   Now enter **10** in the **Tab stop position** box (**cm** is assumed if you don't type it). Click **Set** and then click **OK**.

> Note: Notice a left tab marker (**L**) has appeared on the ruler where each tab has been set (if the ruler is not shown, display the **View** tab and check **Ruler** in the **Show** group).

4.   Press the <**Tab**> key once on your keyboard (usually found above the <**Caps Lock**> key).

5. The cursor moves to the first tab stop. Type the word **Publication** and press **<Tab>** again to move to the next tab marker.

6. Type **Price** and press **<Enter>** to move to the next line.

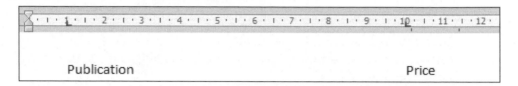

7. With a tab *before* and *after* each publication type, enter the following information:

Hospitality Today	4.99
Journal of Travel and Tourism	5
Theme Park Monthly	3.75
Construction Journal	5.5
Roller Coaster Review	4
Dream Spas Quarterly	5.60

8. You have now created a well-presented and professional-looking list of publications and prices. Save the document as **publication prices**.

9. Next, select all of the text in the document (remember that **<Ctrl A>** lets you do this quickly). Display the **Tabs** dialog box again and click **Clear All** to remove any existing tabs.

10. Click **OK**. Notice that the document has lost all of its tab stops on the ruler.

> **Note:** To quickly set new tabs, click at the required position on the ruler with your mouse.

11. With all of the text in the document still selected, use the mouse to click on the ruler at approximately **0.5 cm** and **7 cm** to set two new tabs. Notice the effect.

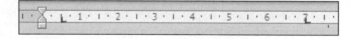

12. Save the document and close it.

13. Open the file **Coasters**. This file contains information about the types of roller coaster cars that are available to buy, but the two columns are too far apart...

14. Select the whole document and display the **Tabs** dialog box again. Before the tabs can be changed, click **Clear All** to remove the original tabs.

15. Set a new left tab by entering **4 cm** in the **Tab stop position** box. Click on **Set**.

16. Create another left tab at **9 cm**, then click **OK** and notice the changes.

> **Note:** You can also change a tab's position by clicking and dragging the tab marker along the ruler to the required place.

17. With all of the document text still selected, click on the left tab stop at **4 cm** on the ruler and drag to **5 cm**. Release the mouse button and observe the results.

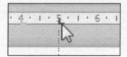

> **Note:** You can also remove a tab quickly by clicking and dragging its marker down, off and away from the ruler.

18. Click on the first tab stop and drag and drop it down and off the ruler. This deletes the first tab stop and the text automatically shifts to the next one.

19. Create a new tab stop at **3 cm** by clicking on the ruler. Observe the results.

20. Practice using the mouse and ruler to add, move and remove tab stops. When you are finished, close the document <u>without</u> saving.

3.8 Right, Center and Decimal Tabs

In the previous exercise you created a number of **Left** tab stops. However, there are a number of other different types of tab that you can use, each of which let you align text in a slightly different way. **Centre**, **Right** and **Decimal** tabs are regularly used in common word processing tasks.

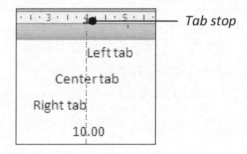

Activity:

1. Open the document **publication prices** which you created and saved earlier. Select the entire document's text and move the tab positions to **4 cm** and **11 cm**.

2. Select the **Home** tab and display the **Paragraph** dialog box and click **Tabs**. From the **Tabs** dialog box, select the **Tab stop position** at **4 cm**. Notice it is left aligned.

3. Click on **Center** from the **Alignment** options and then click **Set**.

4. Repeat this procedure for the tab at **11 cm** but make it **Right** aligned.

5. Click **OK** and observe the effect of the new tab alignment.

6. Experiment by changing the tabs into right, left and centre aligned tabs. When you are finished, close the document <u>without</u> saving.

7.   Next, open the document **Figures**. Notice that there is a left tab at approximately **4 cm**.

8.   Select all the text and remove the current tab by clicking and dragging it down off the ruler. Notice that each line of text returns to its default tab position of **1.27 cm**.

9.   You can also quickly create various tab stops directly on the ruler. Keep clicking the button found to the left of the ruler to cycle through the available tab types.

> Note: The tabs alternate between the useful **Left**, Center, **Right**, and **Decimal**, tab stops. The three other types are rarely used.

10. Change the tab setting to **Right**. With all of the text still selected, click on the ruler at **4 cm**. Notice how the text is now right aligned against the tab stop.

11. Remove the tab stop. Next, change the tab setting to **Decimal**, and click at **4 cm** on the ruler again. Notice how all the numbers line up around their decimal points.

12. Save the document as **figures aligned** and close it.

3.9 Margins

Margins determine the distance between the text and the edges of the paper and are usually the same for the whole document. The top and bottom margins can be used for features such as headers, footers and page numbering (which you will learn more about later).

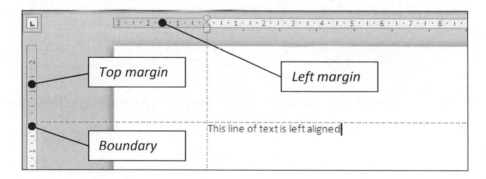

Activity:

1.   Open the document **Progress Report**.

2.   Display the **Page Layout** tab and click the **Margins** button. There are many options shown here, each of which applies a set of preset margins.

3.   For more control over margin settings, select **Custom Margins** at the bottom of the menu. The **Page Setup** dialog box appears.

> Note: The **Top**, **Bottom**, **Left** and **Right** margins are, by default, set to **2.54 cm**. An extra side margin (or **Gutter** margin) can also be added to allow space for binding.

4.   Increase the **Top**, **Bottom**, **Left** and **Right** margins to **6 cm** either by editing the numbers in the boxes or by using the up and down *spinners* (the small arrow buttons).

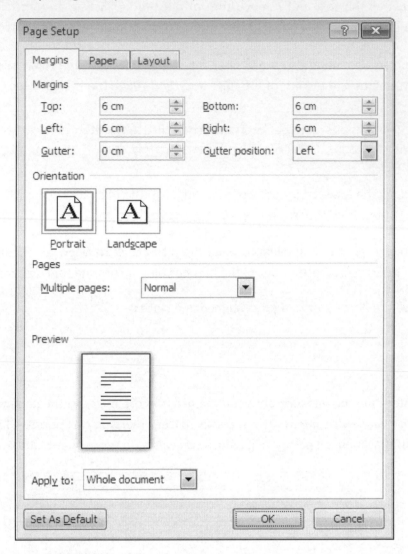

5.   Click **OK**. Notice the effect this has on the document. There is now a **6 cm** space between each side of the text and the edges of the page.

> **Note:**   You can also adjust margins by clicking and dragging the margin boundaries on the top and left rulers.

6.   Move the mouse pointer over the **Top Margin** boundary on the <u>left</u>, vertical ruler. After a moment, it will become a double-headed arrow, ⇕.

7.   The dark area at the top of the ruler indicates the **Top Margin** space. Reduce this margin by dragging the boundary marker up until the margin is about **2 cm** in height.

> Note: You can double click the margins on the ruler to view the **Page Setup** dialog box.

8. Now reduce the **Left Margin** by positioning the cursor over the margin boundary on the top ruler until it becomes a double-headed arrow, ⟺. This will take some care as there are other markers here in virtually the same position. Drag the left margin to **2 cm**.

> Note: Try holding down <**Alt**> while dragging the margin boundaries to position them more precisely.

9. Click the **Margins** button on the **Ribbon** again and select **Normal**. The margins are reset.

10. Close **Progress Report** <u>without</u> saving the changes.

3.10 Paragraph Alignment

Paragraph **alignment** refers to the location where text appears on each line in relation to the margins. *Word* is capable of four types of text alignment: **Left**, **Centred**, **Right** and **Justified** (filling the width of the line). The one that you choose usually depends on the type of document that you are creating. However, left and justified are nearly always best for large paragraphs of text.

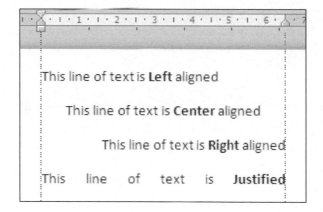

Activity:

1. Open the document **Letter**. All of the text in this document is left aligned, which is the default setting in *Word*.

2. However, this is not how most professional letters look – your address usually appears on the right and the subject line appears in the centre. Highlight the first **4 lines** of the letter.

> Note: Alignment is set by clicking one of the alignment buttons, ≣ ≣ ≣ ≣, which are found in the **Paragraph** group on the **Home** tab.

---

3. Click the **Align Text Right** button, 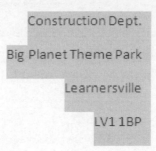. The address is aligned against the right margin.

> Construction Dept.
>
> Big Planet Theme Park
>
> Learnersville
>
> LV1 1BP

4. Use the same technique to right align the date, and then make it **Bold**.

5. Highlight the line **Re: COPY OF INVOICE #CBS01234**. Centre align this text by clicking the **Center** button, ≡, and then apply **Bold** and **Underline**.

6. If only one paragraph is to be aligned, the cursor simply needs to be placed *somewhere* in the paragraph for the effect to take place. Position the cursor anywhere within the main body of the letter (the paragraph starting "**I am writing...**").

7. Justify the text by clicking the **Justify** button, ≡. Each line of the paragraph now fills the width of the page.

> **Note:**   Notice how much clearer and professional the letter now appears. Although it only took a few clicks, the effect of alignment has a real impact on your documents.

8. Save the document as **letter final** and close it.

3.11 Indents

Indents are used to move one or more paragraphs of text away from the left or right margins. The indent markers are shown on the top ruler and can be moved in the same way as tab stops.

Left Indent  *Right Indent*

Activity:

1. Open the document **Agenda**. *Priti* created this simple document (which contains a list of topics to discuss at the next team meeting) and would now like to improve its layout.

2. Place the cursor in the first paragraph below the title **Monthly Meeting Agenda**, and then click the **Increase Indent** button, 📑, in the **Paragraph** group. The entire paragraph is indented.

> **Note:**   Similar to tab stops, the **Increase Indent** button creates indents at **1.27cm** intervals.

3.   Notice the **Left Indent** marker on the top ruler now shows an indent at **1.27 cm**.

4.   Click the **Increase Indent** button again. The indent is increased to **2.54 cm**.

5.   Click the **Decrease Indent** button, ⊞, to reduce the indent back to **1.27 cm**.

> Note: There are key presses for these functions also: to increase an indent press <**Ctrl M**> and to decrease an indent press <**Ctrl Shift M**>.

6.   Display the **Page Layout** tab. In the **Paragraph** group, notice that the **Left Indent** setting is **1.27 cm**. Click once in the **Right Indent** box and enter **1.27 cm**. Press <**Enter**>.

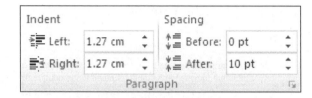

7.   Examine the effect this has on the first paragraph. In particular, notice that the **Right Indent** marker on the ruler has moved inwards **1.27 cm**.

> Note: You can also drag the **Left** and **Right Indent** markers on the ruler. Try holding down <**Alt**> while dragging markers to position them more precisely.

8.   Next, increase the **Left Indent** of the remaining list of items in the agenda to **2 cm**.

9.   Save the document as **agenda final** and leave it open for the next exercise.

3.12 First Line and Hanging Indents

You may be wondering why the **Left Indent** marker appears differently to the **Right Indent** marker? The reason for this is that the left marker can be split into a **First Line Indent** and a **Hanging Indent**.

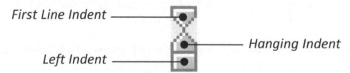

The **First Line Indent** indicates where the first line of each paragraph should start. The **Hanging Indent** indicates where each of the other lines should start.

Activity:

1.   The **agenda final** document should still be open. Place the cursor in the first paragraph and then move your mouse pointer over the **First Line Indent** marker on the ruler.

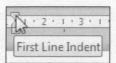

2. Click and drag the indent to the **3 cm** mark. Notice that the first line of the paragraph is now indented further than the others.

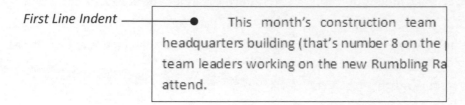

First Line Indent

This month's construction team headquarters building (that's number 8 on the team leaders working on the new Rumbling Ra attend.

3. Next, move your mouse pointer over the **Hanging Indent** marker on the ruler.

4. Click and drag the indent to the **5 cm** mark. Notice that the first line of the paragraph is now indented less than the others.

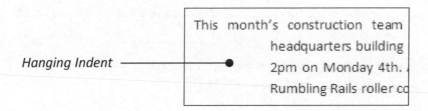

This month's construction team headquarters building

Hanging Indent

2pm on Monday 4th.

Rumbling Rails roller co

> **Note:** Dragging the **Left Indent** marker will move the **First Line** and **Hanging Indent** markers together. Hold <**Alt**> while dragging to position markers more precisely.

5. Click the **Paragraph** dialog box launcher. Precise indent settings can be set under the **Indentation** heading. Set the **Left** marker to **1.27 cm** and the **Special** to **(none)**.

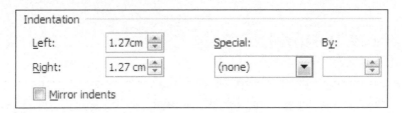

> **Note:** **Special** here can be used to set a **First Line** or **Hanging Indent**.

6. Click **OK** and the indentation changes to a **Left Indent** and **Right Indent** of **1.27 cm**.

> **Note:** Applying bullets and numbering will automatically create a **First Line** and **Hanging Indent**. The first line will feature a bullet or number and then the text. All the remaining lines in the paragraph are indented to line up with only the text.

7. Select all of the items in the agenda's list (from **Apologies** to **Staffing** issues). On the **Home** tab, click the **Numbering** button in the **Paragraph** group.

8. Notice the first line and hanging indents that are created. Experiment by changing the indent markers on the ruler, then save the document and close it.

3.13 Page Breaks and Formatting Marks

From time to time you may need to start a new page without the current page being full. This is known as inserting a **page break**.

Activity:

1. Open the document **Staffing**. This file contains a brief, unformatted memo to the manager of the theme park regarding a number of important issues.

2. Place the cursor <u>before</u> the heading text **Issues** (a little way down the page). You can "force" text onto another page by inserting a page break. Display the **Insert** tab and, from the **Pages** group, select **Page Break**.

> Note: Page breaks can also be inserted by placing the cursor in the correct position and pressing <**Ctrl Enter**>.

3. Scroll down and notice that the heading text **Issues** now starts on page 2.

> Note: The page break appears in your document as a hidden **formatting mark**. To see this and other hidden marks, click the **Show/Hide** button, ¶ , on the **Home** tab.

4. Scroll back up to page 1 and display **Formatting Marks** by clicking the **Show/Hide** button in the **Paragraph** group. Notice that each paragraph ends with a ¶ symbol – this is a **paragraph break** and appears wherever you press <**Enter**>.

> Note: Formatting marks do not appear when you print a document.

5. Notice the page break that you inserted earlier at the bottom of page 1.

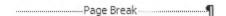
·····························Page Break·····························¶

6. Click and drag to select the page break marker and then press <**Delete**> to remove it. The page break is deleted and the **Issues** header returns to page 1.

7. Insert page breaks for each of the following headers in the document: **Issues**, **Overtime**, and **Capacity of Existing Ride**.

8. Hide **Formatting Marks** again by clicking the **Show/Hide** button in the **Paragraph** group.

9. Leave the document open for the next exercise.

3.14 Line and Paragraph Spacing

You can improve the appearance and readability of a document by changing line spacing – the white space that appears between lines of text. By default, line spacing is **1.15**. Other commonly used spacing is **Single**, **Double** and **1½**.

Activity:

1. The file **Staffing** should still be open from the previous exercise. Select the 5 paragraphs of text underneath the heading **Memo** on page 1.

2. In the **Paragraph** group, click the **Line and Paragraph Spacing** button, 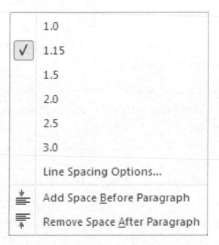.

	1.0
✓	1.15
	1.5
	2.0
	2.5
	3.0
	Line Spacing Options...
≛	Add Space Before Paragraph
≛	Remove Space After Paragraph

3. From the drop-down list that appears, select **2.0** (also known as **Double**) to change the line spacing for the document. Notice that the spacing between lines increases.

> **Note:**   The spacing value refers to how much space is added below each line in a paragraph. For example, **2.0** means add space 2.0 times the height of the line.

4. Use the **Line and Paragraph Spacing** button to set the spacing to **1.0** (**Single**).

5. Display the **Page Layout** tab. The **Paragraph** group contains controls to change the spacing before and after each *paragraph* (this is different from line spacing).

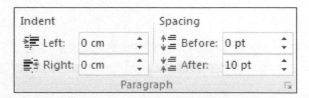

6. To leave space after the selected paragraphs, increase the value in the **After** box to **24 pt**. All selected paragraphs will now gain a **24 pt** space underneath their last line of text.

> **Note:**   As with fonts, line spacing is measured in **points** (shortened to **pt**).

7. Launch the **Paragraph** dialog box. Notice that the settings which have been made are displayed under the **Spacing** heading.

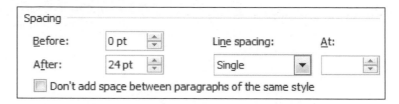

8. Change the paragraph spacing **After** to **0 pt** and the spacing **Before** to **12 pt**. Click **OK**.

> Note: Spacing added after one paragraph and before the next will overlap.

9. Notice the effect of these changes, save the document as **staffing complete** and close it.

3.15 Widows and Orphans

It is very common for a paragraph to start on one page and continue on to another. However, when a paragraph is split across pages, it is considered bad practice to leave one line of text on its own at the bottom or top of a page. A single line of paragraph text left at the bottom of a page is called an **orphan**; the end of a paragraph that appears on a single line at the top of the following page is called a **widow**. Fortunately, *Word* automatically prevents widows and orphans.

Activity:

1. Open the document **Rivets Weekly**. This is a basic newsletter designed for members of the park's construction team.

2. Scroll down to the bottom of the first page and notice that the last paragraph is split over two pages.

> Note: Even though there is space at the bottom of the first page for an extra line of text, *Word* has automatically moved the line to the next page to avoid leaving a widow.

3. Place the cursor anywhere in the final paragraph and launch the **Paragraph** dialog box. Select the **Line and Page Breaks** tab and examine the options that appear.

4. **Widow/Orphan control** is automatically selected by *Word*. Uncheck that option to deactivate automatic control, and then click **OK**. Observe the effect.

5. A widow has been created (a line on its own at the top of a new page). Place your cursor at the start of the header **A Right Dog's Dinner** and press <**Enter**>. An orphan is now created (a line on its own at the end of a page).

6. Place the cursor anywhere in the final paragraph and launch the **Paragraph** dialog box again.

7. Check **Widow/Orphan control** to allow *Word* to automatically prevent widows and orphans, and then click **OK**. Observe the effect.

8. Close the document <u>without</u> saving.

3.16 Styles

For simple, short documents, the basic tools on the **Home** tab are more than sufficient for formatting text. However, for longer or more complex documents, you need to create and use **styles**. Styles are specific combinations of font types, sizes and alignments which help ensure consistent formatting throughout a document (which is very important). When applied, the selected text or current paragraph will adopt all of the style's formatting and alignment settings.

Activity:

1. Open the document **Plan**. This file contains information on the future maintenance of the *Rumbling Rails* ride. Notice that there are a number of bold headers followed by a brief description in plain text.

2. Display the **Home** tab and locate the **Styles** group. The options provided here allow you to apply new styles to the text in your documents.

 — *More*

3. Notice that the style **Heading 1** is currently highlighted. This means that the cursor is placed in a paragraph of text which has the **Heading 1** style applied.

4. Place the cursor on the second line of text containing the date; the style **Heading 2** is highlighted (you may need to click **More** to see this). Next, place the cursor on the third line containing the two lines of introductory text; the style **Normal** is highlighted.

> Note: The highlighted styles are built-in styles that were added when the document was created. It is common practice to use **Heading 1** for main titles, **Heading 2** for sub-titles, and so on. **Normal** is often used for the main body text of a document.

5. With the cursor positioned in the third paragraph, select **Heading 1** from the **Styles** box. The text changes to match the **Heading 1** style.

6. Select **Normal** from the **Styles** box to restore the text's formatting.

> Note: Once you have applied a style it is very easy to change it. Any changes will effect every paragraph of text that has that style applied, which can be very useful.

7. Open the **Styles** task pane by clicking the **Styles** launcher button.

8. Notice that **Normal** is currently selected. Place the cursor in the subheading text **Ride Improvements**. The style **Heading 3** is selected.

9. Move your mouse pointer over the selected style on the **Styles** task pane. Click once on the drop-down arrow that appears and then click **Modify**.

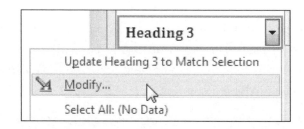

10. The **Modify Style** dialog box appears. From this dialog box you can change all formatting and alignment settings for the selected style.

11. Underneath the **Formatting** heading, change the **Font** to **Arial** and the size to **14**. Select **Underline** and a font colour of **Dark Blue** (from the drop-down labelled **Automatic**).

> Note: Options to alter **Paragraphs**, **Tabs** and **Borders** for the selected style can be found by clicking the **Format** button, Format ▾ , at the bottom of the dialog box.

12. Click **OK**. The style is updated and all paragraphs that are based on it are changed.

13. Use this technique to change the **Normal** style to use the font **Times New Roman** size **14**.

> Note: Styles can be based on other styles. If you change the original style, any style based on it will change too.

14. There are a number of built-in style sets that can be used to give your documents a more professional look. From the **Styles** group, click the **Change Styles** button. From the submenu that appears, click **Style Set**.

15. Move your mouse over each of the style sets shown and the result of applying each will be previewed in the document.

16. Finally, click **Modern** to apply that style set. This replaces the formatting and alignment options for each of the built-in styles (and any text based on them will be updated).

> Note: Completely new styles can be created by clicking the **New Style** button, , on the **Styles** task pane and then specifying font formatting and alignment settings.

17. Close the **Styles** task pane, then save the document as **maintenance plan** and close it.

3.17 Creating a Table

Word's **Table** feature provides a really effective way of presenting data in a clear and easy to read format. Tables consist of **rows** (running from top to bottom) and **columns** (running from left to right) to create a number of **cells** that can contain text. The table can also be formatted to create a more professional, eye catching document.

	Monday	Tuesday	Wednesday	Thursday	Friday
Scaffolding	Mira	Atsu/Alan	Mira/Alan	Atsu	Mira
Train Install	Chen	Chen	Chen	Priti	Priti
System Test	Priti	Priti	Priti	Chen	Chen
Landscaping	Dave	Ali	Dave	Ali	Ali
Labouring	Atsu/Paul	Dave/Mira	Atsu/Paul	Dave/Mira	Atsu/Paul

Activity:

1. Start a new, blank document.

2. To create a new table, display the **Insert** tab and click the **Table** button. When the grid appears, click **Insert Table**.

> Note: A table can also be created directly from the **Table** drop-down button by moving your mouse pointer over the required number of cells on the grid and clicking once.

3. The **Insert Table** dialog box appears.

4. Enter **6** in the **Number of columns** box and **6** in the **Number of rows** box (these numbers can be typed in directly or the up/down spinners can be used).

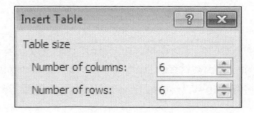

5.   Click **OK** to create the table. It appears at the location of the cursor. Once a table has been created, it is simple to enter text and move around within it.

> Note: It is often easier to enter text into a table first and then format it later (i.e. add colour, adjust text size, correct column widths, etc).

6.   The cursor should be flashing inside the first cell. If it is not, click once in the top left cell to place it.

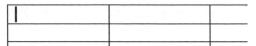

> Note: You can use the <**Tab**> key to move to the next cell in a table and <**Shift Tab**> to move backwards. When entering text, only use <**Enter**> when a new line is required *within* the same cell.

7.   Using the <**Tab**> key to move between cells, enter the following text:

	Monday	Tuesday	Wednesday	Thursday	Friday
Scaffolding	Mira	Atsu/Alan	Mira/Alan	Atsu	Mira
Train Install	Chen	Chen	Chen	Priti	Priti
System Test	Priti	Priti	Priti	Chen	Chen
Landscaping	Dave	Ali	Dave	Ali	Ali
Labouring	Atsu/Paul	Dave/Mira	Atsu/Paul	Dave/Mira	Atsu/Paul

> Note: When the cursor is in the last cell of a row, pressing <**Tab**> will move the cursor to the first cell on the next row.

8.   Save the document as **staff roster** and leave it open for the next exercise.

3.18 Move or Resize a Table

Once a table has been created, you can easily move it to a different position on the page and increase or decrease its size to suit your document.

Activity:

1.   The document **staff roster** created in the previous exercise should still be open.

2.   Without clicking, rest the mouse pointer over the table until the **Table Move Handle**, ⊞, appears at the top left corner.

> Note: If the **Table Move Handle** does not appear, make sure **Print Layout** view is displayed by selecting the **View** tab and then clicking **Print Layout**. This view will show the document as it will appear on the printed page.

3. Now move the mouse over the **Table Move Handle** until a four-headed arrow appears.

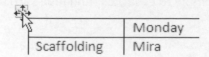

4. You can now move the table anywhere on the page. Click and drag the **Table Move Handle** downward to move the table about half way down the page.

5. Rest the mouse pointer over the table again until the **Table Resize Handle**, ▫, appears at the bottom right corner. This allows you to resize the table to any size you like.

6. Now move the mouse pointer over the **Table Resize Handle** until a double headed arrow appears.

Ali	Ali
Dave/Mira	Atsu/Paul

7. Drag the mouse down a little until the table is about twice its original height.

8. From the **Quick Access Toolbar** at the top left of the screen, click **Undo**, ↺. The table resize is undone.

9. Leave the document open for the next exercise.

3.19 Selecting Cells

You need to be able to select table cells before you can do anything to them, just as a block of text must be selected before it can be formatted. Unfortunately, selecting cells can sometimes be a tricky and frustrating business. Luckily there are a number of useful techniques to help.

Activity:

1. Select the cell containing the word **Scaffolding** by moving inside the left edge of the cell and clicking the left mouse button once when the selection arrow appears, ↗.

2. The entire cell and its contents are now selected. Make the text bold by clicking the **Bold** button, **B**, on the **Home** tab.

3. Move the mouse pointer over the inside left edge of the cell above and double click the left mouse button when the pointer changes to ↗. The entire row is selected.

	Monday	Tuesday	Wednesday
Scaffolding	Mira	Atsu/Alan	Mira/Alan

4. Click the **Bold** button again to make *all* of the cells in the first row bold.

5. Next, move the mouse pointer just below the top edge of the first column until the selection arrow is displayed again. Click once to select the entire column.

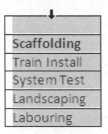

6. Click the **Bold** button. This first removes the **Bold** setting applied to **Scaffolding** earlier, so click again to make *all* of the cells in the first column bold.

7. Now move your mouse pointer over the cell containing the name **Mira**. Click and drag to select this cell and all of the cells below and to the right.

	Monday	Tuesday	Wednesday	Thursday	Friday
Scaffolding	Mira	Atsu/Alan	Mira/Alan	Atsu	Mira
Train Install	Chen	Chen	Chen	Priti	Priti
System Test	Priti	Priti	Priti	Chen	Chen
Landscaping	Dave	Ali	Dave	Ali	Ali
Labouring	Atsu/Paul	Dave/Mira	Atsu/Paul	Dave/Mira	Atsu/Paul

8. Click the **Italic** button, I, to make all of the text in the selected cells italic.

9. To select the entire table, move the mouse over the **Table Move Handle** and click once.

10. Next, use the **Font Color** button's drop-down arrow, to change all of the text to **Dark Blue**.

11. Leave the document open for the next exercise.

3.20 Cell Alignment and Direction

The contents of a cell can be aligned against the left, centre and right edges as well as the top, middle or bottom.

Activity:

1. With the table still selected from the previous exercise, display the **Layout** tab on the **Ribbon**. Notice in the **Alignment** group that the table's text is aligned to the **Top Left**.

2. Click **Align Bottom Right**, to see the difference.

3. Change the text to centre aligned by clicking **Align Center**.

4. Select the top row of the table only. To change the direction of the text click **Text Direction**. The text is rotated 90 degrees and the cell height is increased.

Text Direction

> **Note:** Changing the direction of text can often be a useful way of displaying lots of column headers in a small amount of space (notice that the icons in the **Alignment** group are also rotated).

5. Continue to click the **Text Direction** button to cycle through the available alternatives. Stop when the text is horizontal again (as it was when you started).

6. Leave the document open for the next exercise.

3.21 Resizing Cells

Once you have created a table, it is very easy to resize individual cells or entire rows and columns. You can even automatically adjust rows and columns so that they are equal in size in order to produce a professional look to your finished tables.

Activity:

1. Notice that the height of the top row is now too high. Move the mouse pointer anywhere over the bottom edge of the topmost row (as shown below).

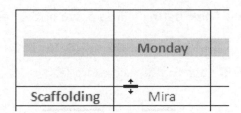

2. The mouse pointer becomes a double headed arrow, ⬍. Click and drag upwards to make the row about the same height as all of the others (then release the mouse button).

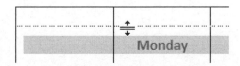

3. To resize the first column, move the mouse pointer anywhere over the leftmost vertical edge. The mouse pointer becomes a double headed arrow again, ↔.

4. Click and drag the border left a little way to increase the width of the column.

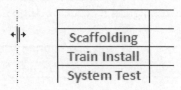

5.   Release the mouse button. The leftmost column is now larger than the rest. To balance the table evenly, select the entire table again.

6.   Display the **Layout** tab and click **Distribute Columns**, ⊞, from the **Cell Size** group. The columns are equally sized.

7.   Click the **Distribute Rows** button also, ⊞, to ensure that each row is the same height.

8.   Save and close the document.

3.22 Merging and Splitting Cells

Sometimes you may need to create a table that contains cells that are bigger or smaller than others in the same table. You can do this by **merging** cells into a single cell or **splitting** cells into two or more smaller cells. Merging and splitting cells is often done to create documents such as invoices, timetables, forms and so on.

Activity:

1.   In a new, blank document, create a table with **5** columns and **10** rows. Select cells 2 and 3 on the first by clicking and dragging.

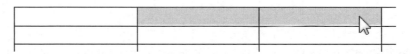

2.   Display the **Layout** tab and click **Merge Cells** in the **Merge** group, ▦ Merge Cells . The cells are merged.

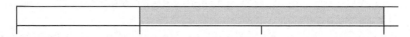

3.   Next, merge cells 3 and 4 (the two cells now at the top right of the table). Then, merge all of the cells on the second row.

4.   Merge cells 1 and 2 on rows 3 to 9. This must be done one row at a time. Then merge cells 1 to 4 on the bottom row.

5.   *Priti* needs to keep a record of building materials ordered for the new ride to send to the accounts department. Enter text into the table so that it matches the picture below.

Date	Name		Department	
Product		Price	Quantity	Total Price
Grand Total				

6. The accounts department has indicated that they need to see product reference numbers in the table. Position the cursor in the cell containing the text **Product** and click **Split Cells** from the **Merge** group on the **Layout** tab, .

7. Make sure **2** columns and **1** row are selected in the **Split Cells** dialog box and click **OK**.

8. Enter **Ref.** in the cell to the right of **Product** and split the cells in the six rows below (you can split the remaining cells one row at a time or all at once).

Date	Name		Department	
Product	Ref.	Price	Quantity	Total Price
Grand Total				

9. This document is now perfect for keeping a record of future purchases. Save the document as **materials** and close it.

3.23 Deleting Cells

Once you have created a table it is very easy to remove individual cells, rows or columns.

Activity:

1. In a new, blank document, create a table with **6** columns and **6** rows.

2. Select the entire second row. To delete this row, click the **Delete** button in the **Rows & Columns** group on the **Layout** tab.

3. From the drop-down menu that appears, select **Delete Rows**. The row is deleted.

4. Next, select the entire last column. From the **Delete** button's drop-down menu, select **Delete Columns**. The last column is removed.

5. Select cells 1 and 2 in the first row only. From the **Delete** button's drop-down menu, select **Delete Cells**. The **Delete Cells** dialog box appears.

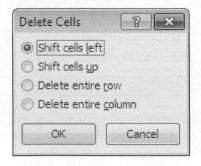

6.   Before individual cells can be deleted, you first have to decide what will take their place. Select **Shift cells left** and click **OK**. The first two cells are deleted and the remaining cells on the row move to the left to take their place.

> Note: Selecting **Shift cells up** will move the cells directly below up to take the place of those deleted.

7.   Select the entire table by clicking the **Table Move Handle**, ⊞.

8.   From the **Delete** button's drop-down menu, select **Delete Table**. The entire table is removed.

9.   Close the document <u>without</u> saving.

3.24 Gridlines, Borders and Shading

There are several effects that you can apply to tables to improve their look or to draw attention to certain parts of it. You can add **borders** to a table or individual rows, columns, or cells, and you can use **shading** to fill in the background of a table.

> Note: Used properly, borders can emphasise information, make it easier to read, and can give your tables a more professional appearance. However, be careful not to go overboard and use too many styles and colours as this can have the reverse effect.

By default, tables in *Word* have a single, thin, black border around all cells. If you remove these, **gridlines** will continue to show the cell boundaries on the screen (but will not be printed).

Activity:

1.   Open the document **materials** that you created earlier. Select the entire table, and then click the **Borders** button drop-down arrow on the **Design** tab.

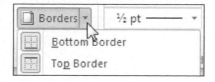

2.   Select **Borders and Shading** from the bottom of the menu. The **Borders and Shading** dialog box appears.

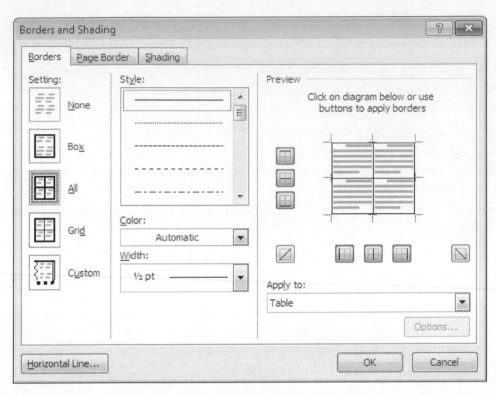

3. With the **Borders** tab displayed, select **None** from under **Setting** and then click **OK**. The table's borders are removed and faint dashed gridlines shown instead.

Date	Name	
Product	Ref.	Price

> **Note:** If gridlines are not shown, select **View Gridlines** on the **Layout** tab. These lines are for guidance only when working with tables and do not print.

4. Select the entire first row of the table.

5. Display the **Borders and Shading** dialog box again and select **Box** from under **Setting**.

6. From the **Style** box, select the first double line, ══════════.

7. From the **Color** drop-down box, select a dark blue colour. Then, from the **Width** drop-down box, select **¾ pt** (this setting represents the thickness of the line).

> **Note:** To apply a border to specific sides of a selected cell or table only, simply click on the table **Preview** where you want the chosen border settings to apply. A second click removes that border.

8. Click **OK**. The entire first row gains a dark blue border.

9. Select the second row. From the **Borders and Shading** dialog box, select the **Shading** tab.

10. From the **Fill** drop-down box, select a light blue colour and observe the effects in the **Preview** panel. Make sure **Clear** is selected under **Style** and then click **OK**.

> **Note:** **Clear** allows for a transparent solid colour. You can also add patterns to cells.

11. Continue to experiment with different table borders, line styles and shading options. Try to reproduce the following picture.

Date	Name		Department	
Product	Ref.	Price	Quantity	Total Price
Grand Total				

12. Save the document using the same name and close it.

3.25 Importing Objects

Various objects from other *Microsoft Office* applications can be imported into a document. For example, if you were producing a report you may want to include a chart or part of a spreadsheet that was created in *Excel*.

Activity:

1. Open the file **Update** which contains a brief report on the *Rumbling Rails* ride. This document is incomplete and a number of items need to be imported from elsewhere. Place the cursor in the space underneath the paragraph starting "**The initial costs...**".

> The initial costs are within the allotted budget and are
>
> |
>
> The tracks are all in place now and the braking system

2. Display the **Insert** tab and click **Object**, Object, from the **Text** group. When the **Object** dialog box appears, display the **Create from File** tab.

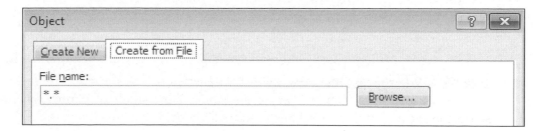

3. To insert a chart created in *Excel*, click the **Browse** button at the right of the **File name** box. The **Browse** dialog box appears.

4. Locate the data folder for this section and select the **Initial Costs** file. Click **Insert**.

> Note: Notice the **Link to file** checkbox. If this is selected any changes made later to the imported file will also be shown in the *Word* document when it is reopened.

5. Select the **Link to file** checkbox and then click **OK**. The contents of the **Initial Costs** spreadsheet are imported (a chart).

> Note: Only the contents of the *default* worksheet are imported. If you need to import another part of a workbook, open it and make the relevant worksheet active and then resave the file. You can also copy and paste items between open files.

6. The imported chart is far too large. Click on the chart to select it, and then drag any corner handle inward until it fits neatly on the page below the text.

7. Centre the chart using the **Center** alignment button on the **Home** tab.

8. Place the cursor below the paragraph starting "**Some technical statistics...**". Import the contents of the spreadsheet **Statistics** (a table) and centre it on the page.

> Note: To change the contents of an imported object you must first double click it. If the object was imported with **Link to file** selected, it will open in its default program; if **Link to file** was not selected, it will open as an embedded object in *Word*. You will learn more about creating and working with spreadsheets in the next section.

> Note: Borders can be added to text, objects and pictures in the same way as tables.

9. Save the document as **update complete** and close it.

10. Next, try to open the **update complete** document again. You will be informed that the document contains links to other files.

11. Select **Yes** and any changes to the linked files (if any had been made) would also be reflected in the document. Leave the document open for the next exercise.

3.26 Inserting Pictures and Clip Art

To make your documents more visually interesting and informative, you can import pictures from files on your computer into a document. Various pictures are also available from the **Clip Art** library that is available online (**Clip Art** images are simple illustrations or photographs provided with *Microsoft Office*).

Activity:

1. Using the file **update complete**, position the cursor below the paragraph starting "**The tracks are all in place now…**".

2. Display the **Insert** tab and then click **Picture**. From the **Insert Picture** dialog box, locate the data files folder for this section and select the file named **Photo**.

3. Click **Insert**. The image appears against the left margin, but it is a little too small. Using a corner handle, click and drag outwards to make the picture about twice its original size. Centre the image in the middle of the paragraph.

> Note: The green handle at the top of the picture, ⚲, can be used to rotate the image.

4. The document is now complete. Save the changes and close it.

5. Next, open the document **Roller Coaster** (ignore any spelling mistakes for now).

6. Position the cursor at the beginning of the paragraph which starts "**The excitement for the rider…**" (under the heading **The thrill of the ride**).

> **The thrill of the ride**
>
> |The excitement for the rider comes from the
> on the body. When the coaster speeds up, th

7. Display the **Insert** tab and click the **Clip Art** button. The **Clip Art** pane appears at the right of the screen.

8. Keyword searches are used to locate relevant **Clip Art** pictures. In the **Search for** box, enter the keywords **roller coaster** and click **Go**. The results are displayed in the pane.

9. Click on any roller coaster image to place it in the document at the cursor's position. If you can find it, we recommend using the image shown below.

10. If the imported picture is too large or too small, resize it using the corner handles, and then click away from the picture to deselect it.

> **Note:** It is important to maintain the **proportions** of pictures and other objects such as charts when resizing them. The corner handles let you do this. However, if you use the other top, bottom or side handles, the object will be distorted.

11. Notice the way the text is laid out around the image – this is known as **text wrap**. Select the **Clip Art** image again.

12. Display the **Format** tab and, from the **Arrange** group, click the **Wrap Text** button.

13. From the drop-down menu that appears, select **Tight**. Notice how the text now wraps around the **Clip Art** picture.

14. With the image still selected, select **Square** wrapping. Notice the effect.

15. Next, select **In Front of Text** wrapping. The picture appears *floating* above the text.

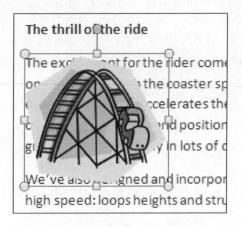

16. Move the mouse pointer over the image until a four-headed arrow appears, ⊹. Click and drag the image into the middle of the page. The text underneath is not affected.

17. From the **Arrange** group, click the **Send Backward** button's drop-down arrow and select **Send Behind Text**.

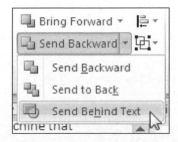

18. The image appears behind the text. Click the drop-down arrow on the **Bring Forward** button and select **Bring In Front of Text** to place the picture in front of the text again.

> **Note:** When an image is placed "in-line" it will appear on the same line as the text around it and will move as you enter, edit and format that text.

19. From **Wrap Text**, select **In Line with Text** to restore the image to its original location.

20. Close the **Clip Art** pane, save the document as **picture** and close it.

> Note: A picture is worth a thousand words. Used properly, images and **Clip Art** can help support information in your document and give it a more professional appearance. However, too many (or inappropriate) pictures can have the reverse affect.

3.27 WordArt, Shapes and Text Boxes

Word has a powerful feature called **WordArt** which allows you to create impressive artwork automatically from the text in your document. This is particularly useful for creating headers for posters, flyers and so on. There are various styles, shapes and colours to choose from.

You can also use *Word's* simple drawing features to add a number of basic shapes to your documents, and even place text inside floating boxes that can be placed anywhere you like.

Activity:

1. Safety inspectors will be visiting *Rumbling Rails* in the next day or two. To direct them to the site office upon their arrival, an eye-catching notice is required for the ride's entrance gate. A simple A4 poster will be ideal.

2. Start a new, blank document. On the first line enter the text **Rumbling Rails**.

3. Select all of the new text, display the **Insert** tab and click **WordArt**, WordArt, in the **Text** group.

4. From the drop-down menu that appears, select any style that you believe looks the most striking (we recommend the one shown below).

A A A A A

5. The text is converted to **WordArt**. Using the **Position** button in the **Arrange** group, move the **WordArt** to the **Top Center** of the page.

> **Note:** The **Drawing Tools - Format** tab can be used to apply a variety of **WordArt** styles and effects. As other *Microsoft Office* programs use **WordArt**, you will learn more about these features in later sections.

6. Display the **Home** tab and, from the **Font** group, set the **WordArt's** text size to **60** (you will need to type this value into the **Font Size** box and press <**Enter**>).

> **Note:** Although useful for creating fancy headings for newsletters, flyers and brochures, **WordArt** and shapes are rarely suitable for use in professional documents.

7. Display the **Insert** tab and click the **Shapes** button in the **Illustrations** group. From the drop-down menu that appears, examine the various shapes that you can select.

8. Under the **Block Arrows** heading, select **Right Arrow**.

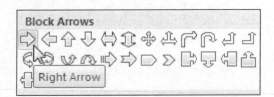

9. The mouse pointer changes to a crosshair, ✛. Underneath the **WordArt**, click and drag to create a shape that fills the width of the page between the margins.

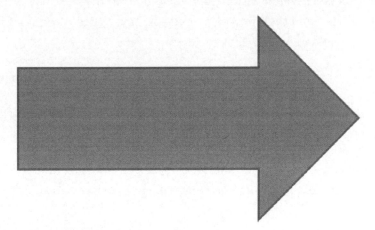

10. With the new shape selected, type the text **This Way**. The text appears in the centre of the arrow.

11. Select the new text and then increase the **Font Size** to **60**. If the text does not fully appear, you may need to resize the shape to accommodate it.

12. Click away from the shape to deselect it.

13. Scroll down to the bottom of the page. Display the **Insert** tab again and, from the **Text** group, click **Text Box**. From the bottom of the drop-down menu that appears, select **Draw Text Box**. The cursor changes to a crosshair again.

14. Using the rulers for reference, click and drag to create a text box approximately **8 cm** wide by **6 cm high** in the middle of the page (it doesn't need to be exact). Type the following text into the text box:

    The Rumbling Rails ride is currently closed to the public. All official visitors must report to the site office.

15. From the **Drawing Tools - Format** tab, click the **Align Text** button,  and select **Middle**. The text is aligned in the middle of the box.

16. Using the **Home** tab, **Center** align the text and increase the font size to **18**.

17. Place your mouse pointer over any edge of the text box until a four-headed arrow appears, and then click and drag the box so that it appears in the middle of the page below the arrow. Resize it if necessary so that you can see all of the text.

> **Note:** **WordArt**, shapes, text boxes and pictures can overlap. To control which object are in front of which, use the **Bring Forward** and **Send Backward** buttons.

18. Save the document as **poster** and close it.

3.28 Columns

Columns can be used to divide a page into two or more vertical sections. Once you fill the first column, text automatically flows into the second. This technique is really useful for creating documents such as newsletters or brochures.

Activity:

1. Open the document **Newsletter**. This file contains basic information about the new *Rumbling Rails* ride.

2. Display the **Page Layout** tab and click the **Columns** button, ⊞ Columns ▾, in the **Page Setup** group. From the drop-down menu that appears, select **Two**.

3. The page is now divided into two columns. The text reads down the first column and then flows into the second automatically. After the first paragraph of body text (starting "**This year...**"), create a new line and insert the image **Photo** from the data files folder.

4. Notice how text that was in the first column has been pushed into the second column. Resize the picture to approximately twice its original size and **Center** align it in the first column, as shown below.

high and will reach speeds of 80 miles per hour.

The ride is built entirely from steel and features a number of jaw-dropping falls,

> **Note:** Columns can be applied to an entire document or to specific parts of it. Once columns have been created they can be resized using the top ruler.

5. Similar to **Page Breaks**, you can also apply **Column Breaks** to force text into the next available column. Place the cursor *before* the subheading **Ride Features**.

6. From the **Page Layout** tab, click the **Breaks** drop-down button, ⊟ Breaks ▾. From the submenu that appears, select **Column**. The remaining text is forced into the second column.

7. Delete the column break. You may need to turn **Formatting Marks** on first, ¶.

8.   Save the document as **newsletter complete** and leave it open for the next exercise.

3.29 Headers and Footers

Headers and **footers** can be added to a document and will appear at the top and bottom of each page. Although often the same across all pages in a document, they can also be set to appear differently on alternate pages. Special automatically updating **fields** such as the date, time and page number can also be easily added.

Activity:

1.   Using the file **newsletter complete** saved in the previous exercise, select the **Insert** tab and click **Header**. From the submenu that appears, click **Edit Header** to reveal the header.

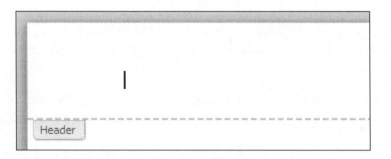

> **Note:**   Notice that the text in the main document becomes ghosted (and can't be directly edited). The **Header & Footer Tools - Design** tab also appears on the **Ribbon**.

2.   Enter the text **Press Release**.

3.   Locate the **Options** group on the **Design** tab and make sure that neither **Different First Page** nor **Different Odd & Even Pages** are checked.

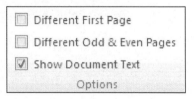

> **Note:**   These useful settings allow you to create a different **Header** and **Footer** for the first page of a document and then for each even and odd page afterwards.

4.   Click the **Go to Footer** button to switch to the footer. Then click **Date & Time** from the **Insert** group to display the **Date and Time** dialog box. Examine the various types of date/time format available.

> **Note:**   Different countries have different ways of presenting information such as the date. If another language or country is selected, the date may not appear correctly.

5. From the list of **Available formats**, make sure the first item (which shows today's date in the form **DD/MM/YYYY**) is selected. **English U.K.** should also be selected in the **Language** drop-down box. If it is not, select it now.

> Note: Notice the **Update automatically** checkbox. If this is selected, the date will be automatically updated on future views of the document. If it is left unselected, only today's date will appear.

6. Click **OK** to insert today's date in the footer. The date is inserted as a **field**.

7. Press <**Tab**> to move to the centre tab stop (headers and footers have a number of tab stops added automatically). From the **Insert** menu, click **Quick Parts** and select **Document Property | Author**. Your name is inserted as an automatically updating field.

> Note: Other document information, which can be seen and edited on the **File** menu's **Info** tab, can also be added as a field (e.g. file size, total page/word count, comments).

8. Press <**Tab**> again to move to the right tab stop. To insert a page number field, click **Page Number** from the **Header & Footer** group. Select **Current Position**, then **Plain Number**.

9. Click **Close Header and Footer** on the right of the **Ribbon** to return to the main document view. Notice that the header and footer are now ghosted (and can't be edited directly).

10. Create a **Column Break** before the heading **More Information** to force the text afterwards onto a new page. Notice that the second page also shows the same header and footer (and the page number has increased).

> Note: Fields can also be used in the body of a document, not just the header and footer.

11. Save the document with the same file name and leave it open for the next exercise.

3.30 Page Orientation and Printing

Page **orientation** simply refers to the direction in which a document is created and printed. It can be in **Portrait** (upright) or **Landscape** (sideways) mode.

 Portrait

 Landscape

> Note: Normally, *Word* documents are created in **Portrait** mode. This is the default setting and the orientation that you will use most often. **Landscape** is useful for creative documents such as brochures.

Activity:

1. To change the current document (**newsletter complete**) to **Landscape**, display the **Page Layout** tab and click the **Orientation** button in the **Page Setup** group.

2. Select **Landscape** from the options shown and all pages in the document are rotated 90 degrees (although the text is not).

3. Use the **Orientation** button to restore the page to **Portrait** mode.

4. Display the **File** tab and select **Print**. A preview of the first page as it will be printed is shown on the right.

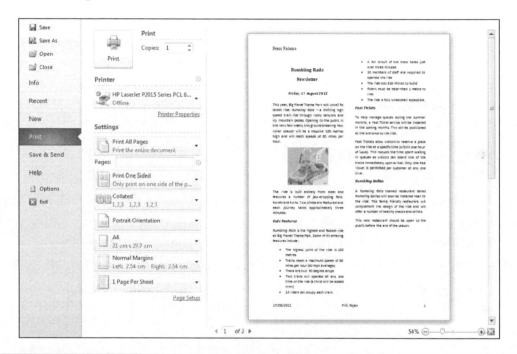

> **Note:** The **Print** screen is also accessible via the keyboard shortcut **<Ctrl P>**.

5. The print options that appear on this screen depend on the printers that you have available to you. Examine the print options on show and notice that you can change page orientation and margins from this screen also.

6. Enter **1** in the **Pages** box to print only the first page of the press release.

7. Make sure **Copies** is set to **1** also so that only one copy of the page is printed.

8. Choose the printer you would like to print to from the **Printer** drop-down button. All printers installed on your computer are visible here.

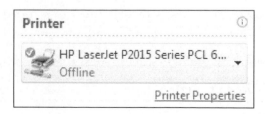

> **Note:** In work and education, you may have access to many printers. Try to find the name of the one closest to you. In some situations you may also be charged for printing, so be careful what you print.

9. Click the large **Print** button to print a copy of the newsletter on your chosen printer. You will automatically return to the main document view.

> **Note:** Alternatively, click the **Home** tab to return without printing.

10. Save and close the document.

3.31 Spelling and Grammar Checking

Word can check the spelling and grammar of any text-based documents that you open, and will even check new text as you type it. Words that are misspelled are shown with a wavy red line underneath them, and grammatical errors are shown with a wavy green line underneath. *Word* makes suggestions to help you correct errors which can either be accepted or ignored.

> A speling error.
>
> A grammar errors.

Activity:

1. Open the document **Roller Coaster**. Wait a moment and spelling errors will appear underlined in red.

> **Note:** If red wavy lines do not appear below at least one word, then the **Automatic Spelling & Grammar** feature is turned off. To turn it back on, click the **File** tab and select **Options**. Click the **Proofing** button and make sure **Check spelling as you type**, **Mark grammar errors as you type** and **Check grammar with spelling** are all selected. Click **OK**.

2. The quickest way of correcting a small number of errors is by using the mouse. Place the mouse over the first item underlined in red, **plavce**, and click once with the right mouse button. A shortcut menu appears with a list of suggestions.

3. Select **place** to correct the error.

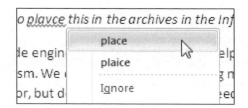

4.   When working with a document, a **Proofing** icon is shown on the **Status Bar** indicating the current spelling status of the document. If there are mistakes, , appears. If everything is correct, , appears.

5.   Locate the next error in the document. Notice that this one is not technically a spelling error but is a repeated word (**the the**). Right click the second word and select **Delete Repeated Word** from the shortcut menu that appears.

> Note: You could continue to correct errors in this way for the entire document. However, the **Spelling and Grammar** checking feature is far quicker.

6.   Place the cursor at the beginning of the document.

ABC
Spelling &
Grammar

7.   Display the **Review** tab and click the **Spelling & Grammar** button. The **Spelling and Grammar** dialog box appears.

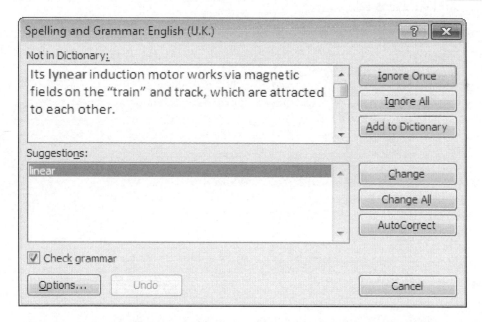

8.   The first spelling error is shown in the top area, **lynear**. Suggested alternatives are shown beneath. Errors can be ignored or changed (or added to the dictionary if they are correct).

9.   Select the alternative **linear** (if it is not already selected) and click **Change**. The error is corrected in the document.

> Note: If the **Suggestions** box does not contain the correct spelling, you can change the error shown in the top box manually. Click **Change** to replace the document text.

10. Work through the remainder of the document making any necessary corrections. A message appears when the check is complete.

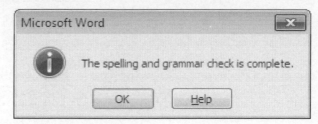

11. Click **OK** and check that the **Status Bar** no longer shows any proofing errors: .

12. Save the document as **roller coaster fixed** and then close it.

> Note: *Word's* spell checking feature only finds words that are not in its dictionary; it will not find mistakes such as **semi detached horse**. For this reason you should always proof read your documents after they have been spell-checked.

13. Open the document **Roller Coaster Grammar**.

14. A number of grammatical errors are underlined in green (it may take a few seconds for the errors to appear after the file is opened). Click the **Spelling & Grammar** button again on the **Review** tab.

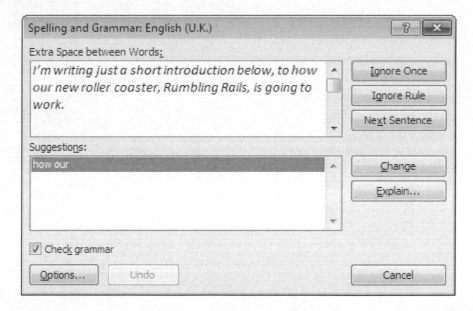

15. The first error is an extra space before **our**. Notice how the buttons at the right of the dialog box are slightly different to those shown when spelling is checked. Click **Change**.

16. The second error is a word at the start of a sentence that does not start with a capital letter. Click **Change** to accept the suggestion.

17. The third error is a little trickier in that a full stop has mistakenly been placed in the middle of a sentence. The problem is shown in the top box; use the keyboard to delete the full stop and then click **Change**.

18. Click **OK** when the check is complete and there are no proofing errors present.

19. Save the document as **roller coaster grammar fixed** and close it.

3.32 Templates

Templates are normal documents that have been saved in a special location to act as a starting point for future documents. They are useful for creating many documents of the same basic type (e.g. letters) as they have all the text and required styles, formatting and layout options preset.

Activity:

1. Open the document **Outline**. This is a normal document which contains a basic outline for a letter but does not contain any specific details.

2. Display the **File** tab and select **Save As**. From the **Save as type** drop-down box, select **Word Template**.

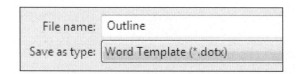

3. Make sure the **Templates** folder is selected in the **Save As** dialog box's navigation panel (this may happen automatically when you choose **Word Template** from the **Save as type** drop-down box).

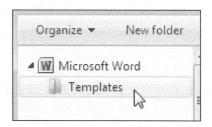

> **Note:** Documents created in *Word* have a **.docx** file extension (or **.doc** in older versions). *Word* **Templates** on the other hand have a **.dotx** (or **.dot**) extension.

4. Click **Save** and the template is saved. Close the **Outline** document.

5. Display the **File** tab and select **New**. Under **Available Templates**, select **My templates**. Notice that **Outline** now appears in the **New** dialog box.

My templates

6. Select **Outline** and click **OK**. A new document is created based upon the **Outline** template created earlier.

> **Note:** There are a number of built-in templates available within *Word* (or downloadable from *Office.com*) which may be of use when creating new documents.

7. You have received a job application from **Kerry Amos** for the role of **Engineer**. She lives at **32 Trent Street**, **Learnersville**, **LV2 3HJ**. Complete the letter by replacing the text in brackets with the applicant's contact information.

8. Save the document as **application** (in the <u>data files folder</u> for this section) and close it.

9. Create another document based on the **Outline** template. Notice that the changes made to the **application** document did not affect the original template.

10. You have received another job application from **Douglas Yorkshire** for the role of **Maintenance Manager**. He lives at **23b Finchale Street, Learnersville, LV3 2WS**. Complete the letter by replacing the text in brackets.

11. Save the document as **application2** and close it.

> Note: If you need to change the template you must open it from the **Templates** folder.

3.33 Mail Merge

Mail Merge is a facility in *Word* that lets you combine a document (e.g. a letter) with a separate "data source" (e.g. a list of names and addresses stored in a database). These two files, when merged, create a personalised copy of the document for everyone on the list.

Activity:

1. *Priti* would like to send a letter to all of the contacts in her building supplies database, inviting them to the opening of the new *Rumbling Rails* ride.

2. Open the document **Event**. Priti needs to create a personalised copy of this letter for each person in the **Builders** database. The database simply contains the contact information for seven people.

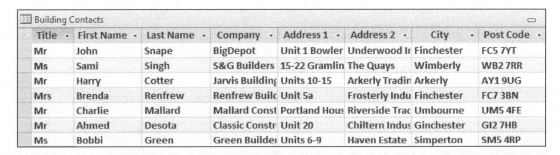

Title	First Name	Last Name	Company	Address 1	Address 2	City	Post Code
Mr	John	Snape	BigDepot	Unit 1 Bowler	Underwood Ir	Finchester	FC5 7YT
Ms	Sami	Singh	S&G Builders	15-22 Gramlin	The Quays	Wimberly	WB2 7RR
Mr	Harry	Cotter	Jarvis Building	Units 10-15	Arkerly Tradir	Arkerly	AY1 9UG
Mrs	Brenda	Renfrew	Renfrew Builc	Unit 5a	Frosterly Indu	Finchester	FC7 3BN
Mr	Charlie	Mallard	Mallard Const	Portland Hous	Riverside Trac	Umbourne	UM5 4FE
Mr	Ahmed	Desota	Classic Constr	Unit 20	Chiltern Indus	Ginchester	GI2 7HB
Ms	Bobbi	Green	Green Builde	Units 6-9	Haven Estate	Simperton	SM5 4RP

> Note: You will learn more about creating and working with databases in section 7.

3. Display the **Mailings** tab and click **Select Recipients** from the **Start Mail Merge** group. From the submenu that appears, select **Use Existing List**.

4. Locate the data files for this section and select the database file **Builders**. Click **Open**.

5.   The database of contacts is now connected to the open document. With the cursor flashing on the first empty line, select **Address Block** in the **Write & Insert Fields** group.

6.   The **Insert Address Block** dialog box appears. You can choose which information from the database you would like to include in the recipient's address. Notice the **Preview** which shows how the address will appear when the mail merge is complete.

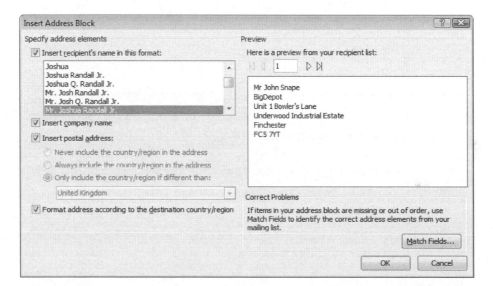

> Note: The **Match Fields** button lets you to fine-tune the address and select/hide details.

7.   The current format of the address is just what *Priti* is looking for. Click **OK** and notice that the text **<<AddressBlock>>** appears in the document. This is a field that will be replaced with personalised information when the mail merge is run.

> Note: **Edit Recipient List** allows you to choose which contacts to include in the merge.

8.   Place the cursor on the empty line <u>below</u> the date and select **Greeting Line** in the **Write & Insert Fields** group. The **Insert Greeting Line** dialog box appears allowing you to customise the letter's greeting. Notice the **Preview** again at the bottom of the dialog box.

9.   The format of the greeting is fine. Click **OK** and notice that the text **<<GreetingLine>>** appears in the document. Again, this will be replaced when the mail merge is run.

> Note: For more control, you can insert any individual field from the database (i.e. **Title**, **First Name**, **Address 1**, etc.) anywhere you like using **Insert Merge Field** button.

10.   You have now created the main mail merge document. Save it as **event complete**.

11. To see the results of the mail merge, click **Preview Results**. Notice that the mail merge fields are replaced with the contact information for the first person in the database, a **Mr John Snape** from **BigDepot**.

12. Finally, to run the mail merge, click **Finish & Merge** and then select **Edit Individual Documents**. Click **OK** at the dialog box (choosing to merge with **All** database records).

13. A new document is created containing a personalised letter for each recipient. Scroll down through the 7 pages and observe the results. Consider how useful the mail merge facility could be if you had hundreds of contacts!

14. Save the new mail merged document as **event letters** and close it. Then close the **event complete** document, saving any changes.

> Note: If you opened the **event complete** document again, you may be prompted to find and reconnect the **Builders** database.

3.34 Sharing Documents

It is very common in business for people to work together on a document, co-authoring and reviewing each others content. In *Word*, the **Track Changes** feature allows you to share your work with others, make comments and suggestions, and keep track of any edits, additions and deletions made. When you get your document back, you can decide whether to accept or reject the changes made.

Activity:

1. Open the document **Plan**. *Priti* created this file but has asked you to help improve it.

2. To track and record the changes that you make, select the **Review** tab and click the **Track Changes** button (not the drop-down arrow). The button is **toggled** (i.e. switched on), indicating that all changes will now be tracked.

> Note: Make sure that **Final: Show Markup** is selected in the **Display for Review**, drop-down box in the **Tracking** group. Other options in this box allow you to show the original document *before* changes and the final document *after* changes.

3. Make the following alterations to the text and notice the tracking highlights:

    - Add a new item to the bottom of the bulleted list: **Extra padding on head rests**.

    - Delete the bullet: **An annual painting of the ride supports**.

    - In the body text underneath the heading **Ride Testing**, make the words **daily**, **weekly** and **monthly** bold.

> Note: Deleted text appears with a line through it (known as **strikethrough**). New text appears underlined. Formatting changes appear as balloon comments.

4. In the **Staff Uniforms** paragraph, highlight the text **themed uniforms** and click the **New Comment** button in the **Comments** group.

> Note: Comments are useful for adding notes without affecting the document's text.

5. A new comment box appears containing a flashing cursor. Enter the following text: **Ideas for themed uniforms are still needed**.

6. Save the document as **interim plan** and close it.

7. The file was sent back to *Priti* and she accepted all of your changes. She also made some extra changes of her own which she would like you to review. Open the file **Revised Plan**.

8. Notice the new changes made by *Priti*. Display the **Review** tab to start accepting or rejecting them.

9. Locate the **Changes** group and click **Next** to select the first item for review (a deleted word). You agree with this change, so click the **Accept and Move to Next** button.

10. The landscaping for the base of the ride still needs a lot of work in your opinion. Click **Reject** to reject the deletion of this bullet and leave it in the document.

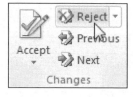

11. A storage box for loose personal items is a good idea! Accept the change.

> Note: To save time, you can use the **Accept** button's drop-down arrow to accept all of the changes in one go.

12. There are a number of minor formatting changes remaining. To accept all of these changes at once, click the **Accept and Move to Next** button's drop-down arrow and select **Accept All Changes in Document**.

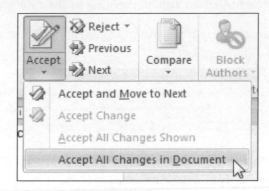

> Note: Notice that *Priti* has left you a comment regarding the staff uniforms.

13. Reviewing is now complete. To turn off tracking in this document, simple click the **Track Changes** toggle button again. No more changes will be recorded.

14. Save the document as **final plan** and close it.

3.35 Protecting Documents

Documents can be **password protected** or made **read-only** so that they cannot be opened by unauthorised people or mistakenly changed.

Activity:

1. Open the document **Sensitive**. This file contains employee information that you are required to keep private and confidential.

2. Display the **File** tab and click the **Protect Document** button. The options shown allow you to protect your document in a number of different ways.

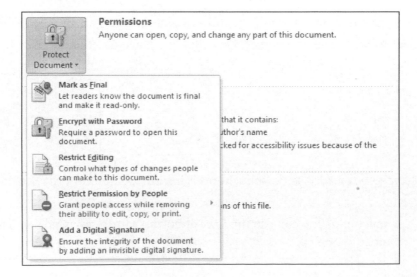

3. Examine the options available, and then click **Encrypt with Password** to display the **Encrypt Document** dialog box. Enter the password **priti12345**.

> **Note:** Encryption is the name given to the process of scrambling the contents of a file so that it cannot be opened and read without permission. It is a useful technique for protecting sensitive documents that you store on portable storage media or send via email.

4. Click **OK**. When prompted, enter the password again (this is to check that you entered it correctly first time) and then click **OK**. The document is now password protected.

5. Close the document and save any changes.

6. Next, try to open the document **Sensitive** again. You are asked to enter a password in order to open the file. Unless you enter the correct password, it is impossible to open and view the file's contents.

7. Enter the password **priti12345** and click **OK**.

> **Note:** To remove the password protection from a document, display the **Encrypt Document** dialog box again, delete the password, and click **OK**.

8. To mark a document as **Final** and allow others to read it without making changes, display the **Protect Document** menu again.

9. Select **Mark as Final** and click **OK**. Read the contents of the information dialog box that appears and then click **OK** to accept it.

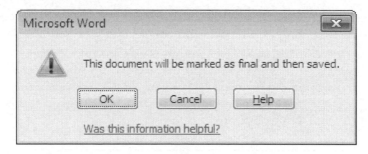

10. The document is now **Read-Only** (i.e. can only be opened and read, not saved), and any future changes must be saved as a different file with a different name.

11. Click the **Home** tab to return to the document. Notice that editing is restricted (a yellow bar appears at the top of the screen) and you can no longer save this file.

12. Close the document and any other open documents without saving.

13. Close *Word*.

3.36 Next Steps

Well done! You have now completed all of the exercises in this section. If you feel you are ready to test your knowledge and understanding of the topics covered, move on to the following **Develop Your Skills** activities. If there are any features of *Microsoft Word* that you are unsure about, you should revisit the appropriate exercises and try them again before moving on.

If you are interested in exploring some of *Microsoft Word's* more powerful features, why don't you use the Internet to find out a little more about the following advanced topics.

Feature	Description
References	*Word* can automatically create a **Table of Contents** and an **Index** page using a document's headers and keywords.
Sections	When certain pages or parts of a document are to be formatted differently from the rest, e.g. columns, page layout or page numbering, the document can be divided into sections. A document can have as many sections as required.
Styles	**Styles** are an extremely useful feature of *Word*. Build on the basic lessons learned in 3.16 and explore the various uses of styles and how they can help to improve your productivity.
Macros	A macro records keystrokes and menu selections and then plays them back exactly as they were recorded. A macro can be created so that frequently repeated tasks can be performed automatically.
Subdocuments	Large documents can be split up into many smaller documents called subdocuments which can be worked on independently. A **Master Document** is used to bring them all together in one place.
SmartArt	**SmartArt** lets you create diagrams from within *Word* using a variety of different layouts and visual styles. This feature is really useful for creating flow and relationship diagrams.
Hyperlinks	Hyperlinks and bookmarks allow readers of a document to jump to a specific place in the text (or to a file or web address) by clicking a single link or button.

At the end of every section you get the chance to complete two activities. These will help you to develop your skills and prepare for your exam. Don't forget to use the planning and review checklists at the back of the book to help organise and review your work.

> Note: Answers to these activities are provided in this section's **Sample Solutions** folder.

Develop Your Skills: Rumbling Rails Mail Shot

In this activity you will be asked to create a simple promotional "mail shot" for *Priti*. You will need to use all of the ICT skills that you have learned in this section to plan, develop and present an appropriate solution.

Activity 1

Did I tell you that our new *Rumbling Rails* roller coaster is a massive 100 metres high and can reach speeds of 80 miles per hour? It's now the biggest and best ride in the theme park, and to celebrate our "grand opening" we are planning to hold a party next week for park staff and suppliers.

To advertise the event, I need to design a simple one page promotional mail shot. I've made a start and entered all the information that I think is needed, but I've not had a chance to format the text and make it look professional. Can you help? The following files are required:

* **Mail Shot**   My incomplete mail shot document

* **Photo**   An image file containing a photograph of the new ride

* **Logo**   An image file containing the theme park's logo

Start by opening the file **Mail Shot** document. Notice that the text formatting is very poor and inconsistent. Correct this first, and then use **WordArt** and header styles to enhance the document and make it look more appealing. Insert and arrange the **Photo** and **Logo** images as appropriate. When you are finished and happy with the design and layout of the mail shot, save the document as **mail shot complete**.

Develop Your Skills: Financial Report

In this activity you will be asked to create a detailed report for *Priti's* boss. You will need to use all of the advanced ICT skills that you have learned in this section to create a suitable solution. To get started, it may help you to break the problem down into smaller parts first.

Activity 2

I've just received the following e-mail from *Monty Spangles*, owner of the park, asking me to create a report on the cost of the new *Rumbling Rails* ride:

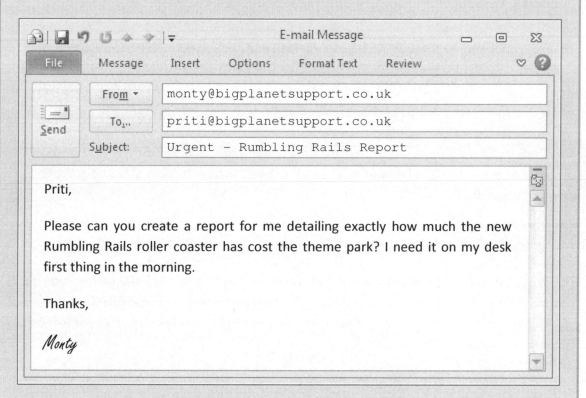

E-mail Message

File   Message   Insert   Options   Format Text   Review

From ▾   monty@bigplanetsupport.co.uk

To...   priti@bigplanetsupport.co.uk

Subject: Urgent – Rumbling Rails Report

Priti,

Please can you create a report for me detailing exactly how much the new Rumbling Rails roller coaster has cost the theme park? I need it on my desk first thing in the morning.

Thanks,

Monty

Can you help me prepare the report? You will need to create a new, well-presented document for *Monty* that looks professional and is easy to read. Include a table showing the financial information stored in the **Final Costs** file. Unfortunately, I forgot to add **Maintenance** to the list which cost **£2500** – will you make sure this is included too?

To help *Monty* understand the contents of the document, describe the table of costs in one or two sentences. Also mention that the reason the cost of **Train components** has increased by approximately **£100,000** was due to the purchase of a third train (which will enter operation next month). If *Monty* has any questions about the report he can contact me on telephone extension **0456**.

It is common practice for all official *Big Planet Theme Park* documents to contain the park logo in the top right corner. Do this now by inserting and arranging the **Logo** file as appropriate. When you are finished, save the document as **cost report**.

Microsoft Excel

4 | Microsoft Excel

Hi, my name's Zak...

I'm a member of the engineering and maintenance department here at *Big Planet Theme Park*. My team and I are responsible for making sure that all of the rides are properly maintained and safe for visitors. Just imagine what would happen if a *Haunted Castle* ride broke down when people were half way through it!

My main role at the park is to reduce costly breakdowns and help develop ways to improve the overall safety and reliability of the rides. I have plenty of mechanical and engineering jobs to keep me busy, but I also spend a lot of time creating spreadsheets to manage my team's budget. We only have a small amount of money to spend, but if we invest it properly, the life of our rides will be extended and the park will save a lot of money.

To help me keep track of my team's spending, I use the program *Microsoft Excel*. Many professionals in various types of organisation use this program – it's really useful for working with numbers and performing calculations quickly and accurately. It also allows me to represent complex data graphically, making it much easier to understand and communicate to others.

What you will learn:

In this section you will use the program *Microsoft Excel* to help *Zak* complete a number of everyday tasks at *Big Planet Theme Park*. You will see how to use simple spreadsheet techniques to enter, develop and organise numerical information for a variety of purposes.

Knowledge, skills and understanding:

* Use *Microsoft Excel* to create spreadsheets and manipulate numerical data

* Learn the best tools and features to solve a range of everyday problems

* Apply a variety of professional editing, formatting and layout techniques

Data files

The files needed to complete the activities in this section are provided in the **Section 4** data folder (see note on page **vii** to download these files). Spreadsheets that you create or edit can be saved to the same folder.

4.1 Using Microsoft Excel

Microsoft Excel is most commonly used to work with figures and is a perfect choice of application for any task that involves numbers. Once a spreadsheet has been set up correctly, it can be used to perform a number of complex calculations quickly and accurately (and any results will be automatically updated when the data is changed). Typically, spreadsheets can be used to help with the following tasks:

* Maths problems, budgets and accounting

* Cash flows and forecasts

* Data analysis

A spreadsheet stores information in a grid of **cells**, which generally contain text, numbers or **formulas**. Cells are arranged in numbered **rows** (going down the screen) and lettered **columns** (going across the screen), forming a **worksheet**. One or more worksheets together are known as a **workbook**, the name *Excel* gives to a saved file.

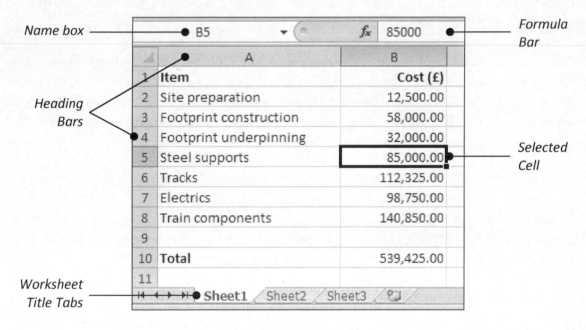

Notice the numbers running down the left side of the spreadsheet and the letters running across the top. These are called **Heading Bars** and are used to **reference** cells. In the picture above, the cell **B5** is currently selected (the location where **Column B** and **Row 5** *intersect*). This is highlighted on the **Heading Bars** and shown in the **Name** box.

> Note: When referring to a cell, the column letter <u>always</u> comes before the row number.

> Note: Although mainly used for working with numbers, people also use spreadsheets for creating and working with simple lists of data (e.g. product lists, stock lists, customer contact lists, etc).

Spreadsheets can also take basic data and present it in a variety of attractive graphs and charts. One important advantage of this is that the graphics created are much easier to understand at a glance. They can also be really useful for including in other documents or presentations.

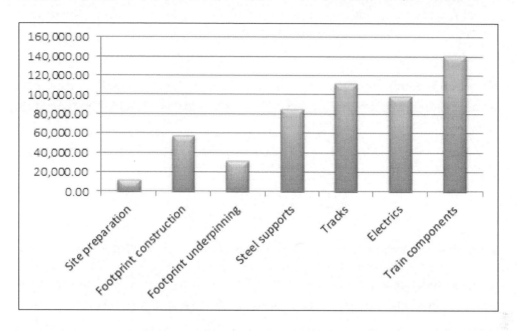

4.2 Creating a Spreadsheet

When creating a spreadsheet you should start on **Sheet1** (the default worksheet) and begin entering data in the top left corner. You should also add **labels** to the top of columns or the start of rows to help describe the contents of the worksheet.

It is <u>very</u> important to enter numbers correctly and accurately. If you make mistakes the spreadsheet will produce the wrong results.

Activity:

1. Start *Excel*. A blank workbook is created by default.

> Note: Notice that cell **A1** is currently selected (it is the **active** cell). The workbook contains three worksheets by default; **Sheet1**, **Sheet2** and **Sheet3**.

2. A useful descriptive label can be entered into a cell by selecting it and typing. With cell **A1** selected, type **Maintenance checks week 7**.

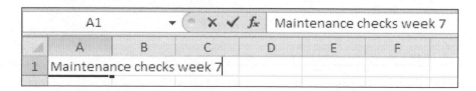

> Note: When entering text into a cell, notice that it also appears in the **Formula Bar**.

3. To complete the cell entry, press <**Enter**>. The active cell moves down to cell **A2**.

> **Note:** The text looks as though it also occupies cells **B1** and **C1**, but this is not the case. A label will expand and appear on top of other cells if – and only if – the other cells are empty. Cells containing numbers do not do this.

4. You can move to other cells by pointing and clicking or by using the arrow keys on your keyboard. Press the down arrow key <↓> to move to cell **A3**, and then type **Staff**.

	A	B	C
1	Maintenance checks week 7		
2			
3	Staff		

5. Next, press <→> to move to cell **B3** (you don't need to press <**Enter**> to confirm an entry).

6. The worksheet that you are creating is to be used to record daily safety checks for the park's engineering and maintenance team. Enter data as shown below.

	A	B	C	D	E	F	G	H
1	Maintenance checks week 7							
2								
3	Staff	Mon	Tue	Wed	Thu	Fri	Sat	Sun
4	Aaron							
5	Adya							
6	Jack							
7	Sun							
8	Zak							

7. The actual maintenance figures now need to be entered. Move to cell **B4** and then enter the number **16**. Continue to input the data below using whichever technique you like to move between cells (note that each employee has two days off).

	A	B	C	D	E	F	G	H
1	Maintenance checks week 7							
2								
3	Staff	Mon	Tue	Wed	Thu	Fri	Sat	Sun
4	Aaron	16	22	9	17	20		
5	Adya	21	16	19	15			12
6	Jack		19	15	14	17	11	
7	Sun		18		32	21	12	10
8	Zak	12	16			24	14	11

> **Note:** Notice that numbers appear right aligned by default. This helps you to tell at a glance which cells contain text and which contain numbers.

> **Note:** You can change a worksheet's name simply by double clicking the relevant tab at the bottom of the screen and typing a new title.

8. Double click the current worksheet's title tab (**Sheet1**) and enter the title **Maintenance**.

Insert Worksheet

9. Press <**Enter**>. The worksheet has been renamed.

10. Click the **Sheet2** tab to display that worksheet. As no data has been entered here, it is empty.

11. Click the **Maintenance** tab again to return to the first sheet.

> **Note:** To add a new worksheet to your workbook, click the **Insert Worksheet** button. It is a good idea to keep all relevant worksheets in the same workbook.

12. Display **Sheet2** again. From the **Cells** group on the **Home** tab, click the drop-down arrow on the **Delete** button and select **Delete Sheet**.

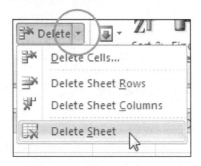

13. The worksheet is deleted and the next available sheet selected. Delete **Sheet3** also, leaving only the **Maintenance** worksheet remaining.

14. Save the workbook as **maintenance** and then close it.

4.3 Resizing Columns and Rows

You may sometimes need to change column widths and row heights to better display the contents of cells and to make your spreadsheets easier to read. This is simply done by dragging the column or row boundaries on the relevant **Heading Bar**.

Activity:

1. Open the workbook **Attendance**. This file contains information on visitor numbers to four specific *Haunted Castle* attractions. Unfortunately, it has been very poorly designed and many of the labels are difficult to read.

2. Move your mouse pointer to the boundary line between column **A** and column **B** in the column **Heading Bar**. The pointer changes to a double-headed arrow, ↔.

Heading Bar

3. Using click and drag, reduce the width of column **A** to approximately **20.00** (the column's width is shown in a **ToolTip** as you drag).

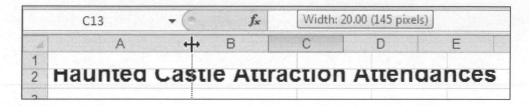

> **Note:** Width is measured in number of characters (20 will show 20 standard characters).

4. Using the same technique, increase the widths of columns **B**, **C**, **D** and **E** to **17.00**.

5. Row 2 is too small (in height) to contain the text contained in **A2**. Place the mouse pointer over the border between row **2** and **3** on the row **Heading Bar**, and using click and drag, increase the height of row **2** to approximately **24.00**.

> **Note:** For more precision, right click a column header and select **Column Width**. You can then enter a precise value. To adjust a row, right click and select **Row Height**.

> **Note:** Similar to *Microsoft Word*, *Excel* also has a **Zoom** feature on the **Status Bar** for zooming into worksheets.

6. Use the **Zoom Slider** on the **Status Bar** to increase the zoom level to **150%**. Explore some of the other zoom levels available.

7. When you are finished, use the **Zoom Slider** to restore the zoom level to **100%**.

> **Note:** You can continue this section using any zoom level that you feel comfortable with.

8. Save the workbook as **visitors** and close it. You will use this file again later.

4.4 Ranges

A **range** is a rectangular collection of cells. Just as single cells are identified by a cell reference, ranges are identified by the first and last cell in the selection. For example, the four cells **B2**, **B3**, **C2** and **C3** can be identified by the range **B2:C3**.

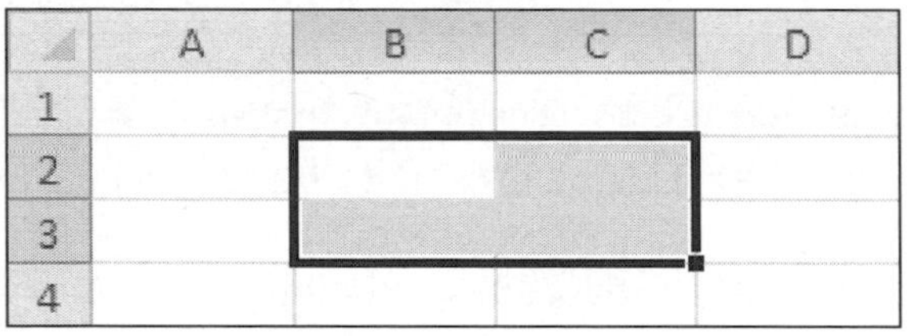

Ranges are selected by clicking and dragging to highlight a number of cells. Entire rows or columns can also be selected by clicking row or column headings.

Activity:

1.   Start a new, blank workbook.

2.   Move your mouse pointer over cell **B2**. Then, click and drag so that a range of four cells (two rows and two columns) is highlighted (as shown above).

3.   Release the mouse button. Notice that the first cell in the range is white and the other cells are highlighted in blue. The first cell is the active cell.

4.   More than one range can be selected at a time by holding down the <**Ctrl**> key while clicking and dragging. Press and hold <**Ctrl**> now and click and drag the range **C5:D6**. There should now be two separate ranges highlighted.

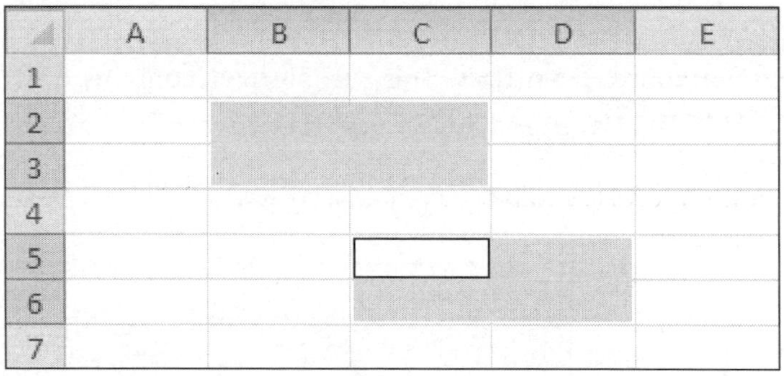

5.   Click anywhere on the worksheet to remove the selected ranges. Next, click on **B** in the column **Heading Bar**. All of column **B** is now highlighted.

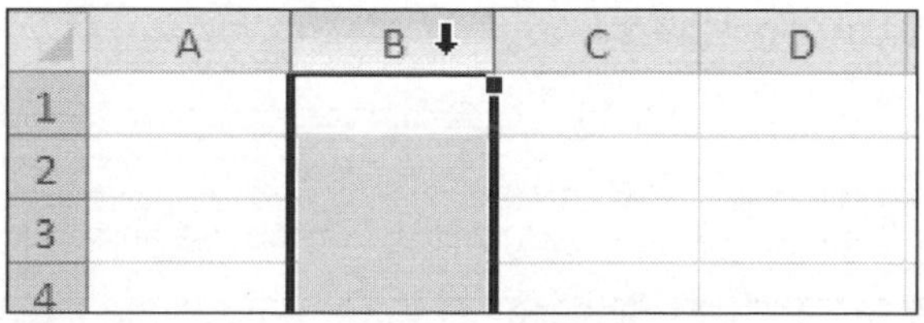

6.   Click on **2** in the row **Heading Bar**. All of row **2** is now highlighted.

7. Click and drag on the row **Heading Bar** to select the row headings from **5** to **7**. Three rows are now selected.

8. A range can also be selected by clicking the first and last cell while holding down the **<Shift>** key. Click on cell **B2**, hold **<Shift>**, and click on cell **F9**. The range **B2:F9** is selected.

9. A range can be extended (or reduced) by holding down the **<Shift>** key and clicking on another cell. Hold **<Shift>** and click on cell **G12**. The range is extended to **B2:G12**.

10. Select the cell **C5** and scroll across to column **Z**. While holding **<Shift>** click in cell **Z5**. The range **C5:Z5** is selected.

> Note: Notice that after column **Z** the headings continue **AA**, **AB**, **AC**, **AD**, and so on.

11. Close the workbook <u>without</u> saving.

4.5 Editing Cells

You can change the contents of an individual cell by simply overwriting the text that is there. This is known as **In Cell Editing**. However, when a cell entry is long or complicated, the changes are sometimes best made by editing the data in the **Formula Bar**.

Activity:

1. Open the workbook **Train Cars**. This spreadsheet contains a list of train cars which are used as part of the **Haunted Castle's** ride *The Viper*.

2. Select cell **A7**, then click once in the **Formula Bar**.

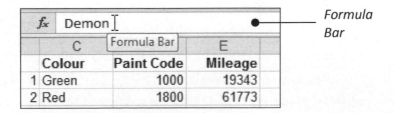

Formula Bar

3. The mode indicator on the **Status Bar** now shows the text **Edit**.

4. Use the **<Delete>** and **<Backspace>** keys to remove the label **Demon**. Enter the new label **Griffin** and press **<Enter>** to confirm the changes.

> **Note:** You can also click the **Enter** button, ✔, on the **Formula Bar** to accept the change.

5. Select cell **E7** which contains the value **23765**. Type **21254** to overwrite this value and then press <**Enter**> to confirm the change.

6. Select cell **E16** and overtype with the value **1200**. Instead of pressing <**Enter**> press <**Esc**>. The change is cancelled and the value in **E16** returns to **3500**.

> **Note:** You can also click the **Cancel** button, ✕, on the **Formula Bar** to cancel the change.

7. The **Kraken** car has been damaged and replaced by the **Harpy**. It has the same **Ref No.**, **Colour** and **Paint Code**, but its **Mileage** is **0**. Make those changes.

15	Harpy		14	Red	1800	0

8. The **Vampire** car is getting old and has been taken out of action. Click on cell **A9** and then press the <**Delete**> key to remove the entry.

9. Click on cell **B9** and then click **Clear** from the **Editing** group, 🖋. Select **Clear All** from the drop-down list that appears.

10. Select the range **C9:E9** and press <**Delete**> to remove the contents of those three cells at the same time.

11. Save the workbook as **train cars updated** and close it. You will return to this later.

4.6 Basic Formulas

Formulas are used to perform calculations using the numbers entered in a spreadsheet. For example, formulas can be used to add a column or row of numbers together to obtain a total. If the data is changed at any time, the formula will automatically recalculate the result.

Activity:

1. Display the **File** tab and start a new, blank workbook. In cell **B2** enter **34** and in cell **B3** enter **16**.

	A	B
1		
2		34
3		16

> **Note:** Although it is common practice to start creating spreadsheets from the upper left corner, you can in fact start in any cell you like.

2. Make **B5** the active cell by clicking on it.

3. To add the contents of **B2** and **B3** together and display the result in **B5**, type in the formula **=b2+b3** and press **<Enter>**.

> Note:　All formulas begin with an equals sign, =. Cell references are used so that results are recalculated if data in those cells change.

4. Cell **B5** now displays the result of adding cells **B2** and **B3** together (**50**).

5. Click cell **B5** and notice that the **Formula Bar** displays **=B2+B3**, the formula for this cell.

> Note:　It is usually quicker to use the numeric keypad on the right of a standard keyboard to enter large amounts of numbers. However, you may need to activate the **Number Lock** feature on your keyboard first by pressing **<Num Lock>** (a light on your keyboard will appear when it is activated).

6. Click in cell **B3** and enter **26** to overwrite the original contents.

7. Press **<Enter>** and the formula updates **B5** to **60**, the new result.

> Note:　You will learn a lot more about formulas as you progress through this section.

8. Close the workbook <u>without</u> saving.

4.7　Performing Calculations

The most basic operations in maths are **add**, **subtract**, **multiply** and **divide**. Similarly, you will often want to perform these calculations in *Excel* (you have already used **add** in the previous exercise). However, the keyboard symbols needed to perform these operations look slightly different to those you may be used to:

+	**Add**
-	**Subtract**
*	**Multiply**
/	**Divide**

> Note:　These symbols usually appear twice on a standard keyboard; one set spread around the main letters and numbers and the other set on the numeric keypad. Many people find that the numeric keypad is easier to use because the keys are closer together and the **<Shift>** key is not needed.

Activity:

1. Open the workbook **Operators**.

2.   Make **B6** the active cell by clicking on it, and then type in **=b4+b5**.

	A	B	C	D	E
1	Mathematical Operations				
2					
3	Number	Add	Subtract	Multiply	Divide
4	First	6	7	3	12
5	Second	3	4	5	4
6	Result	=b4+b5			

Note: Notice that, as you type the formula, the referenced cells are highlighted on the worksheet. Lower case (small) letters will be automatically capitalised.

3.   Press <**Enter**>. This creates a formula to add the contents of cells **B4** and **B5**. The answer is displayed as **9**.

Note: Have you noticed the pop-up menu that appears when you enter formulas? This is used to create more complex formulas which you will learn more about later.

4.   Click in cell **C6** and enter the formula to subtract the two numbers above, **=c4-c5**. Rather than press <**Enter**>, press the right arrow key, →. The answer is displayed as **3**.

5.   In cell **D6**, enter the formula to multiply the two numbers above, **=d4*d5**. The answer is displayed as **15**.

6.   In cell **E6**, enter the formula to divide the two numbers above, **=e4/e5**. Press <**Enter**> and the answer is displayed as **3**.

E6			f_x	=E4/E5	
	A	B	C	D	E
1	Mathematical Operations				
2					
3	Number	Add	Subtract	Multiply	Divide
4	First	6	7	3	12
5	Second	3	4	5	4
6	Result	9	3	15	3

7.   Save the workbook as **operators complete** and close it.

4.8 Brackets

If more than one mathematical operation appears in a single formula, their order can be very important. For the four operations that you have seen so far, *Excel* performs calculations in this order: **Brackets, Division, Multiplication, Addition** and finally **Subtraction** (the **BODMAS** and **BIDMAS** rules in maths). As brackets come first, they can be used to force *Excel* to perform calculations in a specific order.

For example, in the formula **A1+A2/A3**, BODMAS states that the value in cell **A2** should be divided by **A3** first and then added to **A1**. However, brackets can be used to make sure **A1** is added to **A2** first before being divided by **A3**, as the following formula shows: **(A1+A2)/A3**.

Activity:

1. *Zak* has asked you to work out how many people are able to ride the *Haunted Castle's Black Hole* attraction at a time. Start a new, blank workbook.

2. The *Black Hole* ride has two trains which always leave together. Each train has 10 cars and each car can hold a maximum of 4 passengers. Starting in **B2**, enter the following data (and increase the size of the columns so that the labels all fit).

	A	B	C	D	E
1					
2		Passengers per car	Train 1 cars	Train 2 cars	Capacity
3		4	10	10	

3. To work out how many people can ride the attraction – its *capacity* – the number of passengers per car must be multiplied by the total number of cars for both trains.

4. Click on cell **E3** and type the formula **=b3*c3+d3**. Press <**Enter**> and the answer given is **50**. Unfortunately, this is wrong – but can you tell why?

5. Due to the rules of BODMAS, the multiplication was carried out *before* the addition. Click on cell **E3** and press the <**Delete**> key to remove the formula.

6. This time you will use brackets to make sure the addition occurs first. Type in the following formula instead: **=b3*(c3+d3)** and press <**Enter**>.

7. Check that the answer displayed is now **80**; passengers per car multiplied by the total number of cars.

Passengers per car	Train 1 cars	Train 2 cars	Capacity
4	10	10	80

> **Note:** Brackets can also be placed inside of other brackets, giving you even more control.

8. Good job. Save the workbook as **capacity** and close it.

4.9 Functions

Functions are special types of formula that are built into *Excel* to help save you time. There are many functions available that can perform a number of common calculations, but in this exercise you will only look at five of the most useful.

SUM	Adds all the numbers in a range
MIN	Returns the smallest number in a range
MAX	Returns the largest number in a range
AVERAGE	Returns the average (mean) of a range
COUNT	Counts the number of cells in a range

Activity:

1.   Open the workbook **Favourites**. *The Viper* ride has several trains, and each train has 3 cars (each with a unique design and colour scheme). *Zak* recently asked visitors to vote on their favourite type of car and totalled the results in the **Favourite Votes** column.

2.   *Zak* would now like you to complete the spreadsheet by calculating the *total* number of votes received for *all* cars, the *lowest* and *highest* vote, and the *average* vote. He also wants to know the number of cars that were included in the survey.

> **Note:**   It is very difficult to remember all of the functions built in to *Excel*. Luckily, you don't need to – the **Insert Function** feature can be used instead.

3.   Start by clicking in cell **G6**. To add all of the votes for all cars together, click the **Insert Function** button on the **Formula Bar**.

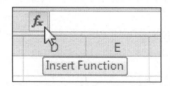

4.   The **Insert Function** dialog box appears. From the category drop-down menu, select each category in turn to see all of the available functions – there are well over 200!

5.   Select the category **Math & Trig**. Then, from the **Select a function** list, find and select the function **SUM** (the function names are in alphabetical order). Notice the brief description of the function that appears towards the bottom of the dialog box.

> **SUM(number1,number2,...)**
> Adds all the numbers in a range of cells.

6.   Click **OK**. The **Function Arguments** dialog box is displayed, prompting for a range of values to send to the **SUM** function.

> **Note:**   **Arguments** are simply the values that you give a function to work with. In the case of **SUM**, the arguments are a range of cell references containing numbers.

7.   In the **Number1** box, click the **Collapse** button, [image], to the right of the **Number1** box. This hides most of the dialog box and lets you select a range in the workbook by clicking and dragging (you can ignore the range that has been automatically found).

8.   Click and drag the range **D5:D18**. The range appears in the collapsed dialog box.

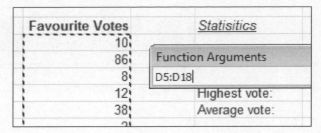

9. Click the **Expand** button, 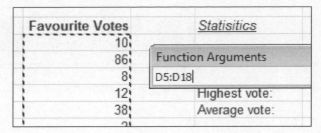, to restore the collapsed **Function Arguments** dialog box.

> **Note:**   You can use more than one range with a function. A second range can be placed in the **Number2** box, then the **Number3 box** (which will appear), and so on.

10. Click **OK**. The function is entered into the worksheet and the result is displayed (**234**), which is all the values in the selected range added together.

> **Note:**   You could also enter this formula the long way by adding each cell individually. However, the **SUM** function is much easier to use and far more practical.

11. Select cell **G7**, and then use the **Insert Function** button to launch the **Insert Function** dialog box. Select the **Statistical** category, then find and select **MIN**. Click **OK**.

12. Once again, the **Function Arguments** dialog box appears. Collapse it using the button in the **Number1** box and select the range **D5:D18**.

13. Expand the **Function Arguments** dialog box and click **OK**. The function is entered into the worksheet and the result is displayed (**2**).

14. Select cell **G8**. Then, use the **Insert Function** dialog box to find and select the **MAX** function and apply it to the range **D5:D18**. The result is displayed (**86**).

15. Select cell **G9**. Again, use the **Insert Function** dialog box to find and select the **AVERAGE** function and apply it to the range **D5:D18**. The result is displayed (**18**).

> **Note:**   If you know a function's name, you can enter it manually into the **Formula Bar**.

16. Select cell **G11**. Then, enter the formula **=COUNT(D5:D18)**. Press <**Enter**> and the result is displayed (**13**).

Statisitics	
Total votes:	234
Lowest vote:	2
Highest vote:	86
Average vote:	18
Cars with votes:	13

> **Note:** Notice that the result of the **COUNT** function is **13**, even though there are 14 cells in the range. This is because **COUNT** only counts cells that contain a number.

17. An error was made by *Zak* when he was inputting the results. The *Harpy* ride received 4 votes. Select cell **D17** and enter **4**. Notice the effect this has on the function calculations.

18. The spreadsheet is now complete. Save it as **favourites complete** and then close it.

4.10 AutoSum

The most common calculation used in spreadsheets is simple addition. To save people time entering the **SUM** function and selecting a range, the **AutoSum** feature can be used instead.

Activity:

1. Open the workbook **maintenance** that you saved earlier.

2. In both cells **A9** and **I3**, enter the label **Total**.

3. Click on cell **B9**. The five cells above need to be added together to find the total. Enter the formula **=SUM(B4:B8)** and press **<Enter>**. The answer should be **49**.

> **Note:** *Why add cells that contain nothing?* Well, if numbers were placed in these cells at a later stage then the formula would still work, but a formula with cells missing from the range would not.

4. Select cell **C9**. Then, click the **Sum** button, Σ, in the **Editing** group on the **Home** tab.

5. *Excel* automatically looks for nearby numbers to add (a feature called **AutoSum**). In this case the five values directly above cell **C9** are found and highlighted.

Mon	Tue	Wed	Thu	Fri
16	22	9	17	
21	16	19	15	
	19	15	14	
	18		32	
12	16			
49	=SUM(C4:C8)			
	SUM(**number1**, [number2], ...)			

6. Press **<Enter>** to place the answer **91** in cell **C9**. Select **C9** again and notice that the formula **=SUM(C4:C8)** appears in the **Formula Bar**.

7. Select cell **I4** and then click the **Sum** button, Σ. *Excel* finds numbers to the left and automatically sums the 7 cells **B4** to **H4**. Press **<Enter>**. The answer is **84**.

> **Note:** **SUM** will automatically look up and down for numbers to sum first and then left to right. If the range it finds is wrong, simply click and drag to select a new one.

8. Formulas for the other cells will be added later by copying. Save the changes to the workbook and then close it.

4.11 IF Functions

The **IF** function checks the contents of a cell and, if a **logical expression** (a test) is true, performs one action; if not, it performs another. **IF** functions may look confusing at first, but they are actually quite easy to understand and use once you try them.

Activity:

1. Open the workbook **Petty Cash**. This spreadsheet contains an incomplete account of all small purchases made by engineering and maintenance staff at the *Haunted Castle*.

2. Notice that the maximum amount of expenses for April is £300 (cell **G4**). *Zak* needs to know if the department has gone over-budget that month and spent too much money. Select cell **D22** and use the **SUM** function to add all the values in the range **D5:D20**.

3. To alert *Zak* if petty cash expenses go over-budget, the word **Yes!** should appear in cell **G6** if – and only if – the value in **D22** exceeds £300. To do this, the useful **IF** function can be used.

4. First, select cell **G6**. Then, click the **Insert Function** button on the **Formula Bar** to display the **Insert Function** dialog box.

5. Select the category **Logical**. Then, from the **Select a function** list, find and select the function **IF**. Click **OK** and the **Function Argument** dialog box appears.

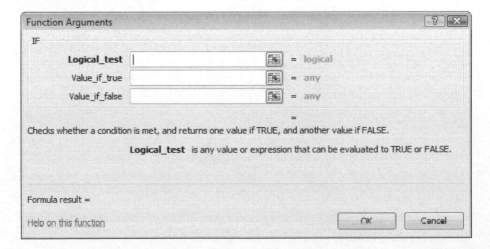

6. The **Logical_test** box is used to enter a **logical expression** (a test) that can be **evaluated** (worked out) as either **true** or **false**. In this case, we are looking to see if the value in **D22** is more than £300. So, enter the following expression: **D22>300**.

> **Note:** Useful logical operators for **IF** functions include equals (=), less than (<), less than or equal to (<=), greater than (>), greater than or equal to (>=), and not equal to (<>).

7. In the **Value_if_true** box, enter **Yes!**. If the **Logical_test** expression is ever evaluated as true, then this value will appear in cell **G6**.

8. In the **Value_if_false** box, enter **No**. If the **Logical_test** expression is ever evaluated as false, then this value will appear in cell **G6** instead.

9. Click **OK**. The **IF** function automatically checks to see if the value in **D22** is more than £300. It is currently not (the logical expression evaluates to false), and so the value **No** appears in cell **G6**. *Zak's* very happy, but...

10. *Sun* has just submitted two claims. Enter **£13.00** in **D17** and **£19.99** in **D19**. This increases the total in **D22** to more than £300, and so the value in **G6** changes to **Yes!** It looks like *Zak's* department is over-budget in April after all!

11. Select cell **G6** and examine the **IF** function in the **Formula Bar**: **=IF(D22>300,"Yes!","No")**.

> **Note:** You can also place **IF** functions *inside* other **IF** functions as **Value_if_true** or **Value_if_false** arguments. These are known as **Nested IF** functions.

12. Save the spreadsheet as **petty cash complete** and close it.

4.12 Cut, Copy and Paste

In the same way that you can cut, copy and paste text in *Microsoft Word*, you can also cut, copy and paste cell contents in *Excel*. You can cut and copy labels, values and formulas. Importantly, any formula that you copy to another location will be <u>automatically adjusted</u> so that it refers to the appropriate cells around it (this does not happen when you cut and paste a formula).

Activity:

1. Open the workbook **Breakdowns**. This spreadsheet contains an account of all ride failures that occurred last year in the *Haunted Castle*.

2. The label in cell **D10** is in the incorrect place. Select the cell and click **Cut**, ✄ , from the **Clipboard** group of the **Home** tab (you can also press <**Ctrl+X**>).

> **Note:** Unlike most other programs, the cut item is not removed immediately. Instead, an animated box is placed around it.

3. Select cell **B13** and click the **Paste** button from the **Clipboard** group (or press **<Ctrl+V>**). The cut cell is then moved to the new location.

4. The result in **C10** needs to be in **B11**. Use cut and paste to move the formula in **C10** to the empty cell **B11**.

5. Copy the formula in **B11** using the **Copy** button, 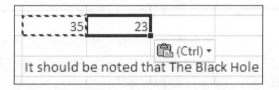 (or press **<Ctrl+C>**). Paste it into **C11**. *Excel* automatically adjusts the copied formula to reference the cells in the new column.

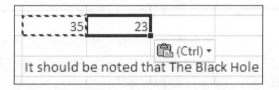

> **Note:** Feel free to examine the contents of cells **B11** and **C11** in the **Formula Bar**. Notice that *Excel* has automatically changed the column reference from **B** to **C**.

6. Select cell **D11** and click **Paste**. The formula is pasted a second time and updated again.

7. Select the range **E11:M11** and click **Paste**. The copied formula is pasted into all cells in the range, and updated to reference the correct cells in each case.

8. Use this powerful technique to copy the formula in cell **N5** to the range **N6:N9**.

9. Save the document as **breakdowns complete** and close it.

4.13 Fill Handle

Cells can be quickly filled with data by using the **Fill Handle**. This appears when the cursor is placed over the bottom right corner of an active cell. The **Fill Handle** is a very useful feature that can be used to quickly copy values or formulas into other cells.

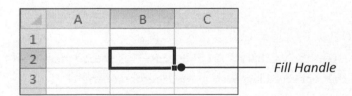

Activity:

1. Start a new, blank workbook and type your first name into cell **B2**.

2. With cell **B2** selected, move your mouse pointer over the **Fill Handle**. The mouse pointer changes to a crosshair, **+**.

3.   Click and drag the **Fill Handle** across to cell **G2**.

◢	A	B	C	D	E	F	G	
1								
2		Zak						✛
3								

4.   Release the mouse and the text in **B2** is copied to all cells in the range **B2:G2**.

> **Note:**   It is only possible to drag in one direction, i.e. along a row or down a column.

5.   In **E4** enter **63**. Use the **Fill Handle** to copy this cell across to **I4**. The entry **63** is repeated.

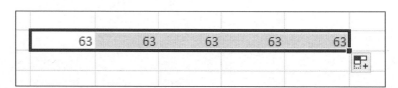

6.   Click the **Auto Fill Options** button, ▦, that has appeared towards the bottom right of the selected range. **Copy Cells** is currently selected which means that the value in **E4** has simply been copied to all other cells in the range.

7.   Select **Fill Series** instead to have *Excel* automatically increase the value of each cell in the range. This technique is very useful for quickly numbering cells.

8.   Click the cell **E4** again. Hold <**Ctrl**> while dragging the **Fill Handle** to cell **E9**. Release the mouse button to fill the cells with increasing numbers up to **68** (holding <**Ctrl**> automatically applies **Fill Series**).

9.   In **A11** enter **January**. Use the **Fill Handle** to copy the cell across to **L11**. *Excel* recognises that the content of **A11** is a date, and then automatically applies **Fill Series** to the contents of each other cell in the selected range.

10.   In **A13** enter **1st**. Use the **Fill Handle** to copy the cell down to **A22**. The automatic **Fill Series** applied is very useful when creating schedules, diaries and calendars.

11.   Close the workbook <u>without</u> saving and then open the workbook **maintenance** that was saved earlier.

12.   To save retyping the formulas in row **9** and column **I**, they can instead be copied using the **Fill Handle**. With cell **C9** selected, drag the **Fill Handle** across to **H9**.

12	16			24	14	11
49	91					✛

13.   When the mouse button is released, the formula contained in cell **C9** is copied to all other cells in the range **C9:H9**.

> **Note:** *Excel* automatically updates the cell references in each copied formula so that each calculation refers to the cells directly above. This is a very useful feature.

14. Click in cell **D9** and check the **Formula Bar** to see that the formula has been updated automatically to sum column **D** instead of column **C** (and so on for each column up to **H**).

15. To complete column **I**, make the active cell **I4** and use the **Fill Handle** to copy the formula down to **I8**. The completed spreadsheet should look the same as that shown below.

	A	B	C	D	E	F	G	H	I
1	Maintenance checks week 7								
2									
3	Staff	Mon	Tue	Wed	Thu	Fri	Sat	Sun	Total
4	Aaron	16	22	9	17	20			84
5	Adya	21	16	19	15			12	83
6	Jack		19	15	14	17	11		76
7	Sun		18		32	21	12	10	93
8	Zak	12	16			24	14	11	77
9	Total	49	91	43	78	82	37	33	

16. Save the workbook using the same file name and close it.

4.14 Checking Formulas

Spreadsheets are not much use if the formulas within them contain errors. All formulas within worksheets should be checked thoroughly to make sure that you have entered them correctly and that they produce the expected results.

In some cases *Excel* will warn you that a formula is incorrect. If so, a formula error value starting with a **#** (hash) symbol is displayed in the relevant cell:

#NULL!	The ranges specified in your formula are incorrect
#DIV/0!	You tried to divide by 0 and this is not allowed
#VALUE!	You tried to apply a calculation with data of the wrong type
#REF!	Cell references are not valid or are missing
#NAME?	A part of the formula has been mistyped
#NUM!	The result created by a formula is too big
#N/A	A value referenced in your formula is missing
######	The result is too long to fit into a cell

Activity:

1. Open the workbook **Totals**. This spreadsheet shows the monthly number of visitors to the *Haunted Castle* in a six month period. Unfortunately, it also contains a number of errors which must be corrected before the results can be trusted and relied upon.

> **Note:** Notice the green triangles in the top left corner of some of the cells. These indicate that there is a possible error in the formulas for those cells.

2. Click once in cell **B5**. This cell contains the error **#VALUE!** indicating that the formula is using data of the wrong type.

3. Notice the **Trace Error** button that has appeared beside the selected cell, ⬦. Place your mouse pointer over this button without clicking to see a brief description of the error.

	Month 1	Month 2	Month 3	Month 4	Month 5
riders	200	300	400	-100	150
#VALUE!		300	700	600	750

A value used in the formula is of the wrong data type.

4. Double click in the cell. The formula is shown within the cell itself, with coloured borders indicating the ranges used in the calculation (this is a really useful way of checking the cells referenced by a formula). Can you tell what the error is?

5. The formula is trying to add the *label* in **A5** to the *value* in **B4**. Edit the formula so that it simply reads **=B4** and press **<Enter>**. The error value disappears and **200** is shown in **B5**.

6. Next, click once in cell **H4** and read the brief description on the **Trace Error** button.

7. *Excel* has detected that the formula contains an unknown function name and has displayed the **#NAME?** error value in the cell. Can you see what the error is?

8. The function **SUM** has been spelled incorrectly. Correct this and press **<Enter>** to remove the error value.

9. The result appears as **0**, which is clearly not correct. Double click **H4** to see the range that the formula refers to.

Month 1	Month 2	Month 3	Month 4	Month 5	Month 6	Total
200	300	400	-100	150	500	=SUM(B7:G7)
200	300	700	600	750	750	SUM(number1,

10. The range **B7:G7** is not correct. You could edit the formula in the cell, but instead try dragging and dropping the blue range rectangle to the correct location, as shown below.

Month 1	Month 2	Month 3	Month 4	Month 5	Month 6	Total
200	300	400	-100	150	500	=SUM(B4:G4)
200	300	700	600	750	750	SUM(number1,

Note: You can also click and drag the corners of the blue range rectangle to expand or contract it.

11. Press **<Enter>** to confirm the change. The formula is now correct.

12. Next, click once in cell **I4** and read the brief description on the **Trace Error** button. *Excel* has detected that the formula is trying to divide by 0 and has displayed the **#DIV/0!** error.

13. As there are six months worth of data, the formula should divide by **6** in order to get the monthly average. Correct this now by editing the formula in the **Formula Bar**.

14. Press <**Enter**> to confirm the change. The average formula is now correct.

15. Although all of the errors that *Excel* warned you about have now been corrected, there are still a few errors remaining in this spreadsheet. Can you find them?

16. Firstly, the cell **C5** should add the contents of **B5** and **C4**. Correct this now.

17. Next, cell **G5** is a copy of **F5**. Correct this now.

18. The cumulative total in cell **G5** now matches the final total in **H4**, which is correct.

> Note: It is important to perform simple visual inspections on your spreadsheets to check that amounts tally and that the results of formulas are as expected.

19. The value in **E4** does not make sense! You cannot have **-100** visitors. *Zak* informs you that this should have been **100**, so correct the error now. The spreadsheet is now complete and correct.

First Half Cumulative Totals								
	Month 1	Month 2	Month 3	Month 4	Month 5	Month 6	Total	Average per month
Number of Haunted Castle visitors	200	300	400	100	150	500	1650	275
Cumulative Total	200	500	900	1000	1150	1650		

> Note: A useful feature of *Excel* is the **Error Checking** facility on the **Formulas** tab. This steps you through each error in a spreadsheet one at a time.

20. Save the workbook as **final totals** and close it.

4.15   Relative and Absolute References

Normally the cell references that you use in your formulas are known as **relative** cell references; they are automatically updated by *Excel* when copied to another cell. For example, if you copy the formula **B2+B3** in column **B** to column **C** it automatically becomes **C2+C3**.

However, if you want to stop *Excel* automatically updating cell references when you copy formulas you can use **absolute** cell referencing instead.

> **Note:** All formulas used so far have been relative. In fact, relative cell referencing is the default and most common way to reference cells in *Excel*.

> **Note:** To make a cell reference **absolute** you simply add a $ symbol before the row and/or column reference (e.g. **A1** will always refer to cell **A1**).

Activity:

1. Open the workbook **Parts** which contains the start of a basic tax calculation. However, the VAT (Value Added Tax) calculations have not been completed yet.

> **Note:** VAT is a government tax charged on most goods and services purchased in the UK.

2. Select cell **C6** and enter the formula for **VAT** (**Price** multiplied by **VAT Rate**): =C5*B15.

3. The result shown in cell **C6** is **£799.58**.

4. As of 2011, the VAT rate in the UK was changed to **20%**. Select **B15** and enter the new **VAT Rate** (you can enter this as **0.20** or **20%**). Notice that the result in **C6** is updated.

5. Use the **Fill Handle** to copy the formula in **C6** to both **D6** and **E6**. The resulting **VAT** for those months is zero.

£4,569.00	£6,408.00	£7,834.00
£913.80	£0.00	£0.00

6. Check the formulas in **D6** and **E6** to find the problem. It has been caused by relative cell referencing. The **VAT Rate** is in a fixed location but the formulas have been automatically adjusted to reference cells that are empty, e.g. the cells **C15** and **D15**.

> **Note:** Relative cell referencing is ideal for most tasks. However, when problems such as this occur, it is useful to know how to use absolute cell referencing.

7. In cell **C6**, enter the formula **=C5*B15**. The $ symbols fix the row and column references as absolute (meaning they will not be updated when copied).

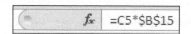

> **Note:** Notice that the reference to **C5** is still relative. When the formula is copied, that reference will be updated but the absolute reference will not.

8. Use the **Fill Handle** to copy the formula in **C6** to both **D6** and **E6** again (overwriting the current contents). Check the formulas in **D6** and **E6**. Even though the relative reference to **C5** has been automatically updated, the absolute reference to **B15** has not.

> Note: You can also make only a column or row reference absolute. For example, **$B15** makes the column reference absolute; **B$15** makes the row reference absolute.

9. Complete the **Total Price** row by adding the **Price** and **VAT** together for each month. Cell **F7** should contain the final overall total **£22,573.20**.

10. Save the workbook as **parts complete** and close it.

4.16 Inserting Rows and Columns

When developing spreadsheets, you will often need to create a new row or column within your data. Columns are inserted to the left of the active cell and rows are inserted above.

Activity:

1. Open the workbook **visitors** that you saved earlier.

2. *The Viper*, an old ride that has recently been refurbished, is to be added to the data. Select all of column **E** by clicking the **Heading Bar** column title.

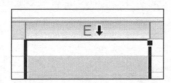

3. Click the **Insert** button, in the **Cells** group on the **Home** tab. The **House of Wax** column is promoted to column **F** and a new column **E** is inserted.

4. Enter the label **The Viper** in cell **E4**. By default, the formatting is the same as the column to the left.

> Note: Notice that the formulas in column **G** have been automatically adjusted to include the new column. It is important to check that any formulas in your spreadsheets are correct after inserting new rows or columns.

5. Enter the attendance figures in column **E** as: **4000, 2500, 3000, 2800, 4200** and **5100**.

6. Copy the formula from **D11** to **E11**. As the formula in **D11** contains relative cell references, they are automatically adjusted when copied to cell **E11**.

7. **Sunday** attendances also need to be included in the statistics. As an alternative to the **Insert** button, right click on row heading **11** to display a shortcut menu.

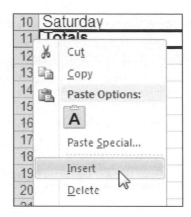

8. From the options available, select **Insert**. Row **11** is promoted to row **12** and a new row **11** is inserted. By default the formatting is the same as the row above.

> Note: This useful shortcut menu technique can also be used to insert columns.

9. Enter **Sunday** in cell **A11** and enter the **Sunday** figures across the new row as: **2000, 4000, 1500, 3000** and **2000**.

10. Check the formula in cell **G11** has been copied from the row above and that its cell references have been adjusted correctly (**=SUM(B11:F11)**).

The Viper	House of Wax	Total
4000	1500	13500
2500	1500	12800
3000	1600	13900
2800	1550	13950
4200	1650	15750
5100	1700	17600
3000	2000	12500
24600	11500	

> Note: Individual cells can also be inserted at the location of the active cell (or range). By default, any existing data within or below the active cell will be moved down.

11. Save the workbook and leave it open for the next exercise.

4.17 Deleting Rows and Columns

Rows and columns can also be deleted easily if they are no longer needed. The rows or columns immediately afterwards are then moved along to fill the space.

Activity:

1. The workbook **visitors** should still be open. *Zak* informs you that you no longer need to include the **Tower of Terror** and **House of Wax** columns.

2. Select the entire **Tower of Terror** column by clicking the **Heading Bar** for column **D**.

3. Click the **Delete** button, 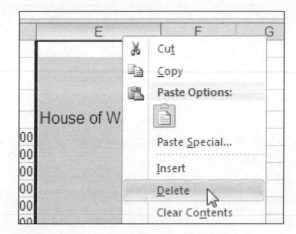, in the **Cells** group on the **Home** tab. The **Tower of Terror** column is removed and the remaining columns move left to fill the space.

> **Note:** It is important to check that any formulas in your spreadsheets are correct after deleting rows or columns.

4. Right click on the **House of Wax** column header and select **Delete**.

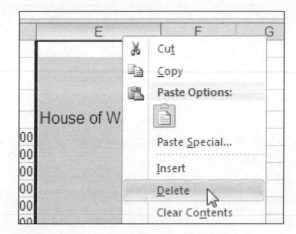

5. The column is removed. *Zak* has also informed you that the row for **Sunday** is not needed any longer. Select all of row **11**.

6. From the **Cells** group, click **Delete**. The row is deleted.

> **Note:** Cells containing formulas can be altered by deleting parts of a worksheet, resulting in **#REF** error values. In this case your formulas will need to be manually adjusted.

7. Save the workbook using the same file name and close it.

8. Open the workbook **train cars updated** that you saved earlier. Using whichever method you prefer, delete row **9** to tidy up the spreadsheet.

9. *Zak* also informs you that column **D** is no longer needed; delete this column.

> **Note:** Entire rows and columns can also be cut, copied and pasted.

10. Save the workbook using the same file name and close it.

4.18 Formatting Text

Formatting text can improve a spreadsheet's appearance and make it easier to read and understand. Cell contents in a spreadsheet can be emphasised using bold, italic and underline, as well as changing the font type, size and colour.

> **Note:** Used properly, basic text formatting can highlight important information and give your spreadsheets a more professional appearance. However, too many different fonts and colours will often have the reverse effect.

Activity:

1. Open the workbook **visitors** again and select cell **B4**. To make the text in the selected cell bold, click the **Bold** button, **B**, in the **Font** group.

2. Click the **Italic** button, **I**, and then the **Underline** button, **U**, to italicise and underline the text.

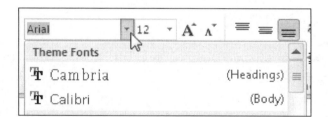

> **Note:** A range of selected cells can be formatted at the same time.

3. To change the font type, click the drop-down button on the **Font** box.

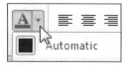

4. Select **Calibri** from the list.

5. The font size can also be changed by clicking the drop-down arrow on the **Font Size** box. Select cell **A2** and change the font size to **16 pt**. Change the **Font** again to **Calibri**.

6. Another useful feature to make text stand out in spreadsheets is font colour. With **A2** still active, click on the **Font Color** drop-down arrow.

7. Move your mouse pointer over any colour in the palette to see the change automatically previewed on the spreadsheet. Finally click a dark blue colour to select it.

> **Note:** To copy the text formatting in a cell, the **Format Painter** tool can be used.

8. Select cell **B4** again. From the **Clipboard** group, click the **Format Painter** button, ![ ]. Then move your mouse pointer over cell **C4**. Notice that the mouse pointer has changed to the **Format Painter** cursor, ⬚⬚.

9. Click once to copy the formatting (not the text) in cell **B4** to **C4**. Use the same technique to copy the formatting of cell **C4** to **D4**.

> **Note:**   You can also select a *range* of cells to apply the **Format Painter** tool to.

Haunted Castle Attraction Attendances			
	Haunted Vault	*The Black Hole*	*The Viper*
Monday	2000	5000	4000

> **Note:**   The useful **Format Painter** tool is also available in other *Office* applications.

10. Insert an empty row above row **11** to separate the attendance data from the final totals. This spreadsheet now looks a lot more professional.

11. Save the workbook using the same file name and close it.

4.19 Cell Alignment

Alignment refers to the positioning of text or numbers within a cell. Content can be aligned to any side of a cell and can even be rotated.

Activity:

1. Open the workbook **maintenance** that you saved earlier and select the range **B3:H3**.

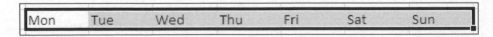

> **Note:**   Cell alignment is set by clicking one of the alignment buttons in the **Alignment** group on the **Home** tab.

2. Click the **Center** button, , to centre the labels horizontally. Click the **Align Text Right** button, , and the labels are moved to the right.

3. Increase the height of row **3** to **60**. Notice that the contents are aligned to the bottom right of the selected cells.

4. Click the **Middle Align** button, , to centre the labels vertically. Click the **Center** button again, , to centre the labels horizontally.

| Mon | Tue | Wed | Thu | Fri | Sat | Sun |

Note: Similar to *Microsoft Word*, you can also **Indent** the contents of cells using the **Increase Indent** button, , and **Decrease Indent** button, .

5. Click the **Orientation** button, . From the drop-down list that appears, select **Angle Counterclockwise**. The text is rotated 45 degrees.

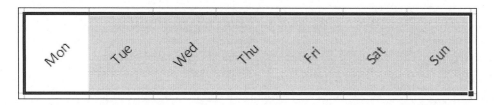

6. Click the **Orientation** button again and select **Rotate Text Up**. The text is rotated 90 degrees.

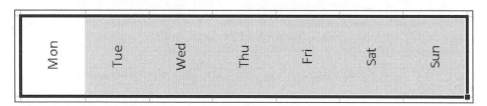

Note: Rotated text is useful where cell widths are small. For more control over alignment, including merging cells and text wrapping, use the **Alignment** dialog box launcher.

7. Save the workbook and leave it open for the next exercise.

4.20 Borders and Shading

Borders are lines around the edges of cells. You can control the style and colour of lines used, and **shading** can be applied to add a background colour or pattern.

Activity:

1. Using the workbook **maintenance**, make sure the range **B3:H3** is still selected. Click on the **Borders** drop-down arrow in the **Font** group.

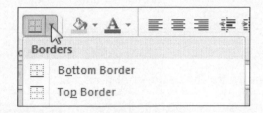

2. Select **All Borders** to add lines *around* and *between* the cells in the selected range. Click away from the selected range to view the results.

3. Click **Undo**, to remove the border (and select the range **B3:H3** again).

4. Drop down the **Borders** button again and select **More Borders**. The **Format Cells** dialog box appears.

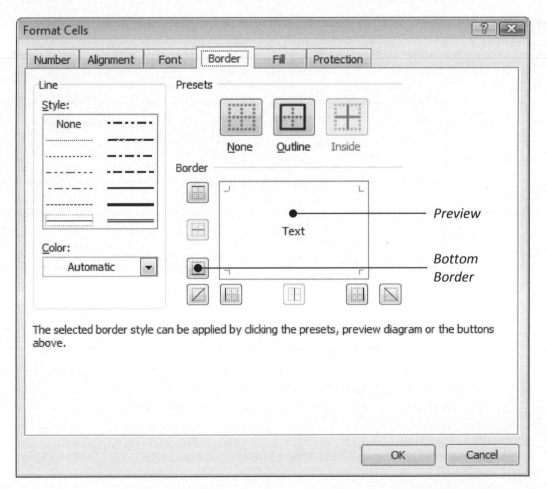

5. To apply a simple single border to the bottom of the selected row (the style selected by default in the **Style** box), click the **Bottom Border** button, , in the **Border** area.

6. Notice that a line now appears along the bottom of the **Preview** pane.

> **Note:** There are many line styles available under **Style**. The three **Presets** buttons can also be used to apply borders around and between cells quickly.

7. To apply the new border click **OK**. Click away from the selected range to view the results.

> **Note:** Borders can often be better seen if the worksheet's gridlines are hidden. To do this, select the **View** tab and uncheck **Gridlines** in the **Show** group. Be sure to check **Gridlines** again before continuing.

8. Shading is added to cell backgrounds using the **Fill Color** button in the **Font** group on the **Home** tab. Select the range **B3:H3** again and make sure the **Home** tab is displayed.

9. Click the drop-down arrow on the **Fill Color** button, , and select a light green colour.

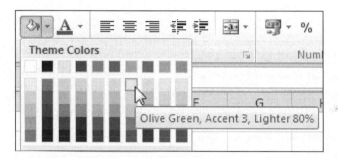

> **Note:** It is often best to use light colours in cell backgrounds; too much colour can obscure the text and make it difficult to read.

10. Apply the same light green colour to the range **A4:A8** and apply a single black border on the right. The spreadsheet should look like that shown below.

	A	B	C	D	E	F	G	H	I
1	Maintenance checks week 7								
2									
3	Staff	Mon	Tue	Wed	Thu	Fri	Sat	Sun	Total
4	Aaron	16	22	9	17	20			84
5	Adya	21	16	19	15			12	83
6	Jack		19	15	14	17	11		76
7	Sun		18		32	21	12	10	93
8	Zak	12	16			24	14	11	77
9	Total	49	91	43	78	82	37	33	

> **Note:** You can reapply the most recent fill colour by clicking the **Fill Color** button.

11. Save the workbook and close it.

4.21 Formatting Numbers

Numbers can be formatted so that they are displayed in a variety of different ways, such as currency, percentage, fraction, etc. The most useful number formats available include:

General	No specific number format (best for most uses)
Number	Plain number formats
Currency	Currency symbols and decimal places
Date	Various date formats
Time	Various time formats
Percentage	A value as a fraction of 100 (followed by %)
Fraction	Decimals expressed as fractions
Text	Plain text with no number formatting
Special	Telephone numbers, postcodes, etc.
Custom	Custom formats that you can design yourself

Activity:

1. Open the workbook **Time**. This is a simple timesheet that *Zak* has created for recording overtime, but many of the cells do not use the correct number format.

2. The **Hours Worked** cells should be displayed to two decimal places. Select the range **E8:E13**. From the **Cells** group on the **Home** tab, click the **Format** button, ▦ Format ▾.

3. From the drop-down menu that appears, select **Format Cells**. The **Format Cells** dialog box appears. Make sure the **Number** tab is displayed.

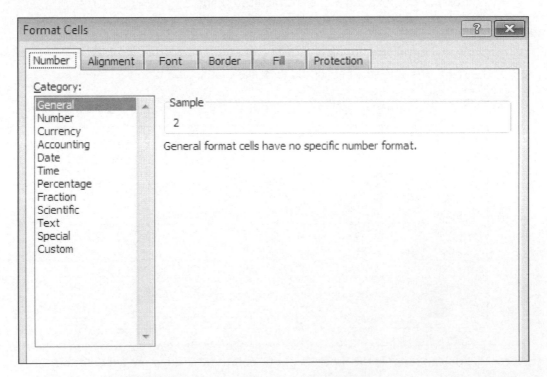

4. Click on each of the different types of number format shown in the **Category** list to see the various types and options available. Finally, select **Number**.

5. Check that the number of **Decimal places** is **2**.

> **Note:**   Notice the **Sample** preview box. This shows the results of the chosen format if it was applied to the first number in the selected range.

6. Click **OK** to apply the chosen format. All the numbers in the selected range are now formatted to two decimal places.

> **Note:**   There are buttons in the **Number** group on the **Ribbon** to **Increase Decimal** places, [icon], and **Decrease Decimal** places, [icon]. This is done one decimal place at a time.

7. Select the range **F8:F13**. Click the **Format** drop-down button and select **Format Cells** to display the **Format Cells** dialog box. This time select **Currency** from the **Category** list.

8. Make sure that **Decimal places** is set to **2**, and then select **£** from the **Symbol** drop-down box (if it is not already selected). A preview is provided in the **Sample** box again.

9. Click **OK** to apply the chosen format. All the numbers in the selected range are now formatted to two decimal places and appear with a **£** symbol.

> **Note:**   The **Number Format** drop-down menu in the **Number** group can be used to select new number formats quickly.

10. Apply the format **Number** (to two decimal places) to cell **D15**. Then apply the **Currency** format with a **£** symbol to cells **D17** and **D19** (to two decimal places).

> **Note:**   When adjusting number formats, it is important to realise that the value in each cell is not changed. It is simply displayed in a different way.

11. With cell **D19** selected, notice that the **Formula Bar** says **10**, but the contents of the cell are displayed as **£10.00**.

12. Overtype the contents of cell **D19** with **9.50**. Press **<Enter>** and the value is automatically formatted as **£9.50**.

> **Note:** If cells display **#######** this means that the cell content is too big for the cell to display. Widening the columns will solve this problem.

> **Note:** Unless you need to change the formatting of a cell for display purposes, the default **General** category format is best for most situations (including text labels).

13. Save the workbook as **timesheet** and leave it open for the next exercise.

4.22 Date and Time

In *Excel*, the date and time are stored as simple numbers that can be formatted to appear however you like. For example, the date is stored as a large number that represents the number of days since **1 January 1900**; however, this can be formatted so that it appears in a more recognisable form (e.g. **21 April 2012**).

Activity:

1. Using the workbook **timesheet**, select cell **D5**. Enter today's date in the form **DD/MM/YYYY** (e.g. 21/04/2012) and then press **<Enter>**.

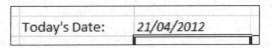

2. Select cell **D5** again. Notice in the **Number Format** drop-down menu that **Date** has been automatically selected by *Excel*.

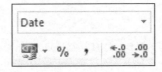

3. Display the **Format Cells** dialog box. Examine each date format available within **Type**. When you are finished, select the **14 March 2001** format and click **OK**.

> **Note:** The keyboard shortcut **<Ctrl ;>** can be used to quickly insert today's date.

4. Select cell **F19** and enter the current time in the form **HH:MM** (e.g. 14:30). Press **<Enter>**.

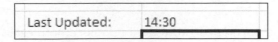

5. Select cell **F19** again. Display the **Format Cells** dialog box and select **Time** in the **Category** list. Examine each time format available within **Type**.

6. When you are finished, select the **13:30:55** format and click **OK**.

> **Note:** The keyboard shortcut **<Ctrl Shift ;>** can be used to quickly insert the current time.

Haunted Castle - Daily Overtime Log

Today's Date: *21 April 2012*

Attraction	Hours Worked	Pay Accrued
The Haunted Vault	2.25	£21.38
The Black Hole	1.00	£9.50
The Tower of Terror	0.50	£4.75
The House of Wax	0.25	£2.38
Concessions	1.50	£14.25
Other:	2.00	£19.00

Total Hours: 7.50

Total Overtime: **£71.25**

Hourly wage: £9.50   Time Completed: 14:30:00

7.   Save the workbook using the same file name and close it.

4.23 Percentages

Percentage means "per hundred" and is a technique used frequently in business and everyday life to describe a fraction out of 100. It is always displayed with a percentage symbol, **%**. For example, **20%** is **20/100** as a fraction or **0.2** as a decimal. In the pie chart below, **20%** has been cut out leaving **80%** remaining.

In *Excel* there is a **Percent Style** button, %, that changes a decimal to a percentage automatically.

Activity:

1.   For a report that *Zak* is creating, you have been asked to work out what percentage of special effects on the *Black Hole* ride are "pop-up ghosts".

2. Create a new, blank workbook. Starting in **B2**, enter the following data (resize any columns as necessary).

	A	B	C	D	
1					
2		Pop-up Ghosts	All Special Effects	Percentage	
3		5	20		
4					

3. To display the number of pop-up ghosts as a percentage of all special effects, enter the formula **=B3/C3** into **D3**. Press **<Enter>**.

4. The result **0.25** appears as a decimal value. To format the answer as a percentage, first make sure **D3** is active.

5. With the **Home** tab displayed on the **Ribbon**, click the **Percent Style** button, 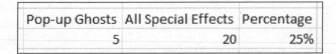, in the **Number** group. The result changes to a percentage, showing that **25%** of all special effects are pop-up ghosts.

Pop-up Ghosts	All Special Effects	Percentage
5	20	25%

6. Change the value in **C3** to **27** and press **<Enter>**; notice that the percentage value changes automatically.

> **Note:**   The **Percentage Style** button only shows percentages in whole numbers.

7. To display percentages to two decimal places, make the active cell **D3** and launch the **Format Cells** dialog box. Make sure the **Number** tab is selected.

8. With **Percentage** selected under **Category**, change the value in the **Decimal places** box to **2** (notice the **Sample** area above which previews the percentage style).

9. Click **OK** to confirm the change. The percentage is now shown more accurately as **18.52%**.

10. Click **Undo**, on the **Quick Access Toolbar** to undo this change. The percentage is shown rounded up to **19%** again.

> **Note:**   **Undo** and **Redo** in *Excel* work in the same way as *Microsoft Word*.

11. Save the workbook as **ghost percentages** and close it.

4.24 Charts

Charts are used to show numerical information in a graphical way that is clear and easy to understand. There are many charts styles available in *Excel*, but the following list includes the five most popular types:

Column	The most commonly used chart in *Excel*, this displays shaded vertical columns that represent values in different categories.	
Line	Specific values are plotted on the chart and are connected by a line. This is useful for displaying how values change over time.	
Pie	Values are shown as slices of a circular "pie", which highlights the contribution that each value makes to the total. This is also a very common type of chart.	
Bar	Similar to a column chart, but the bars are shown horizontally across the page.	
XY Scatter	Specific values are simply plotted on the chart. Different sets of values can have different plot symbols.	

Note: There are many layouts, styles and effects that can be applied to charts. For example, different themed colours or an impressive 3D effect can be applied.

Activity:

1. Open the workbook **visitors** that you saved earlier. This spreadsheet contains information that *Zak* would like to include in a presentation. However, he would rather show this data as a chart so that it is easier for others to understand.

2. Select the cell range **A4:B10**.

3. Display the **Insert** tab and locate the **Charts** group. Many popular charts can be created using the buttons shown here.

4. Click the **Pie** button and select the first type of 2-D chart in the list: **Pie** (a descriptive **ToolTip** will appear when you rest on a chart type).

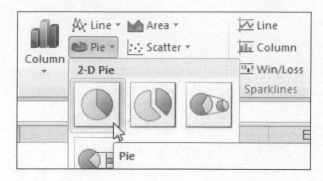

5. A simple pie chart is created from the selected data and each value is shown as a slice of the pie. A **Legend** is automatically created to describe the contents of the chart.

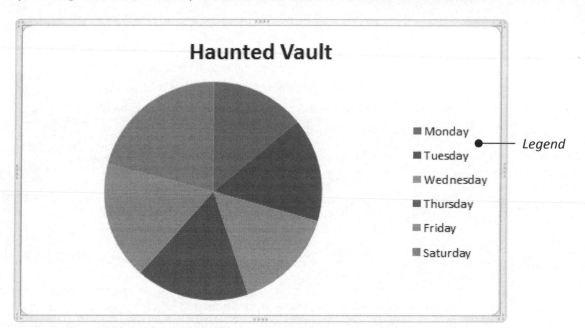

> **Note:** *Excel* automatically obtains chart and legend titles from data labels in the range.

6. Notice the **Chart Layouts** group on the **Chart Tools - Design** tab. Select each layout type in turn to automatically adjust the positioning of elements on the chart.

> **Note:** Each chart type has its own list of chart layouts. You can also reposition elements on a chart manually using drag and drop.

7. Locate the **Chart Styles** group on the **Design** tab. Select a variety of style types to automatically adjust the colours of the chart.

> **Note:** More **Chart Layouts** and **Chart Styles** can be accessed by clicking the **More** button, ⍗, found towards the bottom right corner of both groups.

8. When you have finished exploring the various **Chart Styles** and **Chart Layouts** on offer, press <**Delete**>. The chart is removed.

9.   Next, select the range **A4:D10**. Then, from the **Insert** tab, click the **Column** drop-down button in the **Charts** group.

10. Select the first chart type (**Clustered Column**). A column chart appears with all three rides shown as a separate bar.

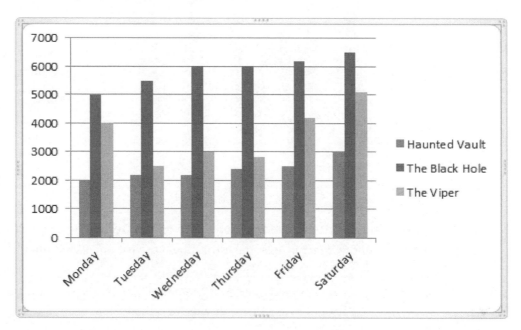

Note: As you can clearly see, **The Black Hole** ride is the most popular attraction, followed by **The Viper** and then **The Haunted Vault**. Notice how much easier it is to draw these conclusions by looking at a chart rather than the raw data.

11. Display the **Layout** tab and click **Chart Title** in the **Labels** group. From the options that appear, select **Above Chart**. Edit the chart title so that it reads **Haunted Castle Visitors**.

Note: Other options on the **Layout** tab allow you to add, edit and remove axis titles, gridlines, legends and data labels.

12. Display the **Design** tab and click **Change Chart Type** in the **Type** group. Select the fourth column chart type on the top row (**3-D Clustered Column**).

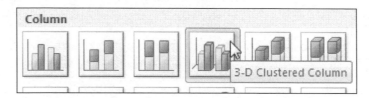

13. Click **OK**. The chart is transformed into a three-dimensional column chart.

Note: The **Move Chart** button on the **Design** tab can be used to move a selected chart to another sheet or workbook. You can also cut/copy and paste charts into other *Microsoft Office* applications.

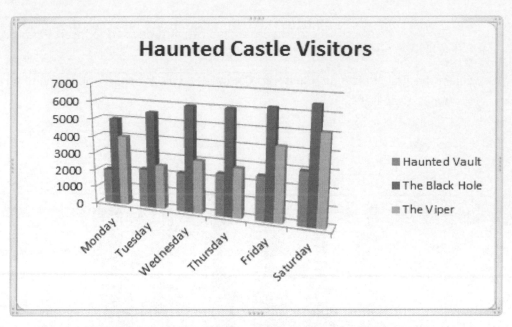

14. Click the **Move Chart** button in the **Location** group on the **Design** tab to display the **Move Chart** dialog box. With **Object in** selected, drop-down the list and select **Sheet2**. Click **OK**.

> Note: A chart can be manually moved or resized using the handles on the chart border.

15. The chart is moved to **Sheet2**. Position it towards the top left of the worksheet, and then return to the **Attendances** worksheet and make sure the range **A4:D10** is still selected.

16. Create a simple 2-D **Line** chart based on the selected range, and add an appropriate title of your choice. Move this chart to the top left of **Sheet3**.

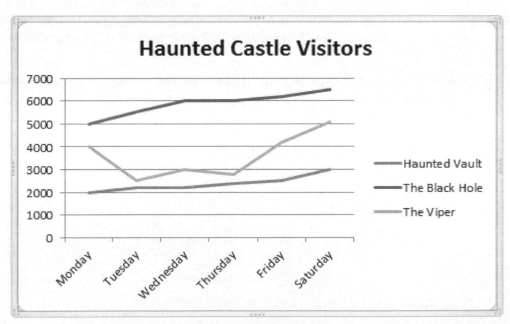

17. Perform the same steps to create a simple **Bar** and **X-Y Scatter** chart. Explore some of the other chart types and formatting options that are available.

18. When you are finished, save the workbook as **visitor charts** and close it.

> **Note:** Similar to *Microsoft Word*, the **Insert** tab can also be used to insert **Pictures**, **ClipArt**, **WordArt** and **Shapes** in *Excel*.

4.25 Printing

Page Setup allows you to modify how a worksheet will look when printed. It can be in **Portrait** (upright) or **Landscape** (sideways) mode. You can also adjust **scaling** and page **margins**.

Activity:

1. Open the workbook **Events** which contains a breakdown of turnover, spending and net profits for special events at the *Haunted Castle*.

2. Display the **File** tab and click **Print**. A preview of the first page as it will be printed is shown on the right. Notice that the worksheet stretches over two pages.

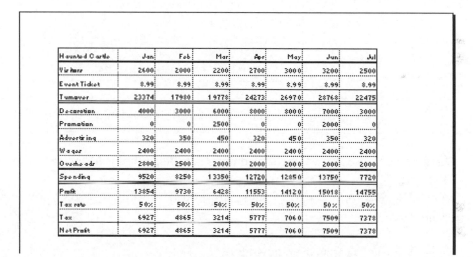

> **Note:** The **Next Page** and **Previous Page** buttons at the bottom of the preview allow you to switch between pages.

3. To rotate the page so that all of the information will fit, click the **Orientation** drop-down button under **Settings**.

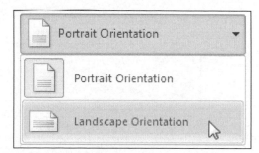

4. Select **Landscape Orientation** from the drop-down menu and the page is rotated 90 degrees (although the contents of the workbook are not).

> **Note:** The worksheet still covers two pages. To fit this on to one, there are two options available to you: **scale** the worksheet down on to one page or use the **Margins** tab to reduce the white space around the edges.

5. Click the **Scaling** drop-down button under **Settings**. Then, select **Fit Sheet on One Page** to shrink the contents of the workbook so that it fits onto one page.

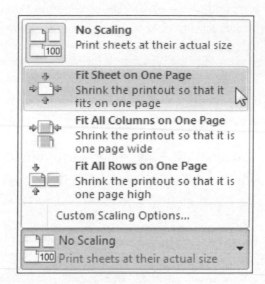

> **Note:** The print options shown depend on your printer and may appear differently.

6. The worksheet has now been scaled down a little so that it fits on to one page.

7. Select **No Scaling** from the **Scaling** drop-down button to return the worksheet to its original size.

8. Next, click the **Margins** drop-down button.

9. Select **Narrow** and observe the effect. The margins are reduced and the worksheet just about fits onto one page again.

10. Select an appropriate printer from the **Printer** drop-down box.

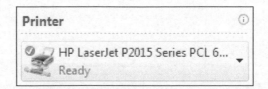

> **Note:** In some situations you may have access to more than one printer. Try to select and use the one closest to you. Remember that you may be charged for printing.

11. Click the large **Print** button to print a copy of the current worksheet on your chosen printer. You will be automatically returned to the main worksheet view.

> **Note:** Alternatively, click the **Home** tab to return without printing.

> **Note:** Notice the dotted line that has appeared on the worksheet. This is called the **Print Area** and shows the boundaries of the cell range that will be printed on each page.

12. Select the range **B5:G9**. From the **Page Layout** tab, click the **Print Area** button in the **Page Setup** group and select **Set Print Area**. The dotted line now surrounds this range.

23374	17980	19778	24273	26970	28768
4000	3000	6000	8000	8000	7000
0	0	2500	0	0	2000
320	350	450	320	450	350

13. Display the **Print** screen and examine the print preview on the right. Notice that only the cells within the custom **Print Area** will be printed. This technique is useful for printing parts of your worksheets.

14. Press <**Esc**> to return to the workbook.

15. From the **Page Layout** tab, click the **Print Area** drop-down button and select **Clear Print Area**. The custom **Print Area** is removed.

16. Save the workbook as **haunted castle events** and leave it open for the next exercise.

4.26 Printing Formulas

When a cell contains a formula, the result of the formula rather than the formula itself is displayed in the cell. However, it is also possible to display the formulas in a worksheet rather than their results, which is very useful when checking for errors.

Activity:

1. The workbook **haunted castle events** should still be open.

2. To display all the formulas present in this worksheet, display the **Formulas** tab and click **Show Formulas**, ⌗ Show Formulas, in the **Formula Auditing** group.

> **Note:** Alternatively, it is possible to switch between formulas and their results by pressing **<Ctrl `>**, i.e. **Ctrl** and the key to the left of **1** on a standard keyboard.

3. The formulas are displayed and the columns are widened to accommodate all of the cell contents.

| =SUM(B5:B9) | =SUM(C5:C9) | =SUM(D5:D9) |

4. If the formulas are to be printed, it is also a good idea to include the row and column **Heading Bars** also. Display the **Page Layout** tab and select **Print** in the **Sheet Options** group (under **Headings**, not **Gridlines**).

5. Display the **Print** screen and notice that the **Heading Bars** will now also be printed.

6. Return to the main view and hide the formulas using the keyboard shortcut **<Ctrl `>**.

7. Save the workbook using the same file name and close it.

4.27 Sorting Data

Sometimes you may need to **sort** the contents of a spreadsheet so that related cells are grouped together or placed in a certain order. For example, you could rearrange the contents of a staff or product list alphabetically by name.

Activity:

1. Open the workbook **Temps**. This spreadsheet contains a list of temporary staff that have worked at the *Haunted Castle* in the past year.

2. Select any cell in column **A** that contains a name and, from the **Home** tab, click the **Sort & Filter** button in the **Editing** group. From the menu that appears, select **Sort A to Z**.

3. The rows in the worksheet are reordered alphabetically using the contents of column **A**.

> **Note:** *Excel* automatically detects data types and their range when sorting. However, if a range is selected first, only the contents of those cells will be sorted. Note also that entire rows are sorted, not just the current column.

4. Select a cell in column **B** containing a name and, from the **Sort & Filter** button, select **Sort Z to A**. The worksheet is reordered again by **Surname** in reverse alphabetical order.

5. Select a cell in column **C** containing a number and click the **Sort & Filter** button. *Excel* recognises that the content of the selected cell is a number. Select **Sort Smallest to Largest** and the worksheet is reordered by increasing **Age**.

6. You can also create more complex, custom sorts. Select any one cell in the range **A5:D20** and display the **Data** tab. Click the **Sort** button in the **Sort & Filter** group.

7. The **Sort** dialog box appears. Select **Column A** from the **Sort by** drop-down box and make sure **A to Z** is selected in **Order**.

> **Note:**   If *Excel* is able to automatically detect the column headings in a worksheet, these will appear instead of **Column A**, **Column B**, and so on.

8. Click **Add Level**, ⬚Add Level , to add another level to the sort. In **Then by**, select **Column B** and again make sure **A to Z** is selected in **Order**.

> **Note:**   It is very common to sort columns of data. However, if you need to sort by row instead, click the **Options** button and select the **Sort left to right** option.

9. Click **OK** to perform the sort. The list is sorted on **First Name** *and then* **Surname**.

> **Note:**   Similar to *Microsoft Word*, you can also search for and replace data in cells using the **Find & Select** button in the **Editing** group. You can choose to search through formulas or the values they calculate.

10. Save the workbook as **temporary staff sorted** and close it.

4.28 Filtering Data

Filtering is a simple technique for selecting records that match certain conditions (these conditions are known as **criteria**). Only the records that match the criteria are displayed; records that do not match are hidden. When a list is filtered, the worksheet is said to be in **Filter Mode**.

Activity:

1. Open the workbook **Research**. This spreadsheet contains the results of a recent visitor survey at the *Haunted Castle*. Select any <u>one</u> cell in the range **A3:G223**.

2. Display the **Data** tab and select **Filter** from the **Sort & Filter** group.

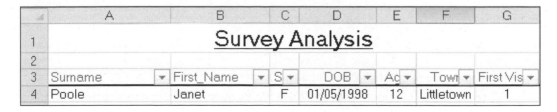

	A	B	C	D	E	F	G
1			Survey Analysis				
2							
3	Surname	First_Name	S	DOB	Ag	Town	First Vis
4	Poole	Janet	F	01/05/1998	12	Littletown	1

> Note: *Excel* automatically detects headers and then fills each drop-down filter list with all of the unique values that can be found in that column.

3.   The worksheet enters **Filter Mode** and drop-down arrows appear in the column headings in row **3**. Click the **Town** drop-down filter arrow.

4.   Uncheck **Select All**, and then click to select **Littletown**.

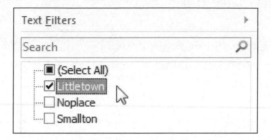

5.   Click **OK** and only the people from **Littletown** are displayed in the worksheet.

> Note: The drop-down arrows gain a filter symbol, 🔽, if the column is currently filtered.

6.   Using the **Town** filter arrow again, click **Select All** and **OK** to restore the entire list.

7.   To display all the males from **Noplace** who were visiting the park for the first time, select *only* **M** from **Sex**, **Noplace** from **Town**, and **Yes** from **First Visit**.

> Note: The number of records found, **9 out of 220**, is shown on the **Status Bar**.

8.   To redisplay the whole list quickly, click the **Filter** button on the **Ribbon** to exit **Filter Mode**. The worksheet returns to its normal state.

> Note: You can also apply custom search criteria for even more advanced filtering.

9.   To only display visitors who are less than 50 years old, enter **Filter Mode** again and select **Number Filters** from the **Age** drop-down list.

10. Select **Less Than** from the submenu that appears and type **50** in the information box.

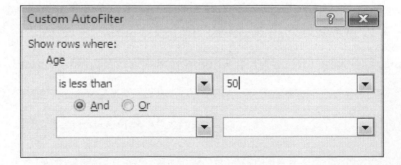

11. Click **OK** to filter the list. Only visitors under 50 years old are now displayed (**148**).

12. To restore the list, click on the **Age** field drop-down. Then click **Select All** and **OK**.

13. Next, create a new filter to show only those people surveyed who are **50** years or *older*. You should locate **72** records.

14. Restore the full list and then create another filter to show only those people whose **Surname** begins with **B**. You should locate **22** records.

15. Restore the full list and then create another filter to show only those people who were born between **01/04/1979** and **01/04/1989** (**11** records). How many of these people were visiting the park for the first time? You should find only **2** records.

> **Note:** Other useful filters include **Top 10**, **Above Average**, **Below Average**, and a wide variety of date criteria. You can also create your own **Custom Filters**.

16. Close the workbook <u>without</u> saving.

4.29 Importing Data

Data can be imported into an *Excel* worksheet from a variety of external sources. In practice, however, it is usually far simpler to only import data contained in plain text files.

Text files must contain information **delimited** (separated) by single characters such as tabs, spaces, or much more commonly, commas.

Activity:

1. Start a new, blank workbook. Display the **Data** tab and, from the **Get External Data** group, click **From Text**. The **Import Text File** dialog box appears.

2. Locate the data files folder for this section and import the file **Concession**.

> **Note:** The plain text file **Concession** is known as a **Comma Separated Values** file (**.csv**). Each value on a row is separated by a comma.

3. The **Text Import Wizard** appears. Notice that *Excel* has already recognised that the file contains data separated by characters (a preview of the file's contents is also shown).

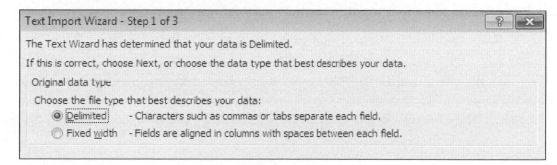

4.   Click **Next** to move to **Step 2** of the wizard. Notice the **Data preview** at the bottom of the dialog box – this shows you the contents of the file that you are importing.

5.   **Tab** is selected as the character which separates values. Change this to **Comma** and notice the effect in the **Data preview**.

```
Concession Sales
                Popcorn  Drinks  Ice Cream  Candy Floss  Smoothies
Black Hole      23.45    340.59  450.45     101.34       34.67
House of Wax    29       609.34  670.98     340.56       56.89
Haunted Vault   134      67      456        2786.9       9.45
```

6.   Click **Next**. The final screen of the wizard allows you to select which type of cell formatting you wish to apply to the new data. **General** is usually always best, so click **Finish**.

7.   The **Import Data** dialog box appears prompting you to enter the cell reference into which the first imported value will be inserted. Make sure that **Existing worksheet** is selected and enter cell **C5** (you can start importing data into any starting cell that you like).

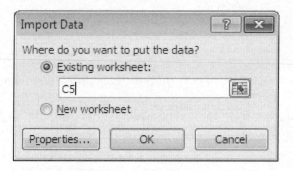

Note: The selected cell represents the top left corner of the imported data block.

8.   Click **OK** and the data is imported. Each value that was separated by a comma in the original file is placed in its own cell.

	A	B	C	D	E	F	G	H
1								
2								
3								
4								
5			Concession Sales					
6				Popcorn	Drinks	Ice Cream	Candy Floss	Smoothies
7			Black Hole	23.45	340.59	450.45	101.34	34.67
8			House of Wax	29	609.34	670.98	340.56	56.89
9			Haunted Vault	134	67	456	2786.9	9.45
10			Tower of Terror	34.56	59	310	34.56	9.99
11			Viper	49.09	45.56	50	53.6	109.45

Note: You can now work with the imported data as normal. Changes made will not effect the contents of the original imported file.

9. Save the workbook as **imported data** and close it.

> Note: You can also open plain text files directly in *Excel*. If the file contains delimited text, it will be automatically separated into cells. However, if you do this, you will need to save the file in *Excel's* **xlsx** format to preserve any formatting or formulas.

10. Display the **File** tab and select **Open**. By default, the dialog box only shows *Excel* files. Click the drop-down button labelled **All Excel Files** and select **All Files** instead.

11. Select the file **Concession** that has now appeared and click **Open**. The contents of the file are automatically placed in cells in the first worksheet (starting in **A1**).

12. From the **File** tab, select **Save**. Read the warning message that appears.

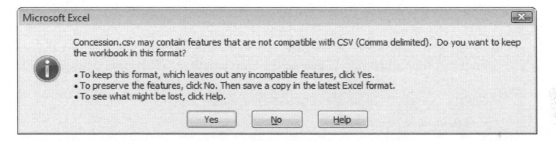

13. To save any formatting or formulas you may later create, the worksheet must be saved as an *Excel* file. Click **No**, change the file name to **concession imported**, and click **Save**.

> Note: In the same way that you can protect documents in *Microsoft Word*, you can also protect workbooks in *Excel*. For instance, your spreadsheets can be password protected or marked as **Final** so that changes are discouraged.

14. Close any open workbooks but leave *Excel* open for the next exercise.

4.30 Modelling Outcomes

Spreadsheets are ideal tools for exploring how changes to data can effect the outcome of your calculations. They allow you to simulate and model situations and, because formulas are dynamic and cells are automatically updated, they let you see at a glance the impact of any changes.

Activity:

1. Open the workbook **Budget**. This spreadsheet shows a list of replacement ride parts that *Zak* must order to complete this month's repairs. The total cost of these parts is £2,416.26 (cell **E14**). Unfortunately, he has a maximum budget of £2000 (**E15**).

> Note: *Zak* obviously cannot spend more money than his budget allows. However, he can experiment with changing the data to see where he can reduce costs.

2.   *Zak* informs you that 6 of the safety harnesses for *The Viper* are worn and must be replaced immediately. However, he wanted to purchase 4 spares too, which aren't essential. Reduce the number of items needed in cell **D5** to **6**.

3.   That has helped, but the total cost is still over-budget by £156.26. *Zak* is sure that, by using a different supplier, the cost of thrust washers can be reduced to £9. To explore what would happen if this was true, change the per item cost in **C10** to **£9.00**.

4.   That didn't make much difference. However, *Zak* has learned that the sliding glass door for the *Haunted Vault* is not an urgent repair; it can wait until next month. To see what effect not having to purchase this item will have, change the number needed in **D7** to **0**.

5.   Finally, the total cost is now within budget! In fact, there's quite a lot of spare cash left over. Maybe *Zak* can order the spare harnesses after all? Change the amount in **D5** back to **10** to find out.

6.   Change the cost of the thrust washers back to **£12.50**. Great — that's all the parts *Zak* needs to order and it has all been done within budget. Well done.

7.   Save the workbook at **budget final** and close it.

4.31 Next Steps

Well done! You have now completed all of the exercises in this section. If you feel you are ready to test your knowledge and understanding of the topics covered, move on to the following **Develop Your Skills** activities. If there are any features of *Microsoft Excel* that you are unsure about, you should revisit the appropriate exercises and try them again before moving on.

If you are interested in exploring some of *Microsoft Excel's* more powerful features, why don't you use the Internet to find out a little more about the following advanced topics.

Feature	Description
Formatting	*Excel* is capable of formatting cells depending on their contents. This means that values which reach a specific value or level can be highlighted so that they stand out. This is called **Conditional Formatting**.
Charts	There are many chart types available in *Excel*. Build on the basic lessons learned in 4.24 and explore the various layouts and styles on offer, including *Excel 2010's* interesting new **Sparklines** feature.
Tracking	It is very common to have another person review and edit spreadsheets that you create. If a workbook has been set up to "track changes", any changes made to a worksheet will be recorded. Once you get the updated workbook back, you can either accept or reject each change.
Macros	A macro records keystrokes and menu selections and then plays them back exactly as they were recorded. A macro can be created so that frequently repeated tasks can be performed automatically.

At the end of every section you get the chance to complete two activities. These will help you to develop your skills and prepare for your exam. Don't forget to use the planning and review checklists at the back of the book to help organise and review your work.

> **Note:**   Answers to these activities are provided in this section's **Sample Solutions** folder.

Develop Your Skills: Haunted Castle Repair Log

In this activity you will be asked to complete a simple spreadsheet for *Zak*. You will need to use all of the ICT skills that you have learned in this section to plan, develop and present an appropriate solution.

Activity 1

My team and I often come across problems during the routine maintenance of rides. To fix these problems before a breakdown occurs, we usually need to buy and fit new parts. To allow us to keep track of spending and make sure we don't go over budget, I plan to start keeping a monthly record of purchases in a spreadsheet.

I've made a start on creating this spreadsheet, but I need you to finish it for me. The information you will need is available in the following file:

✳ **Repair Log**   My incomplete repair log spreadsheet

Start by opening the spreadsheet **Repair Log**, and then enter the most appropriate formulas to calculate results in the following columns:

F (Item Value * Quantity), **G** (Cost * VAT Rate), and **H** (Cost + VAT)

Enter a formula in cell **B24** to *count* the number of repairs, a formula in **B26** to *sum* the items in column **D**, and a formula in **B28** to *sum* the values in column **H**.

The spreadsheet also needs to look professional and be easy to read, so you should apply appropriate text and cell formatting. Add a more descriptive title to the spreadsheet so that it can be more easily identified, and then save the file as **final repair log**.

Develop Your Skills: Maintenance Report

In this activity you will be asked to develop a spreadsheet and create a report for one of *Zak's* colleagues. You will need to use all of the advanced ICT skills that you have learned in this section to create a suitable solution. It may help you to break the problem down into smaller parts first.

Activity 2

I've just received the following e-mail from one of my colleagues in the engineering and maintenance department:

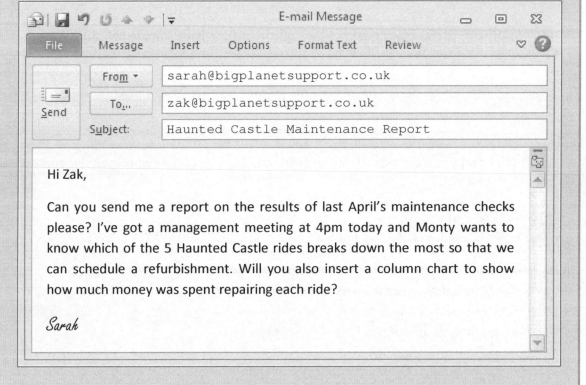

I need to head over to *The Black Hole* to repair yet another breakdown! Will you get this information together for *Sarah*? I've made a start on the report in *Microsoft Word* but I've not included any figures yet. You will need the following files:

* **Report**   My incomplete report document

* **April Checks**   A file containing raw maintenance data for April

Start by opening the file **Report** to see the types of information required to complete the document. Then use the most appropriate application to work out the necessary information and create a chart. You may need to sort and filter the data that you have been given. The spreadsheet also needs to look professional and be easy to read, so you should apply appropriate text and cell formatting. Finally, save the completed document as **maintenance report**.

5 | Microsoft PowerPoint

Hi, my name's Yan...

I'm the head of ride design here at *Big Planet Theme Park*, and it's my job to create the blueprints for new rides and attractions. For my current project I've been asked to redesign *Demon of the Deep*, one of our older and less popular rides.

The *Demon of the Deep* log flume used to be one of the park's best attractions, but times and tastes change. It's now my responsibility to produce new ideas for improving the ride, from initial concepts and rough sketches through to fully developed models and working simulations. As I often work on my own, I need to manage my own time and stay focused to meet my deadlines.

I've already come up with a few new ideas to help improve the ride, and I plan to present these to park managers at a meeting in a few days time. To help me, I will use the application *Microsoft PowerPoint* to create a professional presentation quickly and easily. In fact, as you are here, maybe we can create the presentation together?

What you will learn:

In this section you will use the program *Microsoft PowerPoint* to help *Yan* design, create and edit a presentation. <u>IMPORTANT</u>: as each exercise builds on the last to create a complete presentation, you will need to pay close attention and follow *all* of *Yan's* instructions carefully.

Knowledge, skills and understanding:

* Use *Microsoft PowerPoint* to create and edit eye-catching presentations

* Apply a range of professional formatting and layout techniques

* Choose and display information that is relevant for the audience

* Select suitable animations and themes

Data files

The files needed to complete the activities in this section are provided in the **Section 5** data folder (see note on page **vii** to download these files). Presentations that you create or edit can be saved to the same folder.

5.1 Using Microsoft PowerPoint

In both business and education, people are often asked to give a talk on a specific topic such as a new idea, product or service. People are also frequently required to present the results of their work or the findings of their research to other interested parties. To help lead the delivery of their talk, presentation software can be used.

> **Note:** It is a well known fact that most people do not enjoy public speaking. Fortunately, creating a slide show to accompany a presentation can really help. It can aid your memory and help get important points across to the audience.

Microsoft PowerPoint is an application that is an appropriate choice for any task that requires you to create, edit and give a presentation. It allows you to create a number of **slides** containing key points on one or more topics. When combined in a sequence, the slides form a **slide show** that can be used to accompany your talk.

> **Note:** Presentations are most often displayed using an overhead projector, monitor or digital whiteboard. However, you can also use *PowerPoint* to save a slide show as a sequence of web pages or as printed handouts.

The formatting of text and images is handled easily by *PowerPoint*, as is the ability to include different types of objects such as videos, music and charts. Perhaps more important is the application's ability to present information using a variety of professional text and background styles. To capture your audience's attention, a range of advanced animation effects can also be used to bring your presentation to life.

5.2 Creating a Presentation

PowerPoint features a variety of ready-made templates that you can use to create very impressive and professional presentations. However, it is recommended that you start from a blank template and focus on your presentation's content first. You can then apply formatting later.

Activity:

1. Start *Microsoft PowerPoint*. A new blank presentation appears on the screen.

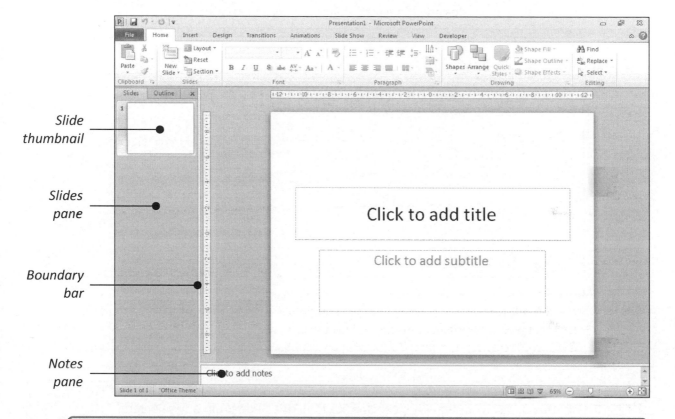

> **Note:** You can also create a new **Blank presentation** using the **File** tab.

2. Examine the *PowerPoint* window. In particular, locate the familiar **File** tab, **Ribbon**, **Status Bar**, **Quick Access Toolbar** and **Zoom** controls.

3. Locate the **Slides** pane on the left of the window. This will display a small preview of all the slides in your presentation (known as **thumbnail** images). Clicking a thumbnail will open the full slide in the main editing window.

4. Locate the **Notes** pane at the bottom of the window. This can be used to add notes to each slide which can be printed and used by a speaker during a presentation.

> **Note:** The various panes can be resized or hidden by dragging their boundary bars.

5. Leave the blank presentation open for the next exercise.

5.3 Slide Layouts

PowerPoint features a number of built-in slide layouts that can be used to quickly create new slides. Each layout features a slightly different arrangement of **placeholders** that you can use to enter your slide's content.

Activity:

1. Examine the layout of the single blank slide currently on-screen. This slide has a **Title Slide** layout (i.e. the slide is designed to be the first screen in a presentation).

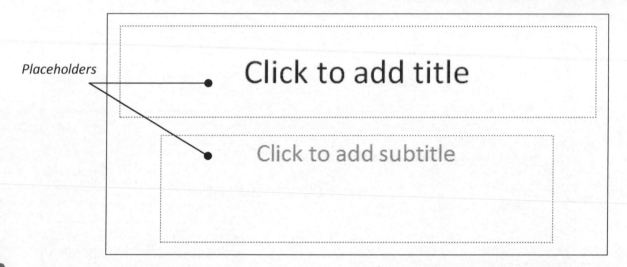

> **Note:** The default text that appears in the placeholders is used to prompt for information. This text will not appear when the slide show is viewed.

2. With the **Home** tab selected, click the **Layout** button, [Layout ▾], in the **Slides** group. A list of other slide layout types appears (notice that **Title Slide** is already selected).

3. Select **Title and Content** from the list. The current slide's layout is changed.

4. Select each of the remaining 7 slide layouts in turn and observe how each one affects the slide. Consider the possible uses for each of the layout types.

> **Note:** The position of placeholders on each slide layout can be changed using click and drag. To restore to the default layout, use the **Reset** button in the **Slides** group.

5. Return the current slide to its original **Title Slide** layout and leave the presentation open.

5.4 Adding and Removing Slides

New slides can easily be added to a presentation at any time using any slide layout you wish. It is also easy to remove any unwanted slides.

Activity:

1. With the default blank presentation open on screen, click the **New Slide** button (not the drop-down arrow) in the **Slides** group on the **Home** tab.

> **Note:** Clicking the drop-down arrow on the **New Slide** button will let you add a new slide using any of the 9 available layout types.

2. A new slide with **Title and Content** layout is created and added to the slide show. It appears on the **Slides** pane and is automatically selected.

3. Use the drop-down arrow on the **New Slide** button to add a slide with **Two Content** layout. There are now 3 slides in the presentation.

> **Note:** Notice that the slides are automatically numbered in the **Slides** pane.

4. Using the **Slides** pane, click once on slide **1**. The slide thumbnail is selected and appears in the main editing window. Use the same technique to select slide **2**.

> **Note:** To delete a slide, simply select it in the **Slides** pane and press <**Delete**>.

5. Using the **Slides** pane, click once on slide **3**. Press the <**Delete**> key on your keyboard to remove the slide (leaving two slides remaining).

6. Select slide **1** and leave it open for the next exercise.

5.5   Entering Text

Text can be added to a slide by simply clicking once within the boundaries of a placeholder and typing. The default "**Click to add…**" prompt will automatically disappear.

Activity:

1. Slide **1** should currently be selected in the **Slides** pane. Click once in the placeholder box labelled **Click to add title**. The default prompt text disappears.

2. *Yan* wants you to help create a presentation for his proposed improvements to the *Demon of the Deep* ride. Enter the presentation title **Demon of the Deep**.

3. Click in the second placeholder to add a **subtitle**, and then type **Redesign Ideas**. Notice that the first thumbnail on the **Slides** pane has been updated to reflect the changes.

> **Note:**   All of the standard text formatting options such as **Bold**, **Italic**, **Underline**, **Font** and **Font Size** are available on the **Home** tab in the **Font** group. Familiar text alignment options such as **Line Spacing** are also available in the **Paragraph** group.

4. Display slide **2**, click once in the top placeholder and enter the text **Project Introduction**.

> **Note:**   In general, most *PowerPoint* slides should only contain brief bulleted points that help to emphasize key points in your presentation.

5. Click once in the lower placeholder and enter the text **Demon of the Deep ride is getting old**. Notice that this slide layout automatically includes bullet points. Press <**Enter**>.

6. Enter the following key points, pressing <**Enter**> after each one.

    Ride suffers from frequent breakdowns
    Gives a bad impression of the park
    Used to be very popular, but not any more
    Too expensive to replace the ride
    Needs a redesign to attract new visitors

7. Save the presentation as **redesign** (in the data files folder for this section) and leave it open for the next exercise.

5.6 Running a Presentation

Once you have created one or more slides, you can "run" a presentation in **Slide Show** view. This will display the presentation as it will be seen by your audience, and is useful for testing that everything works and the presentation appears as you expect.

Activity:

1. Slide **2** should currently be selected in the **Slides** pane. Display the **Slide Show** tab and click **From Beginning** in the **Start Slide Show** group.

2. The presentation runs and slide **1** fills the screen. Click your left mouse button once to move to the next slide (alternatively you can press <**Space**> or <→>). Click once more to reach the end of the slide show where a black screen appears.

3.   Press the <**Esc**> key on your keyboard to close the slide show. You can do this at any time during a presentation.

> **Note:**   You can also run a slide show from the currently selected slide by clicking **From Current Slide**. This option also appears on the right of the **Status Bar**, ⬚.

4.   Leave the presentation open for the next exercise.

5.7   Design Considerations

When creating a new presentation, special care needs to be taken when designing your slides. The following list briefly describes a number of important points that you should consider:

* ✱   Keep things simple. Don't include too much text or too many images on one slide.

* ✱   Stick to key points and statements – avoid long sentences.

* ✱   Don't mix and match too many fonts of different types and sizes.

* ✱   Font sizes should be no smaller than 24 point for general text.

* ✱   Use title case throughout a presentation and avoid block capitals.

* ✱   Avoid dark text on dark backgrounds and light text on light backgrounds.

* ✱   Sans serif fonts (e.g. Arial) are often easier to read that serif fonts (e.g. Times).

* ✱   Don't overdo distracting animations or slide transitions.

* ✱   Use a consistent design theme for your entire presentation.

Visual impact is almost everything in a presentation. In general, try not to use too many different colours, styles or effects as the clarity of your message may be obscured. A simple, consistent design scheme is usually more effective.

> **Note:**   As a guide, 10 slides for a 20 minute talk is considered average. Also remember the "seven by seven rule", which recommends that each of your slides should have no more than 7 lines of text and each line should contain no more than 7 words.

You should also be aware of the value of using pictures rather than lots of text, and simple charts rather than complicated tables of figures. Always consider the emotional implications of certain colours too; reds are believed to be stimulating and representative of energy and danger, while blues are associated with calmness and stability. As some people have difficulty separating certain colour combinations (especially red-green), be careful when using these combinations to describe important information.

> **Note:**   Many businesses, schools, colleges and universities offer professional *PowerPoint* templates to their students and staff for use in formal presentations.

Furthermore, always consider the purpose of your presentation and design your slides accordingly. For example, a presentation to promote a company to potential investors will contain different information than one created to advertise a company to its customers. Furthermore, a presentation intended to run on a big screen in a large hall may need different design features to one which will run on a small screen in a meeting room.

5.8 Themes

It is important for a presentation to have a consistent design style across all of its slides. Although the same text formatting can be copied manually from slide to slide, *PowerPoint* offers several more effective methods to do this automatically. The quickest way is to apply a **theme** to the entire presentation.

> **Note:** A theme is a colour-coordinated set of text styles, backgrounds and graphics.

Activity:

1. The **redesign** presentation should still be open with slide **2** selected. At the moment, both of the slides in the presentation contain simple dark text on a white background. Fairly boring, wouldn't you say?

2. Let's apply a theme to the presentation to make it more interesting. Display the **Design** tab and then examine the theme previews that appear in the **Themes** group.

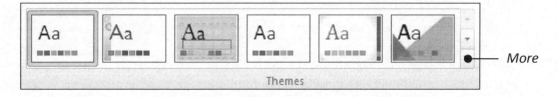 —— *More*

> **Note:** Placing your mouse pointer over a thumbnail will display a **ToolTip** containing the theme's name. The effect of selecting that theme is *previewed* on the selected slide. Notice that the default **Office Theme** is currently selected.

3. Select the *second* theme in the list, named **advent**. Notice how the background colours, graphics, bullet points and text formatting on *all* slides in the presentation change.

4. Select each of the themes currently shown to see their effect.

5. Click the **More** drop-down arrow, , to the right of the theme selection box to view more themes. Locate and select the theme called **Waveform** (you may need to scroll down).

> **Note:** If you are connected to the Internet, an additional selection of themes may be shown from **Office.com**. These will be automatically downloaded when applied.

6. The **Waveform** theme is applied to the entire presentation. Examine both slides to see the effect.

Project Introduction

* Demon of the Deep ride is getting old
* Ride suffers from frequent breakdowns
* Gives a bad impression of the park
* Used to be very popular, but not any more
* Too expensive to replace the ride
* Needs a redesign to attract new visitors

7. Save the presentation and leave it open for the next exercise.

5.9 Colour Schemes

In addition to themes, you can also select a **colour scheme** for your presentation. This is a set of coordinated colours which set your presentation's default font and background styles.

> **Note:** Changing colour schemes is useful when you like the basic design of a theme but not its colours. You can mix and match themes and colour schemes.

Activity:

1. The **redesign** presentation should still be open. Click **Colors**, [Colors ▾], from the **Themes** group. The currently selected colour scheme is highlighted with a border.

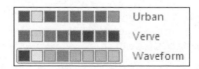

2. Place your mouse pointer over a variety of colour schemes <u>without</u> clicking to preview each style on the selected slide. Notice that the background and text colours change.

3. *Big Planet Theme Park* uses a light purple colour to identify the **Demon of the Deep** ride in all marketing materials. To use a similar approach here, select **Opulent** from the list.

> **Note:**   To customise the selected colour scheme, or create your own from scratch, select **Create New Theme Colors** from the **Colours** drop-down list.

4. Save the presentation and leave it open for the next exercise.

5.10 Slide Master

To customise a selected theme and change the way fonts and designs appear on all slides in a presentation, you can edit the **Slide Master**. Changes to the **Slide Master** will affect all slides in a presentation (including any new slides added to it later).

> **Note:**   A **Slide Master** is particularly useful if you want to change all text and bullet styles in a presentation, or if you want to add a graphic to every slide (e.g. a logo).

Activity:

1. The **redesign** presentation should still be open. Display the **View** tab and click **Slide Master** from the **Master Views** group. The **Slide Master** is now shown.

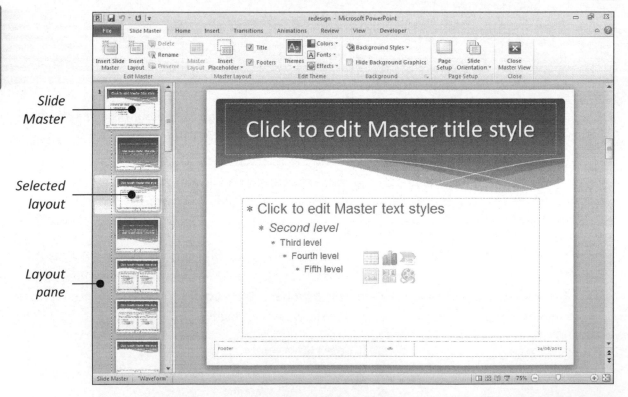

> **Note:**   The **Slide Master** can be found at the top of the **Layout** pane. The slides under this allow you to customise individual slide layouts (e.g. **Title Slide**, **Title and Content**).

2. Click the **Slide Master** thumbnail in the **Layout** pane. Any changes made here to text or bullet styles will apply to every slide in the presentation.

> **Note:**   If a **Layout** slide is selected in the **Layout** pane rather than the **Slide Master**, only slides of that type will be changed.

3. Select all of the text in the first placeholder: **Click to edit Master title style**.

4. Display the **Home** tab and notice that the selected font is **Candara**, size **44**. Change this to **Calibri**, size **48**.

5. Use the **Text Shadow** button, $\boxed{\text{S}}$, to apply a drop shadow effect to the text.

6. Select all of the first bullet's text in the <u>lower</u> placeholder: **Click to edit Master text styles**, then set the font to **Arial** and the size to **28pt**. Leave the other settings as they are.

7. Select all of the next bullet's text: **Second Level**, and set the font to **Arial**, the style to **Italic** and the size to **24pt**.

8. Set the **Third**, **Fourth** and **Fifth** levels to **Arial** size **18** (try selecting all three lines at once).

9. Select <u>all</u> of the bullet text for <u>all</u> levels in the lower placeholder and set the **Font Color** to black (using the **Font Color** button's drop-down arrow).

10. Click **Close Master View** on the **Slide Master** tab to see how the presentation has been changed (the text on both slides has changed to reflect the **Slide Master's** new formatting). Save the presentation and leave it open for the next exercise.

5.11 Bullet Levels

When you add text to a slide you need to be as brief and as concise as possible. Only important facts should be included in the form of **bullet points**. If you would like to expand on a bullet and add extra detail, you can add one or more minor bullets at a different **level** below.

> ✳ This is a level 1 bullet
>   ✳ This is a level 2 bullet
>   ✳ This is a level 3 bullet

There are several levels of bullet point available in *PowerPoint* which can be used to add minor details to major points.

> **Note:** The formatting of bullet points for the whole presentation can also be set in **Slide Master View**. This includes the bullet symbols.

Activity:

1. The **redesign** presentation should still be open. With slide **2** selected, use the **New Slide** button to add a new slide with **Title and Content** layout.

2. Add the slide title **Considerations** (notice that the new slide uses the default formatting set up in the **Slide Master**). Next, add the following bullet points in the lower placeholder:

    Limited budget
    0.5 Million to spend on redesign
    Tight schedule
    Must complete ride redesign in 6 months
    Works must be done in winter season
    Ride must be environmentally friendly

> **Note:** When bullet points are first entered onto a slide, *PowerPoint* assumes they are **first level**. As such, all 6 bullets on the current slide are **level 1** bullets.

3. Place the cursor anywhere in the second bulleted line and click **Increase List Level**, from the **Paragraph** group of the **Home** tab. The bullet's level is increased to **level 2**, making it a sub-point of the **level 1** bullet above.

> **Note:** The second level bullet adopts the **level 2** style set up earlier in the **Slide Master**.

4. The fourth and fifth bullets are really sub-points of the third bullet. Increase both of these to **level 2** also.

> * Limited budget
>   * *0.5 Million to spend on redesign*
> * Tight schedule
>   * *Must complete ride redesign in 6 months*
>   * *Works must be done in winter season*
> * Ride must be environmentally friendly

5. Save the presentation and leave it open for the next exercise.

5.12 Bullet Symbols

You can change the symbols used for the bullet points in your presentation. Although this can be done for each bullet individually, it is *far* easier to apply global changes using the **Slide Master**.

Activity:

1. With the **redesign** presentation open, display the **View** tab and click **Slide Master**.

2. The slide type **Title and Content Layout** is automatically selected. Select **Slide Master** from the top of the **Layout** pane instead.

3. Place the cursor in the first level of bulleted text. Display the **Home** tab and click the drop-down arrow on the **Bullets** button in the **Paragraph** group.

4. Examine the various bullet styles available (selecting **None** would remove the bullet symbol from this level of bullets).

> **Note:** Selecting **Bullets and Numbering** from the bottom of the drop-down menu will allow you to change the colour and size of the bullet or to use a custom image.

5. For now, from the list of bullet symbols that appear, select **Arrow Bullets**, .

6. Place the cursor in the second level of bulleted text. From the **Bullets** drop-down menu, select **Filled Square Bullets**.

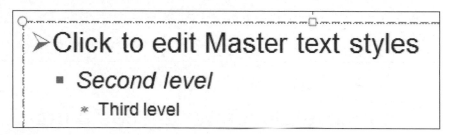

7. Display the **Slide Master** tab and click **Close Master View** to see how the presentation has been affected.

8. Save the presentation and leave it open for the next exercise.

5.13 Rearranging Bullets

Once you have entered a number of bullets onto a slide, it is very easy to rearrange them into a different order using click and drag.

Activity:

1. The **redesign** presentation should still be open. With slide **3** selected, use the **New Slide** button to add a new slide with **Title and Content** layout.

2. Add the slide title **Initial Plan**.

3. Next, add the following bullet points to the lower placeholder in the order shown:

    Close the ride at the end of October

    Refill the ride with water and test for leaks

    Fit new ride features

    Drain the ride of water

    Remove old, unwanted ride parts

    Ride is ready in time for spring season

4. Hold on! The order of events in this list is all wrong. Place your mouse pointer over the fourth bullet point symbol (**Drain the ride of water**). Notice that the pointer changes to a four way arrow.

✥Drain the ride of water

5. Using click and drag, move this bullet below the first line and into second place. Notice that a faint horizontal line appears between bullet points to indicate where the current bullet will be placed when dropped.

6. Use the same technique to reorder the remaining bullets into the correct order, as shown below:

    ➢Close the ride at the end of October
    ➢Drain the ride of water
    ➢Remove old, unwanted ride parts
    ➢Fit new ride features
    ➢Refill the ride with water and test for leaks
    ➢Ride is ready in time for spring season

> **Note:**   You can also **Cut**, **Copy** and **Paste** bullet points.

7. Save the presentation and leave it open for the next exercise.

5.14 Inserting Pictures and Clip Art

To make your presentations more interesting, you can insert pictures or diagrams stored on your computer onto a slide. Various illustrations are also available from the **Clip Art** library that is available online at **Office.com**.

> **Note:** When using a picture in your presentation, always make sure you have permission from the person who owns it. This does not apply to **Clip Art** from **Office.com**.

Activity:

1. The **redesign** presentation should still be open. With slide **4** selected, use the **New Slide** button to add a new slide with **Title and Content** layout. Add the slide title **First Ideas**.

> **Note:** Have you noticed the faded icons in the centre of the slide? These can be used to quickly insert objects such as **Tables**, **Charts**, **Pictures** and **Clip Art**.

2. Click once in the lower placeholder and then display the **Insert** tab. From the **Images** group, select **Picture**. The **Insert Picture** dialog box appears.

3. Locate the data files folder for this section and then select the **Sketch** image file. Click **Insert** to place the picture in the centre of the current slide.

> **Note:** Inserted objects can be repositioned using click and drag, resized using a corner handle, ⬚, or rotated using the green rotation handle, ⬚.

4. Feel free to resize and reposition the image as necessary to match the slide below.

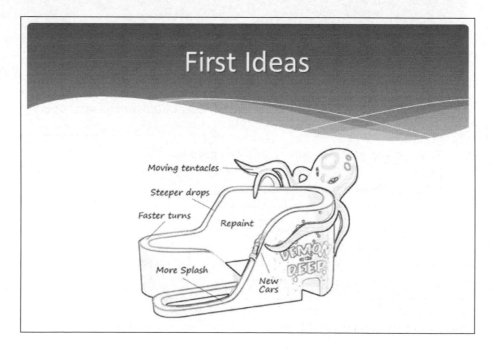

---

5. Next, display the **Insert** tab again and click **Clip Art** from the **Images** group. The **Clip Art** task pane appears on the right of the screen.

6. Type **lightbulb** in the **Search for** box, and check that **All media file types** is selected in the **Results should be** box.

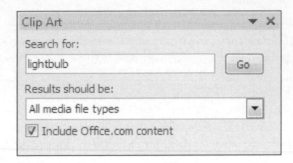

7. Click the **Go** button and, after a short delay, a list of **Clip Art** images matching the **lightbulb** keyword will be displayed.

8. Locate the **Clip Art** image shown below (you may need to scroll down), and click it once. The illustration is placed in the centre of the current slide.

9. Resize the **Clip Art** image and position it to the right of the header text (**First Ideas**), as shown below.

10. Close the **Clip Art** task pane, the save the presentation and leave it open.

> **Note:**   You can add a picture to a slide's background (including solid, gradient, texture and pattern fills) by clicking the **Background Styles** button on the **Design** tab and selecting **Format Background**.

5.15 Inserting Charts

A **chart** can be added to a slide to display complex data in a format that is more meaningful and easier to understand for your audience. The relevant information is entered into a spreadsheet which is then converted into a chart.

Activity:

1. The **redesign** presentation should still be open. With slide **5** selected, use the **New Slide** button on the **Home** tab to add a new slide with a <u>**Blank**</u> layout.

2. *Yan* would like to include a **Column Chart** on this slide containing all of the costs for the ride's redesign.

3. Display the **Insert** tab and click **Chart** from the **Illustrations** group. The **Insert Chart** dialog box appears.

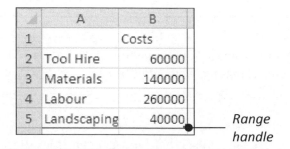

4. The first **Column** chart is selected by default. This is ideal for use in *Yan's* presentation, so click **OK**. *Microsoft Excel* starts alongside the *PowerPoint* window.

5. Replace the sample data in the *Excel* window with the information shown below.

	A	B
1		Costs
2	Tool Hire	60000
3	Materials	140000
4	Labour	260000
5	Landscaping	40000

Range handle

> **Note:** The sample data range includes two extra columns. You will need to use the range handle to reduce the chart data range to include columns **A** and **B** <u>only</u> (**A1:B5**).

6. Close *Excel*. The data range selected is now used to build a **Column** chart on the current *PowerPoint* slide. Click away from the chart to see how it will appear.

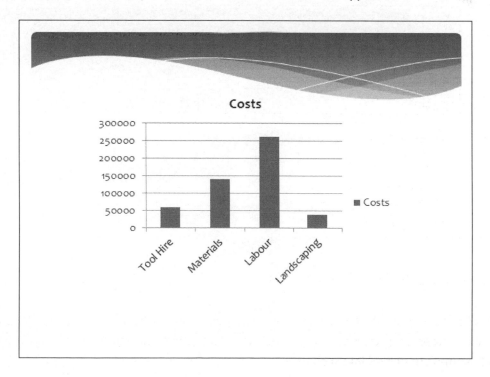

7. Click the chart once to select it and notice the **Chart Tools** tabs appear on the **Ribbon**.

> **Note:** Once a chosen **Chart** type has been selected, you can change your mind and apply another using the **Change Chart Type** button on the **Chart Tools - Design** tab.

8. Display the **Chart Tools - Design** tab now, and click the **Change Chart Type** button in the **Type** group. The **Change Chart Type** dialog box appears.

9. Choose a **Pie** chart instead and select the first type (**Pie**) from the list. Click **OK** and the chart is changed.

> **Note:** Like *Excel*, each chart type has its own list of **Chart Layouts** and **Chart Styles** to choose from (variations on the selected chart type). You can also reposition elements in a chart manually using drag and drop.

> **Note:** Other options on the **Layout** tab allow you to add, edit and remove axis titles, gridlines, legends and data labels.

10. Change the chart type again and select the first **Bar** chart, and then change the title of the chart to **Redesign Costs** (hint: you can right-click the chart's title and select **Edit Text**).

11. Select the chart's **Legend**, ■ Costs, and press <**Delete**> to remove it.

12. By clicking and dragging the chart's border, move the chart down a little so that it is positioned better in the white space available (as shown below).

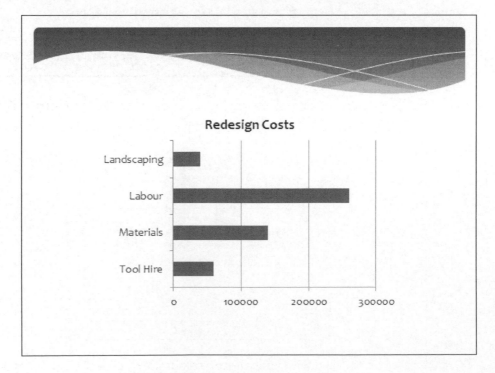

13. Save the presentation and leave it open for the next exercise.

5.16 Inserting WordArt

PowerPoint, like *Microsoft Word*, has a powerful feature called **WordArt** which allows you to create impressive artwork from the text on your slides. There are various styles, shapes and colours to choose from.

Activity:

1. The **redesign** presentation should still be open. With slide **6** selected, use the **New Slide** button on the **Home** tab to add a new slide with a **Blank** layout.

2. Display the **Insert** tab and select **WordArt** from the **Text** group. A drop-down menu appears containing a range of **WordArt** styles (notice that they reflect the presentation's chosen colour scheme). Select the first **WordArt** style in the list.

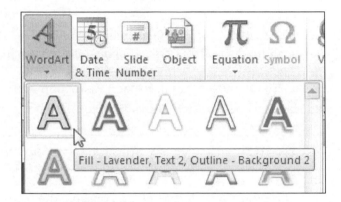

3. A **WordArt** box appears in the centre of the screen with the words **Your text here** already selected. Overtype this with the text **Any Questions?**

> **Note:** Once a chosen **WordArt** style has been selected, you can change your mind and apply another using the **WordArt Styles** selection box. Your text will be preserved.

4. Examine the various formatting features in the **WordArt Styles** group on the **Drawing Tools - Format** tab. These can be used to customise **WordArt** in a number of ways.

5. Select all of the **WordArt** text, then click the **Text Fill** drop-down button and choose a light **Lavender** colour from the list of **Theme Colors**.

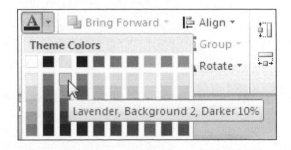

6. The **WordArt** text is filled with your chosen colour. Next, click the **Text Effects** button and examine the various effects that you can apply.

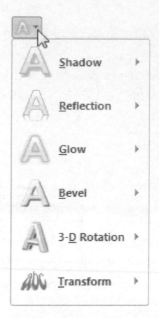

7. Move your mouse pointer over **Shadow**, and then select the first shadow style that appears (labelled with the **ToolTip: Offset Diagonal Bottom Right**).

8. Display the **Text Effects** button again, expand **Reflection** and select the first reflection style (labelled with the **ToolTip: Tight Reflection, touching**).

> **Note:**   You can use **WordArt** and apply these effects in other *Microsoft Office* applications.

9. Click away from the **WordArt** to deselect it and observe the results.

10. Save the presentation and leave it open for the next exercise.

5.17 Inserting Shapes and Text Boxes

PowerPoint offers a number of simple drawing features to add basic shapes to your slides. You can also place text inside floating boxes that can be positioned anywhere you like.

Activity:

1. The **redesign** presentation should still be open. With slide **7** selected, use the **New Slide** button on the **Home** tab to add a new slide with a **Title Only** layout.

2. *Yan* has decided that he would like to include a few interesting quotes from park visitors about the current *Demon of the Deep* ride. Add the slide title **Visitor Opinions**.

3. Display the **Insert** tab and click the **Shapes** drop-down button. Then, from the **Callouts** section, select the first shape, ▢ (**Rectangular Callout**).

4. The mouse pointer changes to a crosshair, . In the centre of the slide, click and drag to create a shape of any size.

5. With the new shape selected, display the **Drawing Tools - Format** tab and locate the **Size** group.

6. By editing the values in the boxes, set the **Shape Height** to **4 cm** and the **Shape Width** to **6 cm**.

7. Using the **Copy** button on the **Home** tab, copy the new shape.

8. Then use the **Paste** button to create two identical copies and arrange them below the slide title as shown below.

> **Note:**   **WordArt**, shapes, text boxes and pictures can overlap. To control which object is in front of which, use the **Bring Forward** and **Send Backward** buttons.

9. Select the leftmost callout shape. Then type the first visitor quote: **"The ride is very old fashioned"**. The text appears in the middle of the shape.

10. Select the text, then use the **Font Size** drop-down button on the **Home** tab to increase the size to **24**.

11. In the second box enter the text: **"It's really slow and boring"**. In the third box, enter: **"It's looking a little run down"**. Increase the **Font Size** to **24** for both shapes.

12. Next, display the **Insert** tab again and select **Text Box**. Click once below the three **Callout** shapes to create a text box, and then type the text: **Quotes collected by a survey on 01/06/2012**.

13. Click and drag the text box's borders to reposition it neatly so that it appears in the middle of the slide underneath the shapes containing the visitor quotes.

> **Note:**   The **Align** button on the **Drawing Tools - Format** tab can be used to position shapes.

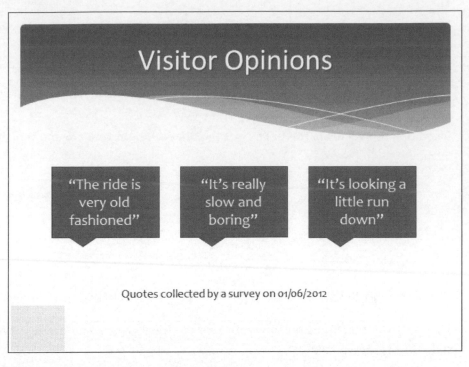

14. Save the presentation and leave it open for the next exercise.

5.18 Inserting Tables

PowerPoint allows you to insert well-designed tables (grids of cells containing text in rows and columns) that can be used to present data in a clear and easy to read format.

Activity:

1. The **redesign** presentation should still be open. With slide **8** selected, use the **New Slide** button on the **Home** tab to add a new slide with a **Title Only** layout.

2. *Yan* would like to include statistics on the drop in visitor numbers on the *Demon of the Deep* ride. Add the slide title **Visitor Numbers**.

3. Display the **Insert** tab and click **Table**. From the drop-down that appears, use the grid to select a table **3x5**.

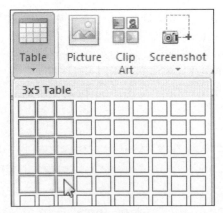

4. A new, blank table appears on the current slide.

> **Note:** Notice that the table matches the presentation's colour scheme. For advanced table options, select **Create Table** from the **Insert Table** drop-down button.

5. Enter the following data into the table. You can use the <**Tab**> key to move from cell to cell (<**Shift Tab**> can also be used to move back one cell).

Quarter/Year	2000	2010
Winter	123000	23000
Spring	89000	31000
Summer	49000	14000
Autumn	78000	11000

6. Move the table, by clicking and dragging its border, into the middle of the slide.

Quarter/Year	2000	2010
Winter	123000	23000
Spring	89000	31000
Summer	49000	14000
Autumn	78000	11000

7. Save the presentation and leave it open for the next exercise.

5.19 Objects on the Slide Master

Any objects such as text boxes, **Clip Art, WordArt,** pictures and shapes can be added to a presentation's **Slide Master**. They will then appear on every slide in the presentation.

Activity:

1. With the **redesign** presentation open, display the **View** tab and click **Slide Master**. Then, select **Slide Master** from the top of the **Layout** pane.

2. Using the **Picture** button on the **Insert** tab, insert the **Logo** image from the data files folder. It appears in the centre of the **Slide Master**.

3. On the **Picture Tools - Format** tab, click the **Align** drop-down button, and select **Align Bottom**. Click the **Align** button again and select **Align Left**.

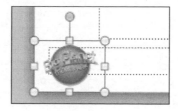

4. The theme park logo now appears in the bottom left corner of the **Slide Master**. Display the **Slide Master** tab and select the **Blank Layout** slide in the **Layout** pane.

> Note: You may notice that the logo does not appear on all **Layout** slides in the **Layout** pane (e.g. **Title** or **Blank Layout** slides). The logo *is* there, but it is hidden.

5. On the **Ribbon**, remove the tick from the **Hide Background Graphics** checkbox in the **Background** group (this feature hides all background images). The logo appears.

6. Click **Close Master View**. The theme park logo now appears in the bottom left corner of all slides apart from the first (recall that we did not remove the tick from the **Hide Background Graphics** checkbox for **Title Layout** slides).

7. Save the presentation and leave it open for the next exercise.

5.20 Changing Slide Order

The order that slides appear in the **Slides** pane is the order that they will appear when a presentation is run. To change this order, individual slides can be moved elsewhere in the slide show sequence. To do this, it is recommended that you use *PowerPoint's* **Slide Sorter** view.

Activity:

1. With the **redesign** presentation open, display the **View** tab and click **Slide Sorter** from the **Presentation Views** group.

> Note: The **Zoom** controls found to the right of the **Status Bar** can be used to resize the slide thumbnails displayed in **Slide Sorter** view.

2. If necessary, use the **Zoom** controls to select a zoom level that allows all 9 slide thumbnails to appear on the screen at once (without needing to scroll).

3. *Yan* would like to move slide **8**, **Visitor Opinions**, between slides **2** and **3**. Click on slide **8** and drag the slide towards slide **2**. A vertical drop bar appears between slides to indicate where the current slide will be placed when dropped.

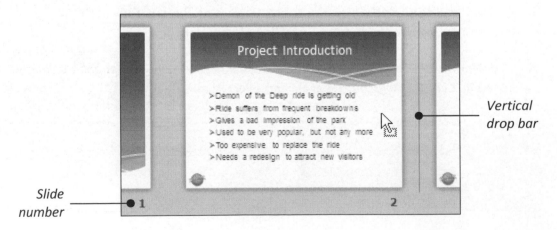

4.   When the vertical drop bar appears between slides **2** and **3**, release the mouse. The **Visitor Opinions** slide is moved and becomes slide **3**.

> **Note:**   To delete a slide, right click its thumbnail and select **Delete Slide**.

5.   Next, move slide **9**, **Visitor Numbers**, between slides **3** and **4**.

> **Note:**   Slides can also be moved using click and drag in the **Slides** pane in **Normal** view.

6.   Switch back to **Normal** view using the button in the **Presentation Views** group. Save the presentation and leave it open for the next exercise.

5.21 Applying Animation

Simple **animations** can very quickly be applied to objects on a slide so that they appear in a variety of fun and interesting ways. Use animation carefully, however, as too many fancy effects can be distracting for the audience.

Activity:

1.   Select slide **2** of the **redesign** presentation in **Normal** view.

2.   Place the cursor anywhere in the title **Project Introduction**, and then display the **Animations** tab. From the list of animations in the **Animation** group, select **Fade**.

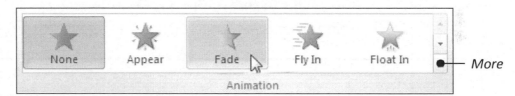

> **Note:**   If a desired effect does not appear in the **Animation** group, click the **More** button to view all available effects.

3.   Next, place the cursor anywhere in the bulleted list below the title and click **Fly In** from the **Animation** group. A preview of the animation may briefly appear on the slide.

> **Note:**   Notice the small numbers that have appeared to the left of both the title and bulleted list. These represent the sequence in which each animation will occur. This order can be changed using the **Reorder Animation** buttons in the **Timing** group.

4.   Display the **Slide Show** tab and click **From Current Slide** in the **Start Slide Show** group. The presentation runs from slide **2**.

5.   Click the mouse button once to activate the first animation: the title text fades in.

6. Click again to activate the second animation: the first line of bulleted text flies in. Click again five more times to display each remaining line of text. Click once more to move on to slide **3**, and then press **<Esc>** to end the show.

7. Select slide **2** again and display the **Animations** tab. Place the cursor in the bulleted text and click the **Effect Options** button in the **Animation** group.

8. Select **From Left** in the list of options available. Display the **Effect Options** again and select **All at Once** from the bottom of the menu.

> **Note:** Notice the effect this has had on the animation sequence. All bullets now have the number **2** next to them and will appear together *after* the first title animation.

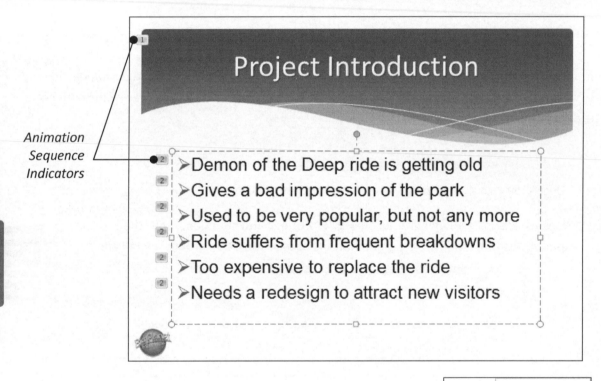

9. In the **Timing** group, click the **Start** drop-down button, ⊳ Start: On Click ▾ , and select **With Previous**. The bulleted list animation will now occur at the same time as the first title animation (notice the effect on the animation sequence).

> **Note:** The **Preview** button can be used to see effects on the slide without needing to run the slide show. The length of an effect (or its initial delay) can also be controlled using the options available in the **Timing** group.

10. Run the slide show from the current slide again and observe the effects (use your mouse or keyboard to move the slide show forward). Press **<Esc>** when finished to end the show.

11. Select slide **2** again and display the **Animations** tab. Select the bulleted list, and then select **None** to remove the animation. Use this technique to remove the animation from the slide's title also.

> **Note:** An easy way to apply animation to all slides is to use the **Slide Master**.

12. Display the **View** tab and click **Slide Master**. Then, select the **Slide Master** from the top of the **Layout** pane.

13. Place the cursor anywhere in the title placeholder containing the text **Click to edit Master title style**. Then display the **Animations** tab and, from the list of built-in animations in the **Animation** group, select **Fade**.

14. From the **Timing** group, drop-down the **Start** button and select **With Previous**. The effect will now happen immediately when the slide is shown during the presentation.

15. Display the **Slide Master** tab and click **Close Master View**.

16. Run the slide show from the beginning and observe the effects (use your mouse or keyboard to move the slide show forward). All slide titles now fade in.

17. Press <**Esc**> when finished to end the show. Save the presentation and leave it open for the next exercise.

5.22 Applying Transitions

Transitions are special effects that appear when you move from slide to slide during a presentation. An impressive selection is available to choose from.

Activity:

1. Select slide **1** of the **redesign** presentation and then display the **Transitions** tab on the **Ribbon**. Examine the various transition options that appear here.

2. From the list of transitions in the **Transitions to This Slide** group, select **Fade**.

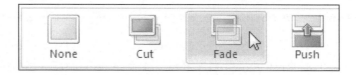

3. Run the presentation from this slide and observe the effect. Press <**Esc**> to end the slide show when you are finished.

4. Apply and then preview some of the other available transitions. The **More** button can be used to access a range of further transitions, including some rather impressive 3D effects.

5. When you are finished, select **Wipe**. Using the **Effect Options** drop-down button, select **From Left**.

> **Note:** The **Effect Options** box can be used to fine tune each of the available transitions.

6. From the **Timing** group, click the **Apply To All** button, , to apply this slide's transition effect to all other slides in the presentation.

> **Note:**   You can apply a different transition effect to each slide. The time it takes for the transition effect to run can be changed using the **Duration** box.

7. Run the presentation from the first slide and observe the effect. The **Wipe** transition appears between each slide. When you are finished, press <**Esc**> on your keyboard to end the slide show.

8. Save the presentation and leave it open for the next exercise.

5.23 Speaker's Notes

To help a speaker deliver a presentation, notes can be added to each slide in a show. The notes do not appear during the presentation, but they can be printed or viewed on another screen.

Activity:

1. Select slide **1** of the **redesign** presentation and make sure **Normal** view is currently selected. At the bottom of the main editing window is an area to add notes.

Boundary bar

Notes pane

Click to add notes

> **Note:**   If the **Notes** pane is not visible or is too small, you can drag the area's boundary bar to increase its size.

2. Click once in the **Notes** pane (the default prompt text disappears). Enter the text: **Demon of the Deep is twenty years old and has broken down 16 times this year already!**

3. From the **View** tab, change the view to **Notes Page**. The new note appears below the slide (and there is more room here to add and format note text).

4. Scroll down to slide **6** (**Initial Plan**), click once in the notes area, and then add the following text: **Mention that October is the beginning of our low season and is an ideal time to close the ride.**

> **Note:**   The **Zoom** controls on the **Status Bar** can be used to zoom in on the text.

5. Return to **Normal** view, save the presentation and leave it open for the next exercise.

5.24 Spelling Check

PowerPoint's spelling check feature can be used to check the spelling of all the words on your slides. *PowerPoint* makes suggestions to help you correct errors which can either be accepted or ignored.

Activity:

1. Select slide **1** of the **redesign** presentation, display the **Review** tab and click the **Spelling** button.

2. *PowerPoint* will now automatically check your presentation. If any errors are found, the **Spelling** dialog box will appear.

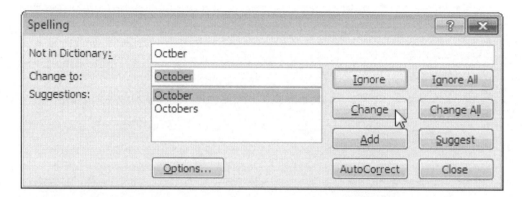

> **Note:** The **Spelling** dialog box is similar to the familiar spell checking feature available in *Microsoft Word*. If an error is found, you can choose to **Ignore** it or **Change** the selected word to one of the **Suggestions** given. Misspelled words will also appear in the presentation with a wavy red line underneath them.

3. When no errors are present in the slide show, a message appears informing you that **The spelling check is complete**. Click **OK** to close it.

4. Save and close the presentation.

> **Note:** Well done! You have now successfully created a presentation for *Yan* to use at his meeting. The ability to follow complex instructions and work accurately is an important skill to learn in business. To check that you followed all of *Yan's* instructions correctly, a model solution is provided in the data files folder named **Sample Redesign**. Compare your final presentation against this solution.

5.25 Templates

Templates are useful *PowerPoint* designs that can be used as a basis for new presentations. *PowerPoint* includes a small selection of built-in templates, but many, many more are available online at **Office.com**.

> **Note:** Some organisations recommend that employees use a specific template for all presentations. These will often reflect the business's corporate image and will include logos, backgrounds and fonts.

Although many templates look very impressive, you should ensure that any design theme you choose is suitable for the target audience. Sometimes less is more, and a simple design with large clear fonts is all that is required for a good presentation.

Activity:

1. Display the **File** tab and select **New** from the options on the left of the screen. Examine the various template types that are displayed.

2. Click once on **Sample templates** and view the small selection of templates that are installed with *PowerPoint*. Select **Training** from the list.

3. Notice the preview, and then click the **Create** button on the right of the screen.

4. A new presentation is created based on the selected **Training** template.

5. Explore the various slides that are available and feel free to alter any default text (the original template will not be affected). The **Notes** area also contains some useful tips.

6. Run the presentation from the start. Notice that many basic designs, animations and transitions have already been set up for you. When you are finished, press **<Esc>**.

7. Close the presentation, selecting **Don't Save** at the prompt if any changes were made.

8. Explore the many other templates available. If you are connected to the Internet, a wide variety of additional templates are also shown in folders in the **Office.com Templates** section on the **New** screen.

9. When you are finished, close any open templates but leave *PowerPoint* open.

5.26 Handouts and Notes Pages

Slides can be printed in various ways, but the most useful formats allow you to create **Handouts** and **Notes Pages**. Handouts can be printed with several slides per sheet for an audience to follow as the presentation is running.

Activity:

1.   Open the **redesign** presentation and select slide **2**. Then, display the **File** tab and select **Print** from the options shown on the left. The **Print** screen appears.

> **Note:**   Familiar settings such as printer selection, number of copies, print range and paper orientation are also available on this screen.

2.   **Full Page Slides** will currently be selected under **Settings**.

3.   Click this button and select **Notes Pages**. A small slide thumbnail will now be printed – one per page – with any notes included below. Use the slide selection buttons at the bottom of the print preview to view other slides and see the notes you entered earlier.

4.   Click the **Notes Pages** button under **Settings** and select **3 Slides**. Three small thumbnails are now shown on each page with space for audience members to take notes.

5.   Click the **Home** tab to return to **Normal** view *without* printing. Save and close the presentation.

5.27 Presentation Tips

You have created a great presentation, memorized your speech, practiced giving your talk, and now the big day has arrived. Before you step up, consider the following suggestions for a successful presentation:

✱   Turn up early to your presentation and give yourself plenty of time to set up

✱   Check all of the hardware that you need to use works correctly

✱   Disable the computer's screen saver (and standby features) to avoid interruptions

✱   Run through your presentation to check that it works as you expect

✱   Leave the presentation on slide 1, ready for your audience as they arrive

✱   Leave plenty of time for questions at the end of your presentation

✱ Try to be confident and enthusiastic; avoid simply reading your slides to the audience

✱ Speak slowly and loudly! Inexperienced speakers tend to talk too fast and mumble

✱ Pause from time to catch your breath and allow the audience to consider your words

5.28 Next Steps

Well done! You have now completed all of the exercises in this section. If you feel you are ready to test your knowledge and understanding of the topics covered, move on to the following **Develop Your Skills** activities. If there are any features of *Microsoft PowerPoint* that you are unsure about, you should revisit the appropriate exercises and try them again before moving on.

If you are interested in exploring some of *Microsoft PowerPoint's* more powerful features, why don't you use the Internet to find out a little more about the following advanced topics.

Feature	Descriptions
Save to Web	A presentation can be saved to the web so that others can access and view it online.
Broadcasting	A presentation can be broadcast via the Internet for others to see. Unlike **Save to Web**, your presentation appears in real-time on other people's computers. When you move from slide to slide or speak using a microphone, these actions are played back immediately in your audience's Internet browser.
SmartArt	**SmartArt** lets you create diagrams from within *PowerPoint* using a variety of different layouts and visual styles. This feature is really useful for creating flow and relationship diagrams.
Advanced Animation	Build on the lessons learned in 5.21 and create your own custom animations using the **Animation Pane**. These give you far greater control over your chosen effects, how and when they occur, and the exact order that they appear. You can also add sound effects to each effect.
Timings	You can apply **Timings** to slide animations and transitions. Instead of clicking the mouse to trigger an event, timings can be used to advance the presentation automatically after a set amount of time. This feature is particularly useful if you want your presentation to run unattended, for example as a promotional slide show in a public space.
Rehearsing	*PowerPoint* can automatically record the time it takes you to move from slide to slide during a **rehearsal**. These durations are then used to create more exact slide timings.
Multimedia	Videos and sounds (including music) can all be imported into *PowerPoint* and added to a slide. Various options allow you to control when and for how long the items are played.

At the end of every section you get the chance to complete two activities. These will help you to develop your skills and prepare for your exam. Don't forget to use the planning and review checklists at the back of the book to help organise and review your work.

> **Note:**   Answers to these activities are provided in this section's **Sample Solutions** folder.

Develop Your Skills: Staff Presentation

In this activity you will be asked to create a simple five-minute presentation for *Yan*. You will need to use all of the ICT skills that you have learned in this section to plan, develop and present an appropriate solution.

Activity 1

The *Big Planet Theme Park* management loved the *Demon of the Deep* presentation that you created earlier and approved my redesign plans on the spot – well done! However, before any work can begin, we need to inform the ride's current staff that we intend to close the attraction for refurbishment.

To do this, I've been asked to give a five minute presentation on our plans. I've already worked out what I need to say and have created an outline for the presentation in *Word*. Will you take this outline and create the presentation for me?

Information for the presentation is available in the following files:

* **Initial Ideas**   A document containing my notes for the new presentation

* **Sketch**   A sketch of the proposed ride changes

Start by creating a new, blank presentation. Then add the contents of the **Initial Ideas** file onto new slides (as suggested in the **Initial Ideas** file). You will need to choose appropriate slide layouts for each individual slide and use two levels of bullets where indicated. Next, insert the **Sketch** image file in a suitable position on slide **4**. As the presentation will be seen by all of the ride team it needs to look professional – apply a suitable theme (I recommend **Flow**) and then save the presentation as **staff presentation**.

Develop Your Skills: Marketing Presentation

In this activity you will be asked to update a draft presentation for *Yan*. You will need to use all of the advanced ICT skills that you have learned in this section to create a suitable solution. It may help you to break the problem down into smaller parts first.

Activity 2

I've just received a telephone call from *Julia* at the *Laser Show*. I've been asked to prepare a presentation on the new *Demon of the Deep* ride for the park's marketing department, including a brief overview of our redesign plans and available budget.

I've made a start on the presentation, but I'd like you to finish it for me. The files that you will need are shown below:

* **Marketing**   The unfinished draft of the marketing presentation

* **Photo**   A photograph of the *Demon of the Deep* ride

* **Logo**   An image file containing the theme park's logo

First, using **Slide Sorter** view, move slide **4** (**Any Questions?**) to the end of the presentation. Next, add a new slide between slides **1** and **2** with a **Title Only** layout.

In **Normal** view, add the slide title **An Old Favourite** and insert the **Photo** image. Reposition and resize the image so that it fits neatly on the page (I recommend a **Shape Height** of around **10 cm**).

Next, rearrange the bullets on slide **6** so that they appear in the correct order. Then, insert a new slide after slide **4** with a **Title Only** layout. Add the slide title **Marketing Budget** and insert a table (in a suitable position) containing the following information:

Item Description	Number	Cost
Mailings	240,000	5,000
Posters & Leaflets	10,000	4,000
Banners	20	1000

Using the presentation's **Slide Master** view, add the theme park's **Logo** to the bottom right corner of <u>all</u> slides. Apply the **Random Bars** animation to the title placeholders (starting **With Previous**), then add a transition effect of **Fade** between each slide.

Finally, run the spell checker on the presentation and correct any mistakes found. Preview the presentation, check it works as expected (correcting any problems that you find), and then save it as **marketing presentation**.

SECTION 6 | Microsoft Publisher

6 | Microsoft Publisher

Hi, my name's Julia...

I'm the manager of the marketing department at *Big Planet Theme Park*. I'm currently working with staff at the *Laser Show* to help advertise their brilliant new attraction, *The Light Fantastic*.

This amazing show uses the latest computer technology to control hundred of lights and lasers in time to music. Lasting 20 minutes, the performance combines pictures and special effects to recreate famous cities and landmarks from around the world – it really is an unmissable event. In fact, as park management expects *The Light Fantastic* to be so popular, they have decided to run the show six times a day!

Working in marketing, it is my job to create an advertising campaign to publicise the new attraction and its show times. To do this, I plan to use the desktop publishing application *Microsoft Publisher* to create a range of eye-catching and informative posters, flyers, brochures, leaflets and newsletters. There's a lot of work to do and a lot of different types of advertising publication to create – maybe you can help?

What you will learn:

In this chapter you will use the program *Microsoft Publisher* to help *Julia* complete a number of everyday tasks at *Big Planet Theme Park*. You will see how to use simple desktop publishing techniques to design, create and edit professional publications for a variety of purposes.

Knowledge, skills and understanding:

* Use *Microsoft Publisher* to create and edit professional publications

* Manipulate graphics and text using a range of editing, formatting and layout techniques

* Understand house styles and recognise best design practices

Data files

The files needed to complete the activities in this section are provided in the **Section 6** data folder (see note on page **vii** to download these files). Publications that you create or edit can be saved to the same folder.

6.1 Using Microsoft Publisher

Desktop publishing programs allow you to create high-quality documents using a range of advanced text and image layout tools. These documents are traditionally printed, but they can also be saved in a simple picture format for use on websites or in e-mail marketing campaigns. Typically, desktop publishing software is useful for creating:

* Leaflets, flyers, greeting cards, business cards and headed letters

* Brochures, magazines, certificates, menus and newsletters

* Advertisements, posters, signs and banners

Unlike word processors, desktop publishing applications place a far greater emphasis on page layout and design, giving you much more control over the positioning and appearance of text and images on the page.

> **Note:** For professional publications, a dedicated printing company is often used to produce large quantities of a publication quickly and cheaply.

Microsoft Publisher is a desktop publishing application which is an appropriate choice for any task that requires an illustration or well-designed document containing a lot of pictures or graphics. The entry, layout and formatting of text is easily handled by such a program, as is the ability to import and arrange different types of object such as images, tables and charts.

> **Note:** *Microsoft Word* and *Publisher* both look and work in very similar ways. However, each application is better suited to creating specific types of document. As a simple rule of thumb, if your planned document is mainly text based, use *Word*; if it is largely visual with lots of images, use *Publisher*.

6.2 Creating a Publication

When you create a new publication, you must first choose a **page size** using one of *Publisher's* built-in templates. The most commonly used page size is **A4**.

> **Note:** Ready-made templates containing professionally designed background illustrations and pictures are also available to use. You will get the chance to explore these templates in a later exercise.

Activity:

1. Start *Microsoft Publisher*. When the application opens, the **Available Templates** window is automatically displayed. Examine the various template types available in the **Most Popular** and **More Templates** groups. You will look at these again later.

2. As part of her advertising campaign, *Julia* would like to create a new poster for the *Laser Show*. She wants it to be A4 in size so that she can print it on her office printer. Select the **Blank A4 (Portrait)** template by clicking it once.

3. A new blank publication is created, ready to add your own text and graphics. Examine the *Publisher* window. In particular, locate the familiar **File** tab, **Ribbon**, **Status Bar**, **Quick Access Toolbar** and **Zoom** controls.

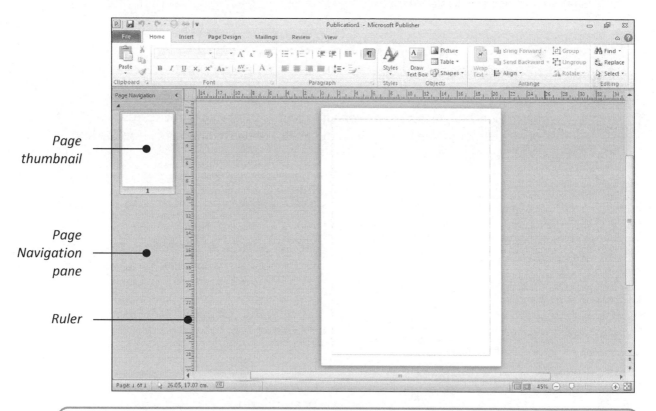

Page thumbnail

Page Navigation pane

Ruler

> **Note:** Of course, once you have chosen a publication template, it is possible to change the size and orientation of the page at a later time using the **Page Design** tab.

4. Locate the **Page Navigation** pane on the left of the window. This will display small previews (or thumbnails) of all of the pages in your publication. Clicking a thumbnail will open the page in the main editing window.

5. Locate the **Rulers** at the top and left of the editing window. These can be used to position objects on the page and control text indentation (similar to *Microsoft Word*).

6. Leave the blank publication open for the next exercise.

6.3 Text Boxes

Unlike *Microsoft Word*, text in *Publisher* is not simply typed directly onto the page. Instead, it needs to be placed in one or more **text boxes**. Each text box can be resized and repositioned any way you like, and there is no limit to the number of boxes that can appear on one page.

Activity:

1. With the blank publication created in the previous exercise still on screen, click the **Draw Text Box** button in the **Objects** group on the **Home** tab.

2. The mouse pointer changes to a crosshair, ✛. In the centre of the current page, click and drag to create a text box of any size. Notice that, as you create the text box, its exact location and size are displayed on the **Status Bar**.

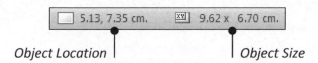

Object Location   *Object Size*

> **Note:**   An object's location, measured by default in centimetres, is the precise location of the *top left* corner of the object in **x** (across) and **y** (down) coordinates. The top left corner of the page is **0, 0**.

3. When you release the mouse button a text box appears on the page with the cursor flashing inside it, ready for text to be entered.

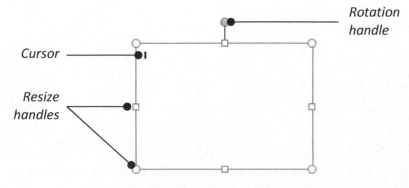

4. Notice that the text box has standard resize and rotation handles. These will always appear when a text box (or any other object) is selected.

5.   By clicking and dragging the text box's border, drag the text box to a new location. As with all objects in *Publisher*, the text box can be placed in any position (and resized to any dimension) that you like.

6.   Display the **Drawing Tools - Format** tab on the **Ribbon** and locate the **Size** group. The options shown here can be used to precisely position and resize any object on a page.

7.   Change the value in the **Shape Height** box to **6 cm** and the **Shape Width** to **17 cm** (press <**Enter**> after each change). Notice the effect that this has on the text box.

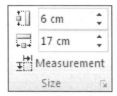

8.   Click the **Measurement** button to display the **Measurement** dialog box. The exact position, size and rotation of a selected object can all be changed here. Change the **x** value to **2 cm** and the **y** value to **1 cm** (press <**Enter**> after each change).

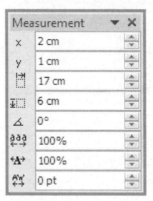

9.   Click the **Close** button, [×], on the **Measurement** dialog box to hide it. The text box has now been precisely resized and positioned on the page. Leave the publication open for the next exercise.

6.4 Zoom Levels

As with other *Microsoft Office* applications, precise zoom levels can be selected on the **View** tab or the **Status Bar**.

Activity:

1.   With the empty text box created in the previous exercise still selected, press the <**F9**> key on your keyboard. The view zooms to **100%** on the current text box.

> Note: Pressing <**F9**> is a really quick and easy way to zoom in on a text box. Pressing <**F9**> again will zoom back out to the *previous* zoom level.

2. Display the **View** tab and locate the **Zoom** group. Examine the various zoom controls available, and then click **Whole Page**.

3. The zoom level is decreased so that the entire current page is displayed in the main editing window.

4. Next, click **Page Width** to zoom in so that the full width of the page fills the editing window.

5. Finally, click **Selected Objects**. The zoom level is increased so that the selected text box fills the editing window (this is the same as pressing <**F9**>).

> **Note:**   Notice that the standard **Zoom** controls, which feature in all *Office* applications, are also available on the **Status Bar**.

6. Leave the publication open for the next exercise.

6.5 Entering Text and Best Fit

When you enter text into a text box, you can edit and format it using a range of standard **Font** and **Alignment** features. Also, a really useful tool called **Best Fit** (sometimes known as **Autofit**) allows you to automatically increase a text box's font size to fill all of the space available.

Activity:

1. With the empty text box created in the previous exercise still selected, type the following text as accurately as possible:

    The Light Fantastic
    An Amazing New Show

2. Display the **Text Box Tools - Format** tab and click the **Text Fit** drop-down button in the **Text** group.

3. From the options that appear, select **Best Fit**. The font size of the text is increased to fill the available space in the text box.

The Light Fantastic

An Amazing New Show

4. Using the bottom **Resize** handle, reduce the height of the text box to *approximately* **2 cm** (remember that you can use the **Object Size** information on the **Status Bar** to help).

5. The size of the text in the text box is automatically reduced to fit. Use **Undo**, , on the **Quick Access Toolbar** to restore the text box's height to **6 cm**.

6. To disable **Best Fit**, display the **Text Box Tools - Format** tab and select **Do Not Autofit** from the **Text Fit** drop-down button.

7. Select the <u>first</u> line of text in the text box and enter the **Font Size** as **58** point. Then, select the <u>second</u> line of text and set the **Font Size** to **36** point.

8. Next, select <u>all</u> of the text in the box and, using the **Font** group, select the font **Impact**.

> **Note:**   It is important to select the right font for the job. **Impact** is a good, strong, sans serif font that will be easy to read from a distance – perfect for a poster.

9. With all of the text still selected, click the **Align Center** button in the **Alignment** group. The text is centred in the box.

> **Note:**   Familiar text alignment and formatting options such as **Bold**, **Italic**, **Underline**, and **Font Color** are all available in the **Font** group on both the **Format** *and* **Home** tabs.

10. Save the publication as **poster** in the data files folder for this section.

11. Leave the publication open for the next exercise.

6.6 Border and Shading Effects

A simple border of any colour or thickness can be added to a text box to mark its boundaries. A variety of shading effects can also be applied to improve the design of a publication.

> **Note:**   Borders can also be added to all *Publisher* objects (e.g. graphics, tables, charts, etc).

Activity:

1. With the **poster** publication open from the previous exercise, adjust the zoom level to **Whole Page**. Then, create a new text box with the following dimensions:

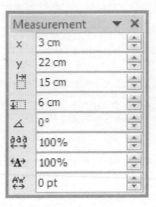

2. Zoom in on the new text box and enter the following text as accurately as you can:

   Now Showing
   at the Laser Show arena
   09:00, 10:30, 12:00, 13:30, 15:00, 16:30

3. Select all of the text and change the **Font** to **Impact**. Then, **Align Center** the text, using the **Alignment** options on the **Format** tab, so that it appears in the very middle of the box.

4. Next, apply a **Font Size** of **36** to the <u>first</u> line, **28** to the <u>second</u> line, and **20** to the <u>third</u> line. Adjust the zoom level to **Whole Page** to see the effect.

5. To apply a border to the selected text box, display the **Drawing Tools - Format** tab and examine the options available.

6. In the **Shape Styles** group, click the **Shape Outline** button's drop-down arrow, [image]. From the **Scheme Colors** available, select any colour of your choice. A border is applied.

7. Display the **Shape Outline** drop-down menu again and expand the **Weight** submenu. From the line weights shown, select **6 pt**. The border's thickness is increased.

8. Next, click the **Shape Fill** button's drop-down arrow, [image], and select any colour of your choice. A background shade is applied to the text box.

9. Display the **Shape Fill** drop-down menu again and expand the **Gradient** submenu.

10. Select any of the options shown to apply that effect (notice that you can create a custom gradient using the **More Gradients** option at the bottom of the **Gradient** submenu).

11. Display the **Shape Fill** drop-down menu again and expand the **Texture** submenu. Select any of the options shown to apply that texture effect (notice that you can access more textures using the **More Textures** option).

> Note: You can also a use a picture as the background for a text box.

12. To apply a built-in shape style, display the **Drawing Tools - Format** tab and expand the **Shape Styles** box using the **More** button.

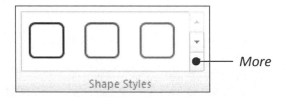

More

> Note: Placing your mouse pointer over a thumbnail will display a **ToolTip** containing the style's name. The effect of selecting that theme is *previewed* on the current page.

13. Explore some of the styles available, and then finally select **Linear Up Gradient - Accent 1**.

14. A simple gradient effect is applied to the text box and a faint border appears around the object. Click away from the text box to see the effect.

Now Showing
at the Laser Show arena
09:00, 10:30, 12:00, 13:30, 15:00, 16:30

15. Select the text box again and display the **Drawing Tools - Format** tab. Click **Shadow Effects** to drop down a menu containing a variety of shadows. From the **Drop Shadow** group, select **Shadow Style 4**.

16. A simple but effective drop shadow is applied to the text box. Save the publication and leave it open for the next exercise.

6.7 Background Effects

Gradients, textures, solid colours and pictures can be used as a page background. In this exercise you will apply a simple, custom gradient (other effects will be covered later in this section).

Activity:

1. Display the **Page Design** tab and examine the available options.

2. Click the **Background** button in the **Page Background** group. Rest your mouse pointer over a thumbnail (without clicking) to preview the background effects on the page.

3. Select **More Backgrounds** to display the **Fill Effects** dialog box. Explore each of the tabs to see the types of effect that can be applied.

4. Display the **Gradient** tab and select **Two colors** from the **Colors** group. Select **Orange** for **Color 1** (from the **Standard Colours** palette), and **White** for **Color 2**.

5. From **Shading Styles**, examine the options available and then select **From corner**. From the **Variants** section, select the bottom right thumbnail.

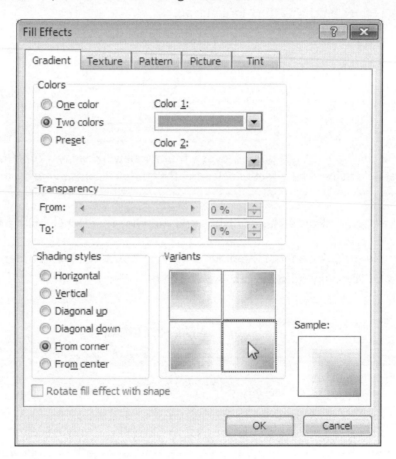

6. Click **OK** to apply the background effect. It fills the entire page.

7. Save the publication and leave it open for the next exercise.

> **Note:** You will get the opportunity to explore other background effects in later exercises.

6.8 Inserting a Picture

Any image file stored on your computer (or accessible from it) can be included in a publication. This includes pictures downloaded from the Internet (assuming you have permission to use them, of course), photos downloaded from your digital camera or mobile phone, or files produced by graphic image programs such as *Adobe Photoshop*.

Activity:

1. To insert a picture on the current page of the open **poster** publication, display the **Insert** tab and click the **Picture** button in the **Illustrations** group.

2. Locate the data files folder for this section, select the **Rocket** image and click **Insert** to import the file. A picture of a rocket appears in the centre of the page.

> Note: As with all objects in *Publisher*, pictures can be moved, resized and rotated.

3. By default, text in a publication is wrapped around an inserted image. From the **Picture Tools - Format** tab, drop down the **Wrap Text** button in the **Arrange** group and select **None**. The automatic text wrapping is disabled.

4. Use the **Size** settings to change the **Shape Height** of the picture to **17 cm**. The width of the picture is automatically **scaled** (resized) to keep the picture in *proportion*.

> Note: It is important to maintain the **aspect ratio** (the relationship between the width and height) of objects such as pictures when scaling them. If you do not they will become distorted. For example, a picture of width 8 cm and height 4 cm will have an aspect ratio of 2:1. If you reduce the picture's width to 4 cm, you would then have to reduce the height to 2 cm to keep the picture in proportion.

5. From the **Arrange** group, click the **Align** drop-down button and select **Align Middle**. Then click the **Align** button again and select **Align Centre** to place the picture in the very centre of the page.

> Note: If the **Align** options are greyed out, first select **Relative to Margin Guides**.

6. The rocket appears on top of the lower text box. From the **Arrange** group, click the drop-down arrow on the **Send Backward** button and select **Send to Back**.

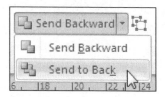

7. The rocket image now appears behind the text box.

> Note: All objects on a page are placed on their own **layer** in a stack, rather like a deck of cards. The items higher up the stack appear on top of all other objects below. To move an object up or down the stack, use **Bring Forward** or **Send Backward**.

8. Well done! *Julia's* poster is now complete. A model solution named **Sample Poster** is available in this section's data files folder for comparison. How well did you do?

9. Save the publication and close it, but leave *Publisher* open for the next exercise.

6.9 Layout Guides

Layout Guides are lines on a page which act as visual aids to help you line up objects. More importantly, you can also **snap** objects to them using drag and drop.

> **Note:** The most useful **Layout Guides** are **Ruler Guides**, **Margin Guides** and **Grid Guides**. **Ruler** and **Margin Guides** are used in this exercise; **Grid Guides** are used in **6.10**.

Activity:

1. Open the file **Layout** from the data files folder. This simple publication features one text box and three shapes on a single page.

2. Display the **Page Design** tab and click the **Guides** button in the **Layout** group.

3. A variety of built-in guides are shown. From the bottom of the drop-down menu, select **Add Horizontal Ruler Guide**. A green dotted line appears across the middle on the page.

4.   This line is known as a **Ruler Guide**, and can be dragged up and down the page. Place your mouse pointer over the guide until it changes to a **Resize** cursor, $\overline{\underline{\overline{}}}$.

5.   Using the left ruler as a reference, drag the **Ruler Guide** up to the **10 cm** mark.

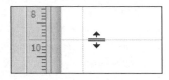

> **Note:**   If the page rulers are not visible, display the **View** tab and place a tick in the **Rulers** checkbox on the **Show** group.

6.   Then, add a *vertical* **Ruler Guide** and place this at the **4 cm** mark using the top ruler as a reference.

7.   By clicking and dragging the object's border, move **Shape 1** left towards the vertical **Ruler Guide**. As the shape touches the guide, it "snaps" and sticks to it.

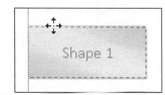

8.   Release the mouse button to drop the shape.

> **Note:**   Notice that the dotted **Layout Guide** line becomes solid when an object snaps and sticks to it. If snapping does not occur, display the **Page Design** tab and place a tick in both of the **Align To** options in the **Layout** group.

9.   Next, carefully move **Shape 3** left towards the vertical **Ruler Guide**. As the shape passes below **Shape 2**, purple vertical bars appear between the objects. These helpful guides make it easier to line objects up with one another.

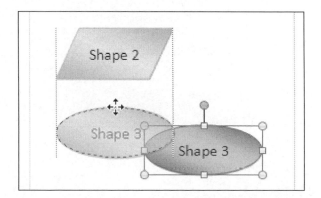

10. Continue to move **Shape 3** left until it touches the vertical **Ruler Guide**; it again snaps and sticks. Release the mouse button, and then drag **Shape 2** left so that it snaps to the guide also. All three objects are now perfectly aligned with each other.

11. Next, drag the text box so that both the left and bottom sides line up with both the vertical <u>and</u> horizontal **Ruler Guides**. Drop the text box.

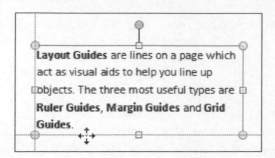

> **Note:** Have you noticed the dotted blue border around the edge of the page? This is a **Margin Guide** and marks the border boundaries of the page.

12. Now, use the top right **Resize** handle to increase the size of the text box. As it approaches both the top <u>and</u> right **Margin Guides**, it again snaps and sticks. Release the mouse button.

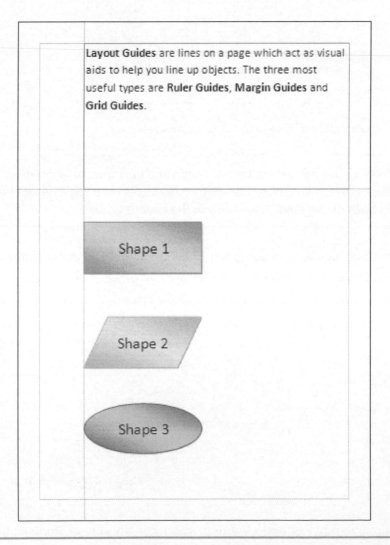

> **Note:** All objects in *Publisher* can be aligned using the techniques described here.

13. Display the **File** tab and select **Print** from the options on the left of the screen. A preview of the page is shown on the right; notice that the **Ruler** and **Margin Guides** do not appear. Click the **Home** tab to return without printing.

14. Save the publication as **guides** and leave it open for the next exercise.

6.10 Working With Pages

Single page publications are useful for creating posters and flyers, but publications such as newsletters and brochures may require more pages.

Activity:

1. The **guides** publication should still be open. Display the **Insert** tab and click the **Page** drop-down arrow (<u>not</u> the icon above it).

2. From the options shown, select **Insert Duplicate Page**. A new page is added containing a *copy* of all of the contents of the first page (including the **Ruler Guides**).

> **Note:**   To select an object, click once on its border – not on the text it contains.

3. With **Page 2** selected in the **Page Navigation** pane, select **Shape 1** on the page and press <**Delete**> on your keyboard to remove it. Notice that the contents of **Page 1** are not affected.

4. With **Page 2** still selected, click the **Page** drop-down arrow and select **Insert Blank Page**.

> **Note:**   Clicking the **Page** button's icon will also insert a blank page.

5. A third, blank page is added to the publication and automatically selected in the **Page Navigation** pane.

> **Note:**   In the previous exercise you learned how to use **Ruler** and **Margin Guides** to help align objects. However, **Grid Guides** are also useful for creating layout guides which split a page into a number of columns or rows.

6. Display the **Page Design** tab, click the **Guides** button in the **Layout** group and select **Grid and Baseline Guides**. The **Layout Guides** dialog box appears.

7. On the **Grid Guides** tab, increase **Columns** to **2** and **Rows** to **3**, leaving the default **Spacing** between columns and rows as **0.2cm**. Notice the **Preview**, and then click **OK**.

8. The page is divided into two columns and three rows, with a small **0.2cm** gap between each "cell". Insert a text box with a black border *within* the boundaries of the top left cell.

9. Next, select the new text box by clicking its border.

> **Note:** You can cut, copy and paste objects in *Publisher* (e.g. text, pictures, tables, charts) in exactly the same way as all other *Office* applications.

10. Copy the selected text box, and then paste one copy in each of the 5 remaining empty spaces created by the layout guides. Then, practice using the layout guides by aligning and resizing each text box so that they line up and fill the "cells" available.

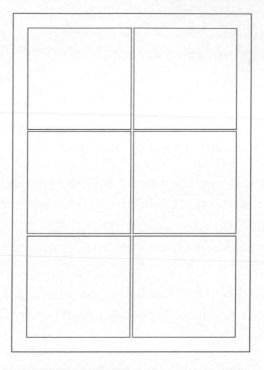

11. Display the **Insert** tab and click the **Page** drop-down arrow. From the options shown, select **Insert Page**. The **Insert Page** dialog box appears, allowing you to add any number of extra pages to the publication.

12. Change the **Number of new pages** to **2**, make sure **After current page** is selected, and then select **Duplicate all objects on page** (**3**).

13. Click **OK**. Two new pages are added *after the current page* containing copies of the objects on page **3**. The publication now contains 5 pages.

14. Select page **5** in the **Page Navigation** pane and then display the **Page Design** tab. From the pages group, click **Delete**. Read the message that appears and then click **Yes**. Page **5** is deleted from the publication.

15. Repeat this action to delete page **4** too.

> **Note:** Multiple pages can be selected in the **Page Navigation** pane and deleted at the same time. A page can also be moved by clicking and dragging its thumbnail; a faint grey line appears between pages to indicate its new position if dropped.

16. Save the publication and close it, leaving *Publisher* open for the next exercise.

6.11 Using Shapes and WordArt

It is possible to use the many design tools available in *Publisher* to create illustrations of your own. Shapes, pictures and **WordArt** can be combined to produce a range of impressive designs.

Activity:

1. Start a new **Blank A4 (Portrait)** publication.

2. *Julia* has had an idea for a logo for the new *Laser Show* attraction. She has sketched the logo on paper:

3. *Julia* would now like you to create this logo in *Publisher*. Using the blank publication currently on-screen, display the **Insert** tab and click the **Shapes** button. Examine the various shape objects available.

> **Note:** *Publisher's* shapes and **WordArt** features are very similar to those you have used in previous *Microsoft Office* applications. If you feel confident using these features, you can try creating the logo without following the instructions in this exercise.

4. Select the **Oval** shape, ⬭, and draw a circle in the middle of the page.

> **Note:** Hold down <**Shift**> when drawing an object to maintain shape proportions (for example, to draw a perfect circle or a perfect square).

5. Use the **Measurement** dialog box to set the **Shape Height** and **Shape Width** to **6.5 cm**.

6. Apply a dark blue **Shape Outline** (**Weight 3 pt**) and select an appropriate **Gradient** from **Shape Fill** (the **From Corner** effects in the **Light Variations** group work well).

7. Next, insert a **Lightning Bolt** shape, ⚡, and position this on top of the circle shape. Set the **Shape Height** to **5 cm** and **Shape Width** to **3.5 cm**.

8. Apply an orange **Shape Outline** (**Weight 3 pt**) and a yellow **Shape Fill**.

9. Next, insert the picture **Rocket** from the data files folder and set its **Shape Height** to **6.5 cm** (allow *Publisher* to automatically adjust the **Shape Width** to maintain proportions).

10. Position the **Rocket** picture on top of the circle and lightning bolt shapes. Then, move, resize and rotate any object in the logo until it best matches *Julia's* sketch.

11. Finally, display the **Insert** tab and click **WordArt**. Select a style from the **Plain WordArt Styles** group (**Gradient Fill - Blue, Reflection** works well).

12. In the **Edit WordArt Text** dialog box that appears, change the contents of the **Text** box to **The Light Fantastic**, and change the **Font** to **Impact** (**Size 36**, **Bold**). Click **OK.**

13. Position the new **WordArt** text below the logo, as suggested in *Julia's* sketch. Well done, the logo is now complete and looks very impressive.

> **Note:**   You can **group** objects together so that they can be manipulated as one.

14. Press <**Ctrl A**> on your keyboard to select all objects that make up the logo.

> **Note:**   Alternatively, hold <**Ctrl**> and click each object separately.

15. From the **Arrange** group, click the **Group** button, ⊞ Group. All of the objects are now grouped into one.

16. Use the **Align** options in the **Arrange** group to position the new logo object in the **Middle** and **Center** of the page (remember to select **Relative to Margin Guides** if these options are not immediately available).

> **Note:** To remove a grouping and separate objects again, use the **Ungroup** button.

17. Save your publication as **new logo** and close it, leaving *Publisher* open.

> **Note:** A model solution named **Sample Logo** is available in this section's data files folder for comparison.

6.12 Picture Placeholders

Picture Placeholders can be used to reserve an area of space in your publication for an image that you want to add later. This allows you to concentrate on creating your publication's layout first, without needing to worry about which pictures you are going to use.

Activity:

1. Open the publication **Prices**. In this simple one page A4 poster publication, *Julia* has created a **Picture Placeholder** where she would like an image to go.

Picture Placeholder

2. *Julia* likes the **Rocket** picture used earlier. Click the **Insert Picture from File** icon, [image], found inside the **Picture Placeholder** (you will need to select the placeholder first).

3. The **Insert Picture** dialog box appears. Insert the **Rocket** picture from the data files folder for this section. The image appears within the boundaries of the **Picture Placeholder**.

> **Note:** Images imported into an existing placeholder will be automatically scaled to fit.

4. Similarly, pictures can also be added to publication backgrounds. Display the **Page Design** tab and click **Background**. From the submenu that appears, select **More Backgrounds**.

5. Display the **Picture** tab and click **Select Picture**. Locate the data files folder for this section and select **Background**. Click **Insert** and a preview of the picture is shown. Click **OK**.

6. The background image fills the page *beneath* all other objects.

> **Note:** If a background image is too small, it will be **tiled** (repeated) to fill all of the space.

7. With the **Rocket** picture imported earlier still selected, copy and paste it to create a duplicate. It appears in almost the same location.

8. Drag the image to the opposite side of the page. Then, click the **Rotate** button, on the **Picture Tools - Format** tab. From the options that appear, select **Flip Horizontal**.

> **Note:** Notice that the picture is flipped over along its horizontal (x) axis. Pictures can also be flipped along their vertical (y) axis, or rotated freely using the rotation handle.

9. Position the image so that it mirrors the other rocket, as shown below.

10. *Julia* would like to include park branding on the poster, but she needs to get permission to use it first. For now, she would like you to simply create a placeholder. From the **Insert** Tab, click **Picture Placeholder** in the **Illustrations** group.

11. A blank placeholder appears in the centre of the screen. With the **Picture Tools - Format** tab selected, set the size of the placeholder to **5 cm** high and **5 cm** wide (**5 cm x 5 cm**).

12. Next, drag the placeholder so that it lines up with the *left* and *bottom* margin guides.

13. *Julia* has just received permission to use the park logo on her poster. Click the **Insert Picture from File** icon found inside the **Picture Placeholder**.

14. When the **Insert Picture** dialog box appears, find and select the **Logo** picture from the data files folder for this section. The image appears within the **Picture Placeholder**.

15. Well done. Save the file as **prices complete** and close it.

6.13 Connecting Text Boxes

A really useful feature of *Publisher* is the ability to **Link** text boxes together. When this is done, the contents of one text box will automatically *overflow* into another.

Activity:

1. Open the publication **Leaflet**. In this two page publication (designed to be printed on both sides of a single A4 page), *Julia* has set up a number of text boxes.

2. Click the second page in the **Page Navigation** pane and select the first text box underneath the header. At the moment, any text entered here will be confined to the dimensions of the box (if too much text is entered it will "fall off" the bottom).

3. To connect the first and second text boxes on this page, display the **Text Box Tools - Format** tab and click **Create Link** in the **Linking** group.

4. Rest the mouse pointer over the second text box on the page. Notice that the mouse pointer changes to a "pouring jug".

5. Click anywhere inside the second text box on the page. The first and second text boxes are now connected, and any text placed in the first box will overflow into the second.

6. Notice the **Go to Previous Text Box** button, ◀, found on the top left border of the second text box. Click this once and the first text box is selected.

7. Click the **Go to Next Text Box** button, ▶, found on the bottom right border of the first text box. The second text box is selected again.

> **Note:**   You will see the effects of entering text into all three boxes in the next exercise.

8. Save the publication as **leaflet final** and leave it open for the next exercise.

6.14   Importing Text

Instead of typing text into text boxes, existing text in different formats can be **imported** into *Publisher*. This is useful if large quantities of text already exists in a different file.

Activity:

1. With the **leaflet final** publication open, select the <u>first</u> text box on the <u>second</u> page.

2. Then, display the **Insert** tab and click **Insert File**, [Insert File], from the **Text** group.

3. The **Insert Text** dialog box appears. Locate and select the *Word* document **Leaflet Text** from the data files for this section and click **OK**. The document's text is imported into *Publisher* (a **Converting** message box may appear for a moment).

4. Zoom in to **Page Width** and notice that the contents of the first text box **overflows** into the second text box (you will need to use the scroll bars to move up and down the page).

> **Note:**   Notice also that the text formatting from the source document has been preserved.

5. Place the cursor in either the first or second text box and press <**Ctrl A**> to select all of the text in *both* boxes. Increase the **Font Size** to **18**. As text "falls off" the bottom of the first text box, it automatically appears in the second.

6. Now the text in the second box has overflowed. As it is not connected to another box, the **Text in Overflow** indicator, ⋯, appears and the text box's handles turn red.

7. With the second text box selected, use the **Create Link** button on the **Text Box Tools - Format** tab to create a link to the third text box. The overflow text now appears here.

> **Note:**   Text boxes can also be linked across different pages. To break a link between text boxes, simply use the **Break** button in the **Linking** group.

8. Select all of the text and, using the **Text Box Tools - Format** tab, click **Align Center** from the **Alignment** group. The text is centred in the middle of each box.

9.   Save the publication and close it, but leave *Publisher* open for the next exercise.

6.15 Font Schemes

A **font scheme** is a set of two fonts that can be applied to any publication. Within each font scheme both a *primary* font and a *secondary* font are specified. Usually the primary font is used for titles and headings and the secondary font is used for body text.

Font schemes are useful for ensuring that all of the fonts in a publication are consistent across pages, which is an important design consideration.

Activity:

1.   Open the publication **Brochure**. This simple publication is designed to be printed on both sides of a single piece of A4 and then folded to create a leaflet. **Grid Guides** have been set up to help you visualise this simple layout.

2.   Examine both pages of the publication and notice that all of the headers use the font **Luclda Sans Unicode** and all the body text uses **Book Antiqua**.

> **Note:**   Notice also that page **2** features a table. As in other *Microsoft Office* applications, tables can be easily created using the **Table** button on the **Insert** tab.

3.   To apply a new **Font Scheme** to the *entire* publication, display the **Page Design** tab and click the **Fonts** drop-down button in the **Schemes** group.

4.   Locate the style **Urban** (you may need to scroll down a little).

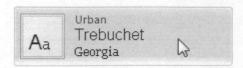

5.   This scheme has **Trebuchet** as the *primary* font and **Georgia** as the *secondary* font. Click it to apply the scheme to every page in the publication; all fonts are updated.

> Note: By default, all new text added to this publication will now use the chosen scheme.

6.   Notice that all of the headers in the publication now use the font **Trebuchet** and all the body text uses **Georgia**.

7.   Leave the publication open for the next exercise.

6.16 Colour Schemes

All publications use a **colour scheme** to set the standard colours of text and objects. By default, *Publisher* uses a colour scheme called **Office**, but this can be changed at any time.

> Note: Colour schemes coordinate all of the text and object colours in your publications, which helps to give them a more consistent and professional look.

Activity:

1.   With the **Brochure** publication open and the first page selected, display the **Page Design** tab. Examine the various colour schemes available in the **Schemes** group.

More

2.   **Tropics** is the currently selected colour scheme. Without clicking, place your mouse pointer over a few of the other schemes to see their styles *previewed* on the page.

3.   Click the **More** button to reveal a vast number of different colour schemes to choose from. Find and select **Cherry**, and notice the effect this has on both pages of the publication.

4.   Click the **More** button again, and this time select a colour scheme that you feel works best with this publication.

5. When you are finished, save the publication as **brochure complete** and close it.

6.17 Columns

Columns can be used to split the contents of a text box into two or more vertical sections, exactly like the columns in a newspaper. This allows space to be used more effectively as you can often fit more words on a page.

> Note: Text placed in columns is usually much easier and faster to read.

Activity:

1. Open the publication **Newsletter**. This simple publication features a number of linked text boxes and is designed to be printed on both sides of a single piece of A4 paper (ignore any spelling errors that are present for now).

2. Click once in the large text box on page **1**. To arrange the contents of this box into two columns, display the **Text Box Tools - Format** tab and click the **Columns** drop-down button in the **Alignment** group.

3. From the options that appear, select **Two Columns**. The text is now divided into two columns (which is far easier to read as the eye has to move less to read a full line).

> Note: Linked text boxes do not need to share the same alignment or formatting settings.

4. Display page **2** and notice that the first two text boxes, although linked to the text box on page **1**, are still arranged using a single column layout. Notice also that the text in the second text box has overflowed due to a lack of space.

5. Use the **Columns** drop-down button to set the first box on this page to use **Two Columns**. The text overflow has now been resolved.

6. Save the publication as **newsletter final** and leave it open for the next exercise.

6.18 Cropping

When a picture is inserted into a publication, only a small part of it may be needed. If this is the case, the picture can be **cropped** to remove any unwanted areas from view.

Activity:

1. With the **newsletter final** publication open, display page **2** and insert the picture **Scanned**. *Julia* scanned this image into her computer from a printed leaflet, but it includes a lot of unwanted detail around the edges.

2. Zoom to **Whole Page**. With the picture selected and the **Picture Tools - Format** tab displayed, click the **Crop** button. Crop handles appear around the image.

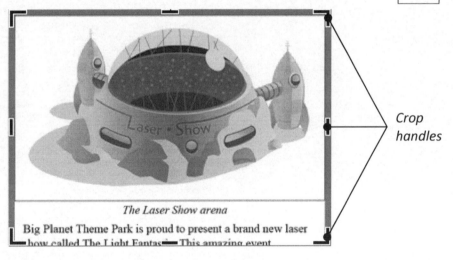

Crop handles

3. Click and drag the *top*, *left*, *right* and *bottom* crop handles inwards to frame the picture of the *Laser Show* arena only.

4.   When you have finished, click the **Crop** button again. The picture is cropped and the unwanted areas removed from view.

> **Note:**   The cropped areas of a picture are not deleted, only hidden. To remove the crop, click the **Reset Picture** button, 🖼, in the **Adjust** group.

5.   Next, use the **Shape Height** box in the **Size** group to set the height of the picture to **7 cm** and press <**Enter**>. Allow *Publisher* to automatically adjust the **Shape Width**.

6.   Position the image in the centre of the page underneath the first text box.

> **Note:**   You can also crop images using this technique in other *Microsoft Office* applications.

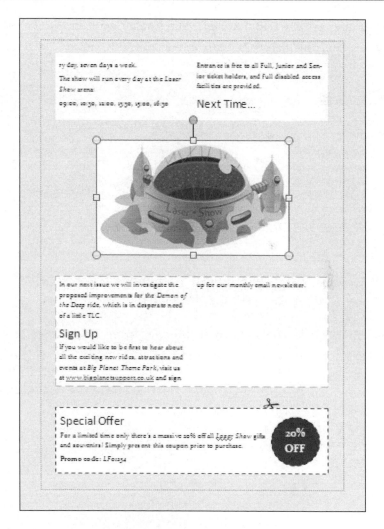

7.   Save the publication and leave it open for the next exercise.

6.19 Clip Art and Text Wrapping

As you have already seen, text in a publication is wrapped *around* an image by default. However, there are many other text wrapping options available.

Activity:

1. With the **newsletter final** publication open, select page **1** and display the **Insert** tab. From the **Illustrations** group, click the **Clip Art** button to display the **Clip Art** task pane.

2. *Julia* would like the newsletter to contain an image of a rocket ship on the first page. In the **Search for** box enter the keyword **rocket** and click **Go**.

> **Note:** Make sure **Include Office.com content** is selected in the **Clip Art** task pane to access the full range of **Clip Art** content that is available.

3. The results are displayed in the pane. Examine the various **Clip Art** illustrations found (notice that you can scroll down the list of results).

4. Select an appropriate **Clip Art** illustration by clicking it once (*Julia* recommends the clip art shown below). The picture appears in the centre of the current page.

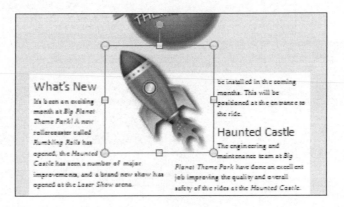

5. Notice that the text "wraps around" the inserted **Clip Art**. Click and drag the **Clip Art** object around the page to see the affect it has on the text.

6. Display the **Picture Tools - Format** tab and, from the **Arrange** group, click the **Wrap Text** drop-down button. Notice that **Square** is already selected.

7. Select **None**. The picture now appears floating above the text. Click and drag the **Clip Art** object around the page to see the effect.

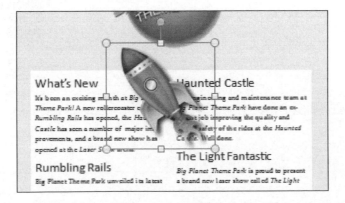

8. Click the **Wrap Text** button and select **Top and Bottom**.

9. Again, click and drag the **Clip Art** object around the page to see the effect it has on the text.

10. Next, use the **Shape Height** box in the **Size** group to set height of the picture to **3 cm**. Press <**Enter**> and *Publisher* will automatically adjust the **Shape Width** value to maintain proportions.

11. Place the **Clip Art** object in the centre of the second column.

What's New

It's been an exciting month at *Big Planet Theme Park!* A new rollercoaster called *Rumbling Rails* has opened, the *Haunted Castle* has seen a number of major improvements, and a brand new show has opened at the *Laser Show* arena.

Rumbling Rails

Big Planet Theme Park unveiled its latest ride this month: *Rumbling Rails* – a thrilling high speed train ride through rocky canyons and icy mountain passes. Now open to the public, this ground-breaking new roller coaster is a massive 100 metres high and reaches speeds of 80 miles per hour.

To help manag queues during the summer months, a *Fast Ticket* service will be installed in the coming months. This will be positioned at the entrance to the ride.

Haunted Castle

The engineering and maintenance team at *Big Planet Theme Park* have done an excellent job improving the quality and overall safety of the rides at the *Haunted Castle*. Well done.

The Light Fantastic

Big Planet Theme Park is proud to present a brand new laser show called *The Light Fantastic*. This amazing event combines pictures and special effects to recreate famous cities and landmarks from around the world!

108 computer controlled lights and lasers

---

12. Close the **Clip Art** task pane, save the publication, and leave it open for the next exercise.

6.20 Spelling Check

Similar to other *Microsoft Office* applications, *Publisher's* spelling check feature can check the spelling of all words in a publication.

Activity:

1. With the **newsletter final** publication open on page **1**, place the cursor at the start of the text in the large text box. Then, display the **Review** tab and click the **Spelling** button.

2. *Publisher* will now automatically check for errors in the *current* "story" only.

> Note: In *Publisher*, a **story** is the name given to the contents of a text box. If two or more text boxes are linked, then they share the same story.

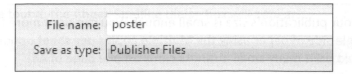

4. Click the **Save as type** drop-down button once to display a list of different file types. Examine the file types available. The most useful at this level are described below.

PDF	Creates a small, compressed document for downloading and viewing on the web. This is the best format to save in if you want to distribute your publication electronically, or if you wish to send it to others who may not have *Publisher* available to open and view your files.
Plain Text	Creates a small file containing only the text in a publication. All images, layout and text formatting are lost.
Web Page, Filtered	Creates a web page out of your publication that can be uploaded to the Internet and viewed by others.
JPEG	Converts your publication into an image that can be used elsewhere in other applications. As this type of file is compressed to save space and make it easier to use online, you may notice the quality of the image decreases a little.
PNG	Converts your publication into an image that can be used elsewhere in other applications. Unlike JPEG, the quality of the file does not decrease, but the file size is usually too large to use online.

5. Select **JPEG File Interchange Format** from the list of file types available. Notice that a **Resolution** area has now appeared below the **Save as type** drop-down.

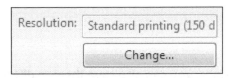

> Note: An image's **resolution** refers to how detailed the image is when printed, and is measured in **Dots Per Inch (DPI)**. The higher the DPI, the better the quality of the printed image but the larger the file size. If you are publishing the image to the web (where files take time to download), a compromise will have to be found between the image's quality and its size.

6. As this preview image of the **poster** publication will only be viewed on screen, you can choose a low resolution; click the **Change** button and select **Web (96 dpi)** and click **OK**.

7. Change the **File name** to **poster preview**. Click the **Save** button to save the publication. This does not affect your original saved *Publisher* file, which remains open on screen.

8. Open your **Documents** library and navigate to the data files folder for this section. Notice that a new picture file, **poster preview**, is present.

9. Double click **poster preview** to open the image in your computer's default picture viewing application. Notice that the text is now part of the image; it can no longer be edited.

10. Close your picture viewing application and return to *Publisher*. Display the **File** tab and select **Save As** again. When the **Save As** dialog box appears, drop down the **Save as type** button to display the list of different file types.

11. *Julia* would also like to save the publication as a web page. From the options available, select **Web Page, Filtered**. Change the **File name** to **internet poster**.

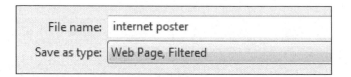

12. Click **Save**. The publication is converted into a web page.

13. Return to your **Documents** library and notice that a new HTML file, **internet poster**, is present. Double click this to open the web page in your computer's default Internet browser application.

> **Note:** Notice that, unlike image files, the text on the web page can still be selected. Other *Office* applications such as *Microsoft Word* can also save and edit files in web page format, although it is perhaps best to use special web-editing software to do this (e.g. *Microsoft Expression Web* or *Adobe Dreamweaver*).

> **Note:** For other people to see the web page, it must be uploaded (using special File Transfer Protocol (**FTP**) software) to a location on the Internet.

14. Close your Internet browser and **Documents** library. Then, close the **poster** publication without saving any changes. Leave *Publisher* open for the next exercise.

6.23 Templates

Templates are useful *Publisher* designs that can be used as a basis for new publications. *Publisher* includes a small selection of built-in templates, but many, many more are available online at **Office.com**. Although many templates look very impressive, you should ensure that any design theme you choose is suitable for the target audience.

Activity:

1. Display the **File** tab and make sure **New** is selected from the options on the left of the screen. The **Available Templates** window is displayed.

2. Examine the various template types available in the **Most Popular** and **More Templates** groups.

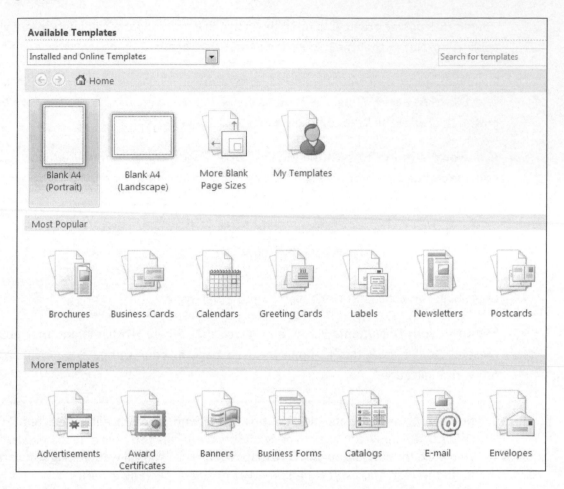

3. Within the **Most Popular** group, click once on **Brochures** to view the selection of templates that are available. Select **Arrows** from the list, and then click the **Create** button on the right of the screen.

4. A new publication is created based on the selected **Arrows** template. Examine the contents of both pages in this publication and feel free to alter any of the default text (the original template will not be affected).

5. Close the publication, selecting **Don't Save** at the prompt if any changes were made.

6. Explore the many other templates available. In particular, view templates for **Business Cards**, **Greeting Cards**, **Award Certificates** and **Resumes** to get a flavour of some of the other designs that you can create with *Publisher*.

7. When you are finished, close *Publisher* along with all open templates <u>without</u> saving any changes.

6.24 Design Tips

When creating your own publications, strong visuals and clear information will help get your message across. Consider the following points of good practice:

* Keep things simple and try not to use too many different colours, fonts and fancy background designs.

* A simple, consistent design should be used *throughout* a publication. Empty areas (known as **white space**) can also make your publication more attractive to the eye.

* As some people have difficulty separating certain colour combinations (especially red-green), be careful when using these colours to describe important information.

* Focus on what is important and do not try to cram too much information onto one page. Long sentences and paragraphs are often boring to read.

* Consider where your publication will be seen. If it will be a poster on a wall, use eye-catching headlines and keep font sizes big enough to see from a distance.

* Avoid dark text on dark backgrounds and light text on light backgrounds.

* Sans serif fonts (e.g. Arial) are often easier to read that serif fonts (e.g. Times).

* Use pictures and simple charts rather than complicated tables of figures.

* Use guides to line up objects and help maintain consistency between pages.

6.25 House Styles

A **house style** (also known as a "style sheet") is a set of rules that specifies exactly how promotional materials such as publications, presentations and documents should look. A company will frequently have a house style linked to their corporate image or range of products. This helps to make sure that a recognisable, consistent brand is communicated to customers.

House styles can include guidelines on the following:

* Font types, sizes, alignment, positions and colours

* Background designs and colours

* Margins, spacing and page sizes

* Position and size of company logos

* Spelling preferences (e.g. US or UK) and the format of times, dates and currencies

* Addresses and other contact details

House styles also help to reduce the amount of time you need to spend creating a design as all of the hard decisions have already been made for you. If you are asked to follow a house style in your own work, make sure you find and follow the relevant guidelines for your publication type.

6.26 Next Steps

Well done! You have now completed all of the exercises in this section. If you feel you are ready to test your knowledge and understanding of the topics covered, move on to the following **Develop Your Skills** activities. If there are any features of *Microsoft Publisher* that you are unsure about, you should revisit the appropriate exercises and try them again before moving on.

If you are interested in exploring some of *Microsoft Publisher's* more powerful features, why don't you use the Internet to find out a little more about the following advanced topics.

Feature	Description
Building Blocks	**Building Blocks** are ready-made illustrations such as calendars, sidebars, borders and advertisements that you can use in your own publications.
Business Information	*Publisher* has a feature which allows personal information to be recorded, which can then included in any publication created from a template. This is called **Business Information** and it can be edited to suit your own needs.
Styles	Similar to *Microsoft Word*, *Publisher's* **Styles** are specific combinations of font types, sizes and alignments. When they are applied, text will adopt all of the style's formatting settings. This helps ensure consistent formatting throughout a publication.
Master Pages	When each page in a publication has common elements (e.g. the same background, headers, footers, logos, etc.) then creating a **Master Page** is useful. Whatever appears on the **Master Page** will also appear automatically on every page in that publication.
Headers and Footers	**Headers** and **Footers** are text areas which appear at the top and bottom of every page in a publication (and are set on the **Master Page**). They can contain fixed items of text such as publication title or author name, or **fields** such as the date and time or page number.
Pack and Go	This useful feature can be used to prepare your publication to be sent to and printed by a commercial printing company.
Design Checker	Once a publication has been created it can be automatically checked for common problems such as low quality images, poor use of colour, layout issues, and badly aligned or resized objects.
Hyphenation	To improve the layout and readability of text, *Publisher* can hyphenate single words at the end of lines. This splits the words in two (using a hyphen, -) so that space is used more efficiently.
Mail Merge	*Publisher's* **Mail Merge** feature is used to combine a main publication (a flyer, for example) with a separate list containing names and addresses. These two files, when merged, create a personalised copy of the main publication for everyone on the list.

Develop Your Skills...

At the end of every section you get the chance to complete two activities. These will help you to develop your skills and prepare for your exam. Don't forget to use the planning and review checklists at the back of the book to help organise and review your work.

> **Note:** Answers to these activities are provided in this section's **Sample Solutions** folder.

Develop Your Skills: Advertising Poster

In this activity you will be asked to create a simple advertising poster for *Julia*. You will need to use all of the ICT skills that you have learned in this section to plan, develop and present an appropriate solution.

Activity 1

The *Laser Show* arena has a special offer running at the moment: 20% off all souvenirs and gifts. I've sketched an idea for an *A4* poster to advertise the promotion, but I need you to create it for me in *Publisher*.

Start with a new, **Blank A4 (Portrait)** publication. Use three separate text boxes for the "**Special Offer**", "**20% Off**" and "**All Gifts and Souvenirs**" text.

For the illustration in the middle of the page, use an **Explosion** shape. The following picture of a space rocket can be inserted from the data files folder:

✳ **Rocket**

Apply an orange outline colour to the explosion shape and fill it with a white/yellow gradient. Finally, save the publication as **advertising poster** in the data files folder for this section.

7 | Microsoft Access

Hi, my name's Zahra...

I'm manager of the *Active Leisure* team here at *Big Planet Theme Park*. My staff and I are based in the *Pirate's Cove* section of the park, which is a fun leisure pool and fitness area for visitors of all ages and abilities.

Starting next week, we will begin offering a range of exciting new activities for visitors to take part in. Although some will be based in the pool, most will take place in one of our popular health and fitness halls. All of the activities will also be run by highly trained and experienced trainers and will occur at the same time every day, Monday to Friday. However, due to limited availability, we expect that visitors will need to book their places well in advance.

Of course, this means there is going to be a lot of booking information to keep track of. Visitor and trainer details will need to be recorded along with all of the activities and their times. To help make sure that both trainers and visitors meet up in the right place and at the right time, I'm going to use the application *Microsoft Access* to create a database to manage bookings. Maybe you can help me?

What you will learn:

In this section you will use the program *Microsoft Access* to help *Zahra* create a new, fully functional database. You will then move on to use a range of database techniques to enter, store, edit and analyse large amounts of complex information.

Knowledge, skills and understanding:

*   Use *Microsoft Access* to design and construct a simple database for a purpose

*   Enter, maintain and work with large amounts of data

*   Build and run queries to retrieve information and create reports

Data files

The files needed to complete the activities in this section are provided in the **Section 7** data folder (see note on page **vii** to download these files). Databases that you create can be saved to the same folder.

7.1 Using Microsoft Access

A **database** is a simple storage system designed to hold large amounts of information. Often used in business, they allow lots of data – usually in the form of plain text – to be recorded, accessed, edited, sorted and searched through quickly and easily. Although the possible uses of a database are endless, they are most often used for storing:

* Staff, customer and student records

* Stock, product, order and shipping details

* Lists, diaries and schedules

* Website content and user login data

Microsoft Access is a program that allows you to design and build databases. It is known as a **Database Management System** because it also allows you to access and update the information held in a database and to display that data in a variety of useful ways.

> **Note:** If you are new to the world of databases, you may find them a little overwhelming at first. Don't worry – most beginners experience the same difficulties when they first start out. However, with a little time and practice, you'll soon be able to create and use databases like a professional.

In this section you will create a new database to store visitor booking information at *Pirate's Cove*. You will also get the opportunity to open and explore a few ready-made databases.

7.2 Tables, Fields and Records

If you were to crack open a database and take a look inside, you would find all of the information stored within one or more **tables** (which appear very similar to worksheets in *Excel*).

Employee Name	Date of Birth	Department	Salary
Jack Grimes	27/03/87	Fitness	£15000
Shona Piquet	03/12/90	Aqua	£13500
Tariq Hussan	15/06/84	Sport	£18000
Ivan Hendle	15/08/82	Sport	£13500

In those tables, information is split up into a number of columns known as **fields**. Each field represents a single, separate piece of information (such as the four fields in the example above: **Employee Name**, **Date of Birth**, **Department** and **Salary**).

> **Note:** As all data held in a database is stored within tables, it makes sense that all databases must contain *at least one* table.

© CiA Training Ltd 2012

Information is added to a table in rows known as **records**, where each record represents a single complete set of fields. In the previous example, the four fields containing information for **Jack Grimes** make up a single record:

Jack Grimes	27/03/87	Fitness	£15000

Activity:

1. Start *Microsoft Access* and open the database **Staff Members** from the data files folder. This is a working database containing information about staff members and their jobs.

2. Locate the **Navigation** pane on the left of the screen, labelled **All Access Objects**, which lists all of the objects present in the current database. One table called **Trainers** is listed.

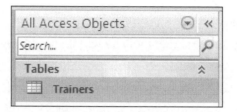

> **Note:**   In *Access*, any item contained in a database (such as a table) is called an **object**. You will learn more about other types of object later in this section.

3. Double click on the **Trainers** table object. It is opened in the main part of the window and all of the records contained are shown in a list. This is known as **Datasheet View**.

Staff ID	FirstName	Surname	Area	Speciality	Date of Birth
002	Jack	Grimes	Fitness	Gymnastics	27/03/1987
003	Shona	Piquet	Aqua	Aerobics	06/10/1990
005	Tariq	Hussan	Sport	Golf	12/08/1984
009	Ivan	Hendle	Sport	Tennis	22/07/1982
011	Rajesh	Kumar	Fitness	Yoga	24/11/1961
014	Yoshio	Kosugi	Sport	Judo	03/06/1975
015	Zahra	Johnson	Aqua	Swimming	13/07/1991
017	Noleen	Stewart	Fitness	Aerobics	18/05/1989

4. The table contains records for each of the trainers in the *Active Leisure* team at *Pirate's Cove*. Records can easily be added, altered and deleted from here.

5. On the **Home** tab, click the drop-down arrow on the **View** button and then select **Design View**. This view allows you to edit the structure of the table by defining the various fields that should appear in it.

> **Note:**   Clicking the **View** button instead of the drop-down arrow will switch directly from **Datasheet View** to **Design View** (and vice versa).

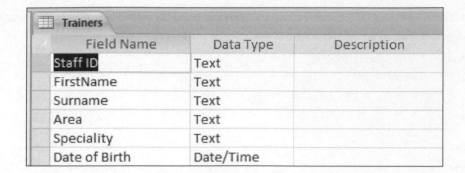

> **Note:** You will learn more about a field's **Data Type** and **Description** in a later exercise.

6. Click the drop-down arrow on the **View** button and select **Datasheet View** to view the table's data again.

7. Close the database (this is an option on the **File** tab). As no changes have been made to the design of any objects, there will be no prompt to save changes.

> **Note:** Other *Microsoft Office* programs such as *Excel* can be used to store information in tables, so why use a database? The answer is simple: a well-designed database allows you to record, update, manage and search through vast amounts of information very quickly and efficiently.

7.3 Creating a Database

In most *Office* applications, files are created during the **Save** process (for example, saving a new document in *Word* will create a document file). In *Access*, however, a blank database is created and saved <u>before</u> any changes are made to it.

Activity:

1. With the **File** tab displayed, make sure **New** is selected on the left (**Available Templates** will be displayed) and that the **Blank database** template is highlighted.

2. The panel on the right allows you to name the new database and specify where it will be located (your default file name and path may appear differently).

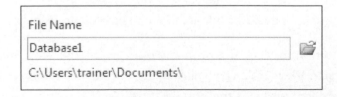

> **Note:** The default is to create your new database in your **Documents** library.

3. Click the **Browse** button, 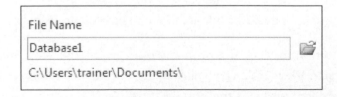, to display the **File New Database** dialog box.

4. Navigate to the data files folder for this section, and then replace the default database **File name** with **activity list**.

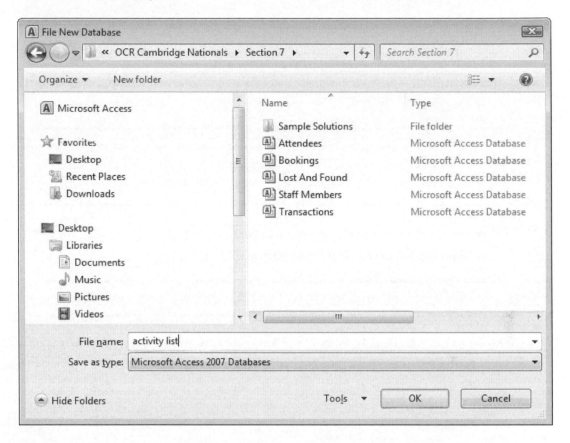

5. Click **OK**. Notice that the **File Name** and file path have both been updated.

6. Click the **Create** button. A new database is created and saved (even though there is no content yet). A new default table is created and opened in **Datasheet View**.

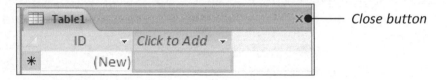

Close button

7. In order to demonstrate the general method for creating new tables in a database, close the default table by clicking the **Close** button found to the right of the **Table1** tab.

8. Leave the **activity list** database open for the next exercise.

7.4 Creating a Table

Before creating a new database table you first need to consider all of the fields that it will contain. As you will learn more about in later exercises, this is a very important stage in the design of a database as the chosen fields will define the *exact* types of information that can be stored.

For example, if you want to record information about customer telephone numbers, at the very least you will need a field for their name and another for their telephone number.

> **Note:** Fields can be added, edited and deleted in a table at *any* time in **Design View**.

Activity:

1. With the **activity list** database open, display the **Create** tab and click the **Table Design** button. A new table appears in **Design View**, which allows the structure of the table to be created.

Table Design

> **Note:** The **Design View** is divided into two main areas. The upper half of the screen allows you to specify the name and data type for each field in the table; the lower half shows more details about the currently selected field.

2. In the first row, enter **Code** as the **Field Name**. Then press <**Enter**> to move to the **Data Type** column. The default type **Text** appears.

> **Note:** You will learn more about the various data types in the next exercise.

3. Move to the **Description** column and enter **Activity code**. **Description** text is displayed on the **Status Bar** whenever this field is selected in **Datasheet View** (recall that **Datasheet View** is used to view and enter records in a database).

Field Name	Data Type	Description
Code	Text	Activity code

4. Click in the **Field Name** column for the second row (which confirms the changes made in the first row). Enter the following fields, choosing a default **Data Type** of **Text** for each.

Field Name	Data Type	Description
Activity	Text	Activity name
Staff ID	Text	Trainer for this activity
Location	Text	Activity location
Time	Text	Starting time (daily)
Cost	Text	Cost per person
Discount	Text	Big Planet Club discount
Maximum	Text	Maximum participants

> **Note:** You can use the <**Tab**> or <**Enter**> key to move to the next column/field.

5. Leave the table open for the next exercise.

7.5 Data Types

Each time you add a new field to a table you must also select an appropriate **Data Type**. There are many different **Data Types** available to choose from, and each can be used to restrict the type of information allowed in a field (a form of data **validation**). The most useful types are listed below:

Data Type	Description
Text	Any combination of letters, numbers or punctuation can be entered into fields of this type.
Number	Only numbers can be entered into fields of this type. Letters and punctuation are rejected.
Date/Time	Only accepts values in time or date format (e.g. 08:00:00).
Currency	Only accepts values in currency format (e.g. £12.50).
AutoNumber	Fields of this type include a single number that is automatically increased by 1 each time a new record is added to the table.
Yes/No	Displays a checkbox which can be either on or off.

Activity:

1. The **activity list** database currently contains 8 fields. For each field, a **Data Type** of **Text** has been selected (the default).

2. Click once in the **Data Type** column for the **Time** field, and then click the drop-down arrow that appears to right of the selection. Examine the various **Data Types** available.

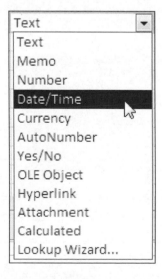

3. Select **Date/Time**. Now only valid dates and times can be entered into this field (e.g. **08:00:00** or **04/04/2012**). Any invalid dates or times will be rejected.

4. For the **Cost** field and **Discount** field, choose a **Data Type** of **Currency**. Now only valid money amounts can be entered into this field (e.g. **£15.50**).

5. Finally, for the **Maximum** field, choose a **Data Type** of **Number**. Now only numbers can be entered into this field.

Field Name	Data Type	Description
Code	Text	Activity Code
Activity	Text	Activity name
Staff ID	Text	Trainer for this activity
Location	Text	Activity location
Time	Date/Time	Starting time (daily)
Cost	Currency	Cost per person
Discount	Currency	Big Planet Club discount
Maximum	Number	Maximum participants

6. Leave the table open for the next exercise.

7.6 Saving Tables

When a table, or any other database object, has been created or edited in **Design View**, it must be saved so that the changes are applied.

Activity:

1. To save the newly created table, click on the **Save** button on the **Quick Access Toolbar**.

Save button ———

2. As the table has not yet been saved, the **Save As** dialog box is displayed. Enter the **Table Name** as **Activities**.

3. Click **OK** to confirm the table name and close the dialog box. A message box will appear warning you that no primary key has been defined. Click **No** to continue.

> **Note:** A **primary key** is a field that contains unique values for all records in a table. If used, each record can be referred to individually. As you will only use simple tables in this section, you do not need to worry about primary keys for now.

4. The table is saved. Notice the new **Activities** table now appears in the **Navigation** pane, and the tab for the table now displays the table's saved name.

5. The design of the table is now complete. Using the **View** button, return to **Datasheet View**. The table's fields, as created by you, appear across the top of the screen.

6. Leave the database open for the next exercise.

7.7 Entering Records

Once you have finished designing the structure of a table, records can be entered. A simple way to do this is in **Datasheet View**. It is important to enter data accurately – records added to a table are *automatically* and *immediately* saved in the database.

Activity:

1. The **Activities** table should currently be open in **Datasheet View**. There are no records saved in this table yet, but *Zahra* wants you to test the database with some dummy data.

> **Note:** Dummy data is really useful for testing if a database works as expected. However, once you are finished testing, this data must always be removed.

2. Click in the first field (**Code**) and type **A001**.

3. Press <**Enter**> to move to the next field (**Activity**). Type **Aqua Fit** and press <**Enter**>.

4. Using <**Enter**> (or <**Tab**>) to move between fields, enter the **Staff ID** as **003** and the **Location** as **Large Pool**.

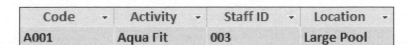

5. In the **Time** field, enter **800** and press <**Enter**>. An error message appears because this is not a valid entry for the data type (recall that a data type of **Date/Time** was selected and **800** is not a valid time).

> **Note:** Depending on the **Data Type** of a selected field, *Access* will automatically reformat any values you enter.

6. Select **Enter new value** from the options. Then, type **8.00** and press <**Enter**>. *Access* displays this as **08:00:00** (hours, minutes and seconds).

7. In the **Cost** field, type **15.5** and press <**Enter**>. *Access* displays this as **£15.50** because a data type of **Currency** was chosen for this field.

8. In the **Discount** field, type **2** and press <**Enter**>. Again, *Access* displays this as **£2.00**.

9. In the **Maximum** field, type **Ten** and press <**Enter**>. An error message appears as only numbers are allowed in a **Number** field. Select **Enter new value** and type **10**.

10. Press <**Enter**>. This is the last field in the table and so the record is complete. The first field in the next record is automatically selected.

Time	Cost	Discount	Maximum
08:00:00	£15.50	£2.00	10

> **Note:** New records are always added at the bottom of a table and are automatically saved by *Access*. There is no need to save manually.

11. Let's try another one. Enter the following field values for the next record:

Code	Activity	Staff ID	Location	Time	Cost	Discount	Maximum
Y001	Starting Yoga	011	Hall 2	8:00	10	1.5	12

12. There are now 2 records stored in the table. Leave it open for the next exercise.

7.8 Editing Table Design

The design of a table can be easily altered after it has been created. However, if records have already been added to the table, there are two important issues which must be considered:

✱ If an existing field is deleted, any data in that field will be permanently lost for <u>all</u> records

✱ If a new field is added to the table, it will be empty for all existing records

Activity:

1. The **Activities** table should be open. Use the **View** button to switch to **Design View**.

2. The **activities list** database also needs to keep track of the minimum number of people allowed on each activity. In the first empty row at the bottom of the table, click once in the **Field Name** column and type **Minimum**.

3. Set the **Data Type** to **Number** and **Description** to **Minimum participants**.

| Maximum | Number | Maximum participants |
| Minimum | Number | Minimum participants |

4. In the next row, enter a **Field Name** of **Fully Booked** and select a **Data Type** of **Yes/No**. Leave the **Description** field empty.

5. To see the effect of these changes, click the **View** button to switch to **Datasheet View**. A message is displayed before the **Datasheet View** is shown.

![Microsoft Access dialog box: "You must first save the table. Do you want to save the table now?" with Yes and No buttons]

> **Note:**   To take effect, tables must be always be saved after making design changes. If you click **No**, any changes will be lost.

6. The table's design has been changed and must be saved to take effect. Click **Yes**. The table is saved and **Datasheet View** is displayed.

7. The **Datasheet View** now has 2 extra field columns on the right (you may need to use the horizontal scrollbar to see these).

> **Note:**   Notice that the two new fields for all existing records are empty. This may seem obvious and of little concern, but if the table had thousands of records it may have to be considered.

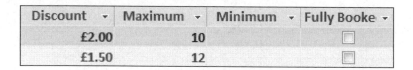

Discount	Maximum	Minimum	Fully Booke
£2.00	10		☐
£1.50	12		☐

8. It is just as easy to remove fields from a table. Switch back to **Design View** and click in the **Fully Booked** row to select it (if it is not already selected).

9. With the **Design** tab displayed, click the **Delete Rows** button, . A warning message is displayed.

![Microsoft Access warning dialog: "Do you want to permanently delete the selected field(s) and all the data in the field(s)? To permanently delete the field(s), click Yes." with Yes and No buttons]

10. All data in this column of the table will be permanently lost. Again, this is not really a problem here but in a large table with lots of pre-existing data it must be considered.

11. Click **Yes**. The field is deleted.

12. Switch to **Datasheet View**. You will have to click **Yes** to save the table design changes again. The **Fully Booked** column is no longer shown.

13. Leave the table open for the next exercise.

7.9 Column Widths

In **Datasheet View**, values or field names are sometimes longer than the default column width of a table. This causes the data display to be **truncated** (cut off). The truncated data is not lost; it is just hidden. Fortunately, it is an easy matter to display all of the content by simply changing the width of the columns.

Activity:

1. The **Activities** table should be open in **Datasheet View**. Let's add another record. Click in the first field of the first blank record in the table and enter the following values:

    Z001, Introduction to Judo, 014, Small Sports Hall, 19:00, 12, 2, 8, 2

2. Depending on your screen resolution, the **Activity** and **Location** fields may not be fully displayed (if they are fully displayed, you can simulate this problem by reducing the size of the *Access* window). There are two ways to deal with this.

3. First, place the cursor on the bar between the column headers **Activity** and **Staff ID** as shown below. The cursor changes to a double-headed arrow.

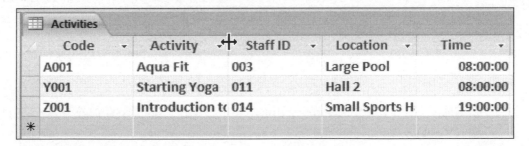

4. Double click and the column width will increase automatically to accommodate the largest value in this field.

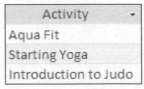

5. Column widths can also be adjusted manually. Place the cursor on the bar between the column headers **Location** and **Time** so that it changes to a double-headed arrow.

6. Click and drag to the right to increase the column width by a small amount. Release the mouse button to see the effect. You may need to repeat the process until all of the text in all of the fields can be seen.

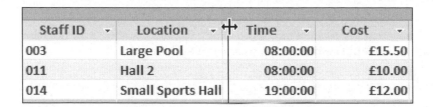

7. Leave the table open for the next exercise.

7.10 Editing Records

In addition to adding new records, one of the strengths of *Access* is that it is also easy to amend or remove records that already exist. Remember, data changes made in **Datasheet View** are automatically saved as they happen.

Activity:

1. The **Activities** table should be open in **Datasheet View**. Click in record **2** for activity **Y001** (**Starting Yoga**). Then, find the **Record** navigation buttons which are located at the bottom of the table.

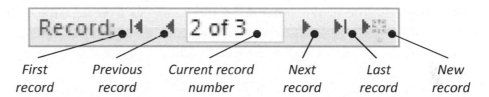

2. Click the **Next record** button to move to record **3**, then click the **First record** button to move to record **1**. Finally, click the **Next record** button again to move back to record **2**.

3. Move the mouse pointer over the start of the **Staff ID** field for record **2** until it changes to a large cross icon.

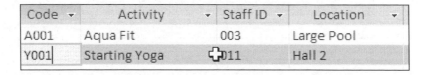

4. Click with the mouse to select the whole of the field. Press the <**Delete**> key. The entire contents of the field are deleted.

5. Click the **Undo** button, ![undo icon], on the **Quick Access Toolbar**. The action is reversed and the **Staff ID** field returns to its original value.

6. A data entry error has been made: the starting time of **Starting Yoga** should be **10:00**. Click in the field and edit the value to **10:00:00**. Press <**Enter**> to confirm the change.

> **Note:** Standard editing functions such as **Cut**, **Copy**, and **Paste** may also be used.

7. It has been decided that all activities should be priced at **£8.00**. First, change the value in the **Cost** field for record **1** to **£8.00**.

8. Next, highlight the new value using click and drag.

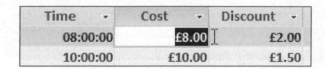

Time	Cost	Discount
08:00:00	£8.00	£2.00
10:00:00	£10.00	£1.50

9. Click the **Copy** button, 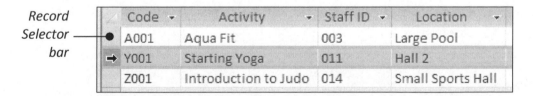, in the **Clipboard** group of the **Home** tab.

10. Highlight the activity cost in the record below and click the **Paste** button. The copied price replaces the original value. Repeat this for record **3**.

> **Note:** Standard **Find** and **Replace** techniques also work for databases.

11. Leave the table open for the next exercise.

7.11 Deleting Records

Records can easily be deleted in **Datasheet View**. Deleting a record removes it and all of its field data from the table. There is a warning prompt and then the record is removed permanently.

Activity:

1. The **Activities** table should be open in **Datasheet View**. Move your mouse pointer over the **Record Selector** bar until an arrow pointer appears, ➡. Click once on record **2** (**Code Y001**) to select the whole of that record.

Record Selector bar

Code	Activity	Staff ID	Location
A001	Aqua Fit	003	Large Pool
Y001	Starting Yoga	011	Hall 2
Z001	Introduction to Judo	014	Small Sports Hall

2. Click the **Delete** button, ✕ Delete , in the **Records** group of the **Home** tab.

Microsoft Access

You are about to delete 1 record(s).

If you click Yes, you won't be able to undo this Delete operation. Are you sure you want to delete these records?

Yes   No

3. Read the confirmation message that appears and then click **Yes** to permanently remove the record. Use the same technique to delete the other two dummy test records.

4. Well done. The database is now ready to be used by staff at *Pirate's Cove* to record new activities. *Zahra* thanks you for your help.

5. Close the database, saving any changes that have been made to the table's design.

7.12 Sorting Records

In a large table it can sometimes be useful to **sort** all of the records into a specific order. For example, you could sort all employee records alphabetically by name or numerically by age. This technique allows you to group records in a way that helps you find the information you need quickly and easily.

Records can be sorted in **ascending** or **descending** order using any field in a table. Ascending sorts for a text field will be alphabetical, A-Z. For a numeric field it will be lowest to highest, and for a date field will be oldest to newest. Descending order applies the opposite sort.

Activity:

1. Open the **Attendees** database.

> **Note:** If a yellow **Security Warning** appears under the **Ribbon**, simply click **Enable Content** to remove it. Because of the risk of viruses, always be careful enabling content if you do not fully trust the source of the database.

2. Using the **Navigation** pane, double click to open the **Visitors** table. This table contains details of park visitors who have recently attended activities at *Pirate's Cove*.

3. Move your mouse pointer over the field header **Last Name** until it changes to a downward arrow, ↓.

Last Name ↓	Ticket Type
McKnight	Full
Robson	Junior

4. Click once to select this field, and then click the **Ascending** button, 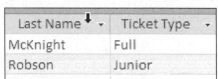, in the **Sort & Filter** group on the **Home** tab. The table is instantly sorted into ascending (alphabetical) order of name.

Visitor	Title	First Name	Last Name	Ticket Type
HC173	Mr	Saeed	Akram	Full
HC168	Mr	Jahved	Ali	Junior
HC145	Miss	Brenda	Appleby	Full
HC106	Mr	Tariq	Assiz	Senior

> **Note:** Entire records are sorted, not just the contents of the selected field.

> **Note:** A small icon, ↑, in the **Last Name** heading indicates a sort is active on this field.

5. With the **Last Name** field still selected, click the **Descending** button, 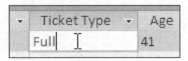. The table is now sorted in reverse order of name (notice the arrow icon has reversed).

6. Click the **Remove Sort** button, [A↓ Remove Sort], from the **Home** tab. The sort is removed and the records are displayed in their original order.

7. Next, select the **Age** field and select **Ascending** from the **Ribbon**. The table is sorted by increasing age. Select **Descending** to reverse the sort.

8. Click the **Remove Sort** button, [A↓ Remove Sort], and leave the table open for the next exercise.

7.13 Filtering Records

Filtering is a quick way to find records in a table that match certain selection criteria. Only the records that match the criteria are displayed (the records that do not match are hidden).

Activity:

1. The **Visitors** table of the **Attendees** database should be open in **Datasheet View**. Place the cursor in the first record's **Ticket Type** field (**Full**).

Ticket Type	Age
Full	41

2. From the **Sort & Filter** group on the **Home** tab, click the **Selection** button, [Selection ▾]. Examine the various options that are listed based on the selected field.

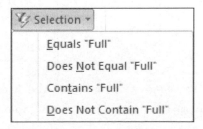

3. Select **Equals "Full"**. Only records with **Ticket Type** fields containing the text **Full** are displayed. The **Record** navigation buttons at the bottom of the table show the number of filtered records (**Record 1 of 34**) and the text **Filtered**.

4. From the **Home** tab, click **Toggle Filter**, 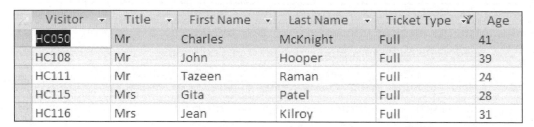. This switches off the filter but does not delete it.

5. Click the **Toggle Filter** button again. The last filter used is reapplied.

Visitor	Title	First Name	Last Name	Ticket Type	Age
HC050	Mr	Charles	McKnight	Full	41
HC108	Mr	John	Hooper	Full	39
HC111	Mr	Tazeen	Raman	Full	24
HC115	Mrs	Gita	Patel	Full	28
HC116	Mrs	Jean	Kilroy	Full	31

> **Note:** A small icon, ▼, in the **Ticket Type** heading indicates a filter is active on this field.

6. To remove the filter completely, click **Advanced** on the **Home** tab and select **Clear All Filters**. All 65 records appear again.

7. Next, place the cursor in the first record's **Age** field (**41**). Click the **Selection** button and select **Less Than or Equal to 41**.

8. Only visitors whose age is 41 or under will now appear (47 records). Click **Advanced** and select **Clear All Filters**.

9. Using the same technique, apply a filter so that only visitors whose age is **Greater Than or Equal to 41** are displayed (21 records). Click **Advanced** and select **Clear All Filters**.

10. Using the same technique again, apply a filter so that only visitors whose age is **Equal to 41** are displayed (3 records). Click **Advanced** and select **Clear All Filters**.

11. You can also apply more specific *custom* filters. Click the drop-down arrow on the **Visit Date** field header, ▼, and move your mouse pointer over **Date Filters**.

Sort/Filter button

12. From the submenu that appears, select **Before**.

13. A **Custom Filter** dialog box appears. Place the cursor in the **Visit Date is on or before** box.

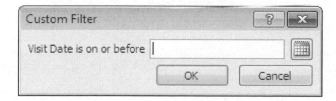

14. Enter **13/05/2011** and click **OK**. Only records with a **Visit Date** on or earlier than May 13, 2011 will be displayed (21 records).

> **Note:** You can also apply more than one filter at a time.

15. With the previous filter still active, click the drop-down arrow on the **Ticket Type** field header and move your mouse pointer over **Text Filters**.

16. Select **Contains**. In the **Custom Filter** dialog box enter the text **Full** and click **OK**. Only records with a **Visit Date** on or earlier than **13/05/2011** <u>and</u> with a **Ticket Type** of **Full** are now displayed (9 records).

17. Click **Advanced** from the **Home** tab and select **Clear All Filters**. Examine the various filter types available for other fields in the table. Feel free to try out a number of different filters, but make sure you select **Clear All Filters** before continuing.

18. Leave the table open for the next exercise.

7.14 Queries

For more control over sorting and filtering in a table, you can use a **query**. A basic query **selects** specific fields and records from a database table and then displays them in another table. The original table is not affected by the query.

One of the biggest advantages of a query is that it is saved as a separate object in *Access* and can be opened and used again at any time. Of course, every time you open the query, it will always show the most current information stored in the database.

Activity:

1. The **Visitors** table should still be open in **Datasheet View**. *Zahra* wants to quickly produce a list of all **Junior** visitors to *Pirate's Cove*, showing their **First Name**, **Last Name**, **Ticket Type** and **Age**. The results should be shown in order of **Age** with the oldest visitors first. This can be done easily using a simple query.

2. Display the **Create** tab and select **Query Design** from the **Queries** group.

3. A query design tab (**Query1**) is displayed and the **Show Table** dialog box appears on top.

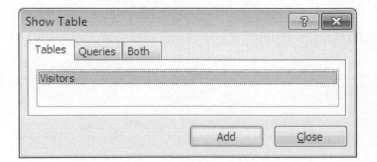

4. The **Show Table** dialog box is used to select which tables should be used as the basis for the query. With the **Visitors** table highlighted, click **Add** to add the table to the query.

5. Click **Close** in the **Show Table** dialog box to close it.

6. Examine the contents of the **Query1** tab. The top half contains a list of all fields in the **Visitors** table; the lower half allows you to select which fields to include in the query.

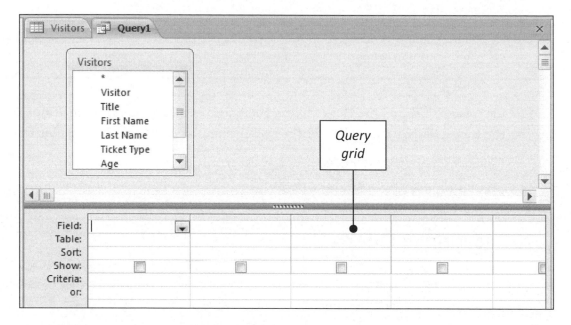

7. In the lower query grid, click the drop-down arrow button on the first column's **Field** property box. From the list of fields displayed, select **First Name**.

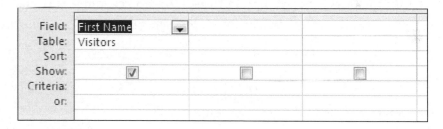

8. Use the same method to select **Last Name** in the second column.

> **Note:** An alternative method for adding a field to your query is to double click the field name in the field list at the top of the page. The field is added in the next column. You can also drag and drop fields from the field list to an available query column.

9. Add the fields **Ticket Type** and **Age** to the query using whichever method you prefer.

Field:	First Name	Last Name	Ticket Type	Age
Table:	Visitors	Visitors	Visitors	Visitors
Sort:				
Show:	✓	✓	✓	✓
Criteria:				
or:				

> **Note:** The query will display fields in the order that they appear in the query design. This can be different to the order that they occur in the original table.

10. With the **Query Tools - Design** tab displayed, click **Run** to run the query. All 65 records contained in the **Visitors** table are shown (in **Datasheet View**), but only the four selected fields appear.

Run

> **Note:** Queries simply provide a different view of a table's data. However, editing values in the results of a query will also change the original table's content.

11. Click **Save**, , on the **Quick Access Toolbar** to save the query. Enter **Visitor Query** as the **Query Name** and click **OK**. Notice that the new query now appears on the **Navigation** pane.

12. Leave the query open for the next exercise.

7.15 Sorting in Queries

Records selected using queries can also be automatically sorted (in either ascending or descending order) based upon the contents of one or more of the included fields.

Activity:

1. Using **Visitor Query**, switch back to **Design View**. Click in the **Sort** box of the **Last Name** field, then click the drop-down arrow on the right and select **Ascending** from the list.

Field:	First Name	Last Name	Ticket Type	Age
Table:	Visitors	Visitors	Visitors	Visitors
Sort:		Ascending		
Show:	☑	☑	☑	☑
Criteria:				

2. Run the query. All 65 records are shown again, but now they are sorted alphabetically by **Last Name**.

3. Switch back to **Design View**. Change the **Sort** field of **Last Name** to **(not sorted)** and then select **Descending** in the **Sort** box for the **Age** field.

4. Run the query again. The selected fields are now displayed in descending order of **Age** (eldest first). Save the query and then close it.

5. A saved query can be run at any time. Double click the **Visitor Query** object in the **Navigation** pane. The query runs automatically and once again selects and sorts all records in the **Visitors** table.

6. Leave the query open for the next exercise.

Note: It is important to remember that a query can be run at any time. If new records are added or removed, the query will always show the most up-to-date information.

7.16 Selection Criteria

Queries are of most use when used to filter records based on specific selection criteria. When used, only the records that match those criteria are shown.

Activity:

1. **Visitor Query** should be open in **Datasheet View**. Use the **View** button on the **Home** tab to switch to **Design View**.

2. Click in the **Criteria** box for the **Ticket Type** field and type **Junior**. Press **<Enter>**. This will now restrict the query to records which contain the text **Junior** in the **Ticket Type** field.

Note: In queries, **junior** is the same as **Junior** or **JUNIOR**. The speech marks, if not entered manually, will be added automatically by *Access*.

3. Click **Run** on the **Query Tools - Design** tab again to run the query. 21 records are selected.

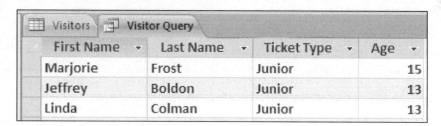

4. Click the **View** button on the **Home** tab to return to **Design View**.

5. When the **Show** checkbox is ticked for a field, ☑, it indicates that the field will be displayed in the query. Click the checkbox for the **Ticket Type** field to remove the tick.

Field:	First Name	Last Name	Ticket Type	Age
Table:	Visitors	Visitors	Visitors	Visitors
Sort:				Descending
Show:	☑	☑	☐	☑
Criteria:			"Junior"	

6. Run the query. The **Type** field is no longer displayed, but it is still used in the query to select records.

7. Switch back to **Design View** and replace the tick in the **Show** checkbox for **Ticket Type**.

8. This now completes *Zahra's* query – well done. Save and close the query and then close the **Attendees** database.

7.17 Numerical Criteria

When creating a query to select records, a number of useful mathematical operators can be used with numeric fields (i.e. fields with number, currency or date/time data types). These include:

<	less than
>	greater than
>=	greater than or equal to
<=	less than or equal to
<>	not equal to

Activity:

1. Open the database **Transactions** and double click on the **Invoices** table to open it. This table contains records of supplier invoices (bills) that *Zahra* has recently received. Running *Pirate's Cove* is an expensive business!

2. Display the **Create** tab and select **Query Design**. Add the **Invoices** table to the query and then close the **Show Table** dialog box.

3. Place the fields **Company Name**, **Town**, **Amount**, **Date** and **Type** into the query grid in that order.

Company Name	Town	Amount	Date	Type
Invoices	Invoices	Invoices	Invoices	Invoices
✓	✓	✓	✓	✓

4. Position the cursor in the **Criteria** box for **Amount** and type **=500**.

Town	Amount	Date
Invoices	Invoices	Invoices
✓	✓	✓
	=500	

Note: Currency symbols such as £ or $ do not need to be included when entering query criteria. Only the value itself is required.

5. Run the query. All invoices for *exactly* **£500** will be selected (only 1 record).

> **Note:** Technically, the **equals** operator, **=**, is not required if only used by itself. It will simply be assumed when you enter a value directly into a field's **Criteria** box, as you saw earlier in Exercise 7.16 (e.g. **Junior** could have been entered as **=Junior**).

6.   Switch back to **Design View**.

7.   Change the criteria in the **Amount** field to **<>500** and run the query. All orders *not equal to* **£500** will now be selected (79 records).

8.   Switch back to **Design View**.

9.   Next, try changing the selection criteria in the **Amount** field to each of the following **Criteria** values, running the query after each change to observe the result:

Criteria	Result
<500	All orders with amounts worth *less than* **£500** will now be selected (16 records).
>500	All orders with amounts worth *more than* **£500** will now be selected (63 records).
<=500	All orders with amounts worth *less than or equal to* **£500** will now be selected (17 records).
>=500	All orders with amounts worth *more than or equal to* **£500** will now be selected (64 records).

10. Switch back to **Design View** and remove the selection criteria in the **Amount** field.

11. Enter the following **Criteria** for the **Date** field: **>=03/01/2011**. Press **<Enter>**.

Amount	Date	Type
Invoices	Invoices	Invoices
☑	☑	☑
	>=#03/01/2011#	

> **Note:** The **#** symbols are added automatically by *Access* to indicate that the selection criteria is based on a date value.

12. Run the query. All orders dated *on or after* 3rd Jan 2011 will be selected (49 records).

13. Experiment using numerical criteria to select records. When you are finished, save the new query as **Criteria Query** and close it.

14. Close the **Invoices** table but leave the **Transactions** database open for the next exercise.

7.18 Multiple Criteria

Multiple query criteria can be combined with an **AND** relationship. For example, you can select records where the **Type** field is **Supplies** <u>AND</u> the **Amount** is **>2000**. Each extra **AND** criteria will usually narrow the selection and produce fewer results.

Criteria can also be combined with an **OR** relationship. For example, you can select records where the **Type** field is **Supplies** <u>OR</u> the **Amount** field is **>2000**. In this case, each extra **OR** criteria will usually widen the selection and produce more results.

Activity:

1. In the **Transactions** database, create a new query in **Design View**. Add the **Invoices** table, close the **Show Table** dialog box, and then add the fields **Type**, **Company Name**, **Town**, **Amount** and **Date** to the query.

2. Position the cursor in the **Criteria** box for the **Type** field and enter **supplies**. In the **Criteria** box for **Amount** type **>2000**. Press <**Enter**>.

Field:	Type	Company Name	Town	Amount
Table:	Invoices	Invoices	Invoices	Invoices
Sort:				
Show:	☑	☑	☑	☑
Criteria:	"supplies"			>2000
or:				

3. Run the query. Only 1 record is found where the **Type** is **Supplies** <u>AND</u> the invoice **Amount** is more than **£2000**.

4. Switch back to **Design View**. Delete the query selection criteria from the **Amount** field and enter **training** in the **or** row for **Type**. Press <**Enter**>.

Field:	Type	Company Name	Town	Amount
Table:	Invoices	Invoices	Invoices	Invoices
Sort:				
Show:	☑	☑	☑	☑
Criteria:	"supplies"			
or:	"training"			

5. Run the query. 27 records are now found where the **Type** is **Supplies** <u>OR</u> **Training**.

Note: You can also use the **OR** and **AND** operators to enter multiple criteria.

6. Switch to **Design View** and remove <u>both</u> selection criteria from the **Type** field. Next, enter **<2000 or >3000** in the **Criteria** box for **Amount**. Press <**Enter**>.

7. Run the query. 74 records are now found where the invoice **Amount** is *less than* **£2000** <u>OR</u> *more than* **£3000**.

8.   Switch to **Design View**. Next, remove the selection criteria for the **Amount** field and replace it with **>2000 and <3000**. Press <**Enter**>.

9.   Run the query. 6 records are now found where the invoice **Amount** is *more than* **£2000** AND *less than* **£3000**.

10. Save the query as **Multiple Criteria** and close it.

7.19 Not and Between

Two particularly useful operators for use in query selection criteria are **Not** and **Between**. The **Not** operator can be used to select records that *do not* match a certain criteria. The **Between** operator can be used to select values *within* a specific range.

> **Note:**   The **Not** operator is the same as the **<>** (not equals) numeric operator.

Activity:

1.   In the **Transactions** database, create a new query in **Design View**. Add the **Invoices** table, close the **Show Table** dialog box, and then add the fields **Type**, **Company Name**, **Town**, **Amount** and **Date** to the query.

2.   In the **Criteria** box for the **Type** field, enter **not supplies** (i.e. not equal to supplies).

Field:	Type	Company Name	Town	Amount
Table:	Invoices	Invoices	Invoices	Invoices
Sort:				
Show:	✓	✓	✓	✓
Criteria:	Not "supplies"			
or:				

3.   Run the query. All invoices that are <u>NOT</u> for supplies will be selected (61 records).

4.   Switch back to **Design View**. Change the criteria to **<> supplies** and press <**Enter**>. Run the query. All invoices that are <u>NOT</u> for supplies will again be selected.

> **Note:**   In practice, you can use either the **Not** or **<>** operators to achieve the same result.

5.   Switch back to **Design View**. Delete the selection criteria from **Type** and, in the criteria for the **Amount** field, enter **between 500 and 900**. Press <**Enter**>.

Field:	Type	Company Name	Town	Amount
Table:	Invoices	Invoices	Invoices	Invoices
Sort:				
Show:	✓	✓	✓	✓
Criteria:				Between 500 And 900
or:				

7.22 Quick Reports

Printing queries (or tables) does not allow any real control over the appearance of the final printed document. To produce more professional looking output it is better to create a **Report**.

> **Note:**   Basic reports always provide a **list** of all records in simple **tabular** (table) form.

Reports are separate objects in *Access* – just like tables and queries – and once created can be run at any time. Importantly, you can create a report based on the contents of a table or the results of a query (in practice, creating a report based on the results of a query is usually more useful).

Activity:

1. In the **Transactions** database, click <u>once</u> to select the **April Invoices** query in the **Navigation** pane (do not open it).

2. Display the **Create** tab and select **Report** from the **Reports** group. A new report is generated based on the currently selected query.

3. Notice the new **Report Layout Tools** tabs that have appeared on the **Ribbon**. You can use these to customise the look of the report. Make sure the **Design** tab is selected.

> **Note:**   Similar to *Microsoft Publisher*, **Themes** can be applied to reports.

4. Click the **Themes** button to reveal a variety of report design schemes. Rest your mouse pointer over each one (without clicking) to see a preview on the report tab.

5. When you are finished, select **Angles** to apply that theme (themes are listed alphabetically and **ToolTips** appear when you rest the mouse pointer on a thumbnail).

> **Note:**   Standard **Font** type, size and alignment features are available on the **Format** tab.
> **Color** and **Font** schemes, set when choosing a **Theme**, can also be customised.

6. You can edit default report headers. Click on the report title, **April Invoices**, to select the text box. Click again to select the content. Replace the text with **April Invoice Report**.

Page margins ───────•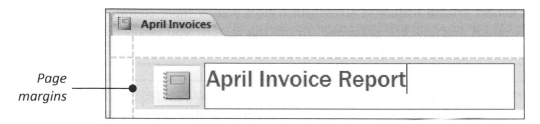

7. Then, using the same technique, change the column heading **Company Name** to **Supplier Name** (the original field name will not be changed).

8. Using the formatting features available in the **Font** group on the **Format** tab, make the header **Supplier Name** bold, underlined and coloured red.

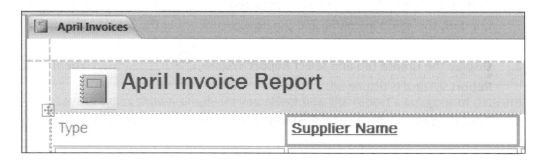

9. The broken lines that appear on the report indicate the boundaries of the page margins. It currently looks like the report will overflow the right edge of the paper (and go onto a second page). Display the **Page Setup** tab on the **Ribbon**.

> **Note:** **Show Margins** must be selected in the **Page Size** group to see margin boundaries.

10. Select **Landscape** from the **Page Layout** group. The orientation of the page is now changed (notice the effect this has on the page margin boundaries).

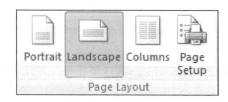

11. Display the **Design** tab and click the **Views** drop-down button. Select **Print Preview** to see how the report will appear when printed. Notice the useful page setup options available on the **Ribbon**, such as **Page Size**, **Margins**, **Page Layout** and **Columns**.

12. Click **Close Print Preview**. Save the report as **April Invoice Report** and close it, leaving the database open for the next exercise.

> **Note:** Notice that the report, **April Invoice Report**, now appears on the **Navigation** pane.

14. Close **Print Preview**. The report is displayed in **Design View** (any aspect of the report's layout can be changed here by adjusting the size, position and formatting of the text boxes shown).

15. Close the report, saving any changes.

16. Next, *Zahra* would like to create a brief summary report for all invoices submitted in *April*. She only wants to see the company name, invoice type and invoice amount. Display the **Create** tab and select **Report Wizard**.

17. From the **Tables/Queries** drop-down, make sure that the previous **Query: April Invoices** is selected.

> **Note:** Recall that **April Invoices** already selects the records required for this report.

18. From the **Available Fields** box, move **Type**, **Company Name** and **Amount** to **Selected Fields** box. Click **Next** and then **Next** again (skipping the grouping options).

19. Select **Company Name** again in the first drop-down box, and leave the sort order as **Ascending**.

20. Click **Next**. This time choose a **Columnar** layout and an **Orientation** of **Portrait**. Make sure the **Adjust the field width...** check box is ticked and click **Next**.

21. On this final screen, change the report title to **April Invoice Summary** and click **Finish** to automatically create the report and **Print Preview** the results.

22. Examine the report. All chosen fields for records selected by the **April Invoices** query are shown one at a time, sorted in alphabetical order by **Company Name**.

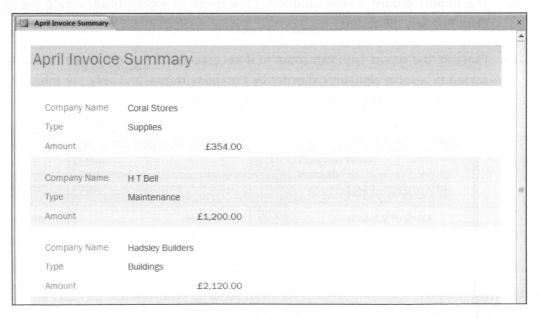

23. Close the report, saving any changes, and leave the **Transactions** database open for the next exercise.

7.24 Grouped Reports

The **Report Wizard** is particularly useful for producing reports where the records are **grouped** together based on shared values. For example, a report created on a table of staff members could have records grouped together by surname, age or department.

Activity:

1. *Zahra* would like a report containing a list of all companies in the **Transactions** database that have submitted an invoice. She only wants to see the invoice type, invoice number, the company name and the invoice amount in the report. She also wants the records to be grouped together by the type of invoice (e.g. **Training, Maintenance, Supplies**).

2. With the **Transactions** database open, display the **Create** tab and select **Report Wizard**.

3. Click the **Tables/Queries** drop-down button and select **Table: Invoices** to select the whole **Invoice** table. From the **Available Fields** area, move the fields **Type**, **Invoice**, **Company Name** and **Amount**.

4. Click **Next**. This screen can be used to group records in the report.

5. With **Type** selected, click [>]. Records will now be grouped by invoice **Type** (meaning that records will be grouped together wherever their **Type** values are the same).

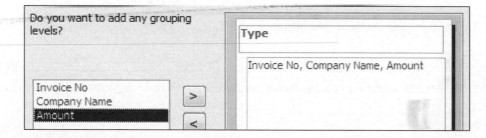

> **Note:** You can group records by more than one field. Records are initially grouped based on the <u>first</u> selected field. Then, *within each grouping*, records are grouped further based on the second selected field, and so on.

6. Click **Next** and then sort records by **Company Name** in **Ascending** order.

7. Click **Next**. Try selecting each **Layout** type and observing the preview. Notice that the layout types are different from those available for non-grouped reports.

8. Choose a **Layout** of **Stepped** (the most commonly used) and an **Orientation** of **Landscape**.

9. Make sure the **Adjust the field width...** check box is ticked and then click **Next**. On the final screen, change the report title to **Invoices By Type**.

10. The **Report Wizard** is now complete. Click **Finish** to automatically create the report and **Print Preview** the results.

11. Examine the report. All invoices of the same type are grouped together and *then* sorted (in ascending alphabetical order) by **Company Name**.

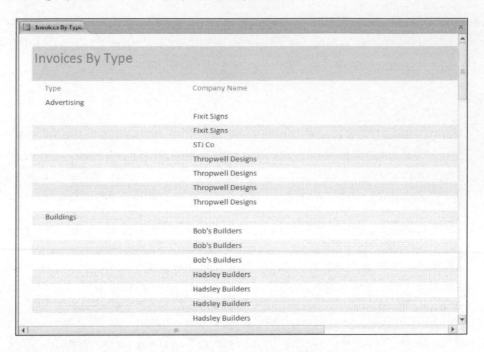

12. Close **Print Preview**, then close the report, saving any changes.

13. Close the **Transactions** database.

7.25 Report Summaries

When creating a report, it is possible to add useful summarised statistics for each of the numeric fields included (i.e. summed values, mean average values, and minimum/maximum values).

Activity:

1. Open the **Attendees** database. *Zahra* would like to create a report showing the age of all visitors to the *Pirate's Cove*, grouped by the type of ticket bought. She is also interested to find out the average, minimum and maximum ages of visitors.

2. Display the **Create** tab and click **Report Wizard** again. Select **Table: Visitors** from the **Tables/Queries** drop-down box.

3. From the **Available Fields** box, move **Ticket Type** and **Age** into the **Selected Fields** box.

4. Click **Next**, and then group the records based on **Ticket Type**.

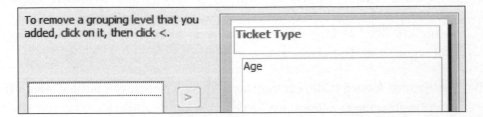

5. Click **Next**, and then click the **Summary Options** button at the bottom of the dialog box. From here it is possible to calculate summary statistics for each of the selected numeric fields in your report.

6. Place a tick in the **Avg** (average), **Min** and **Max** boxes for the **Age** field.

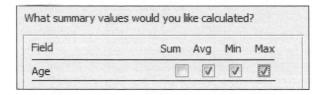

7. Click **OK**.

8. Then, click **Next** on the **Report Wizard** dialog box. This time, choose a layout style of **Block** (to see the effect of this layout type) and an **Orientation** of **Portrait**.

9. Click **Next**.

10. Change the report title to **Visitor Summary Report** and click **Finish**. The report is created and the results shown in **Print Preview**.

11. Examine the report. All invoices are grouped together by **Ticket Type** with summary statistics at the bottom of each group (you may need to scroll down to see these).

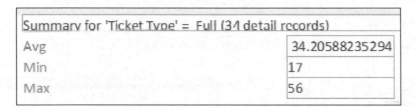

> **Note:**   *Access* is not always perfect in its report layout. For example, some fields may be displayed as ######## which means there is not enough space allocated to a field to display all of its contents. If this happens, you can adjust the size of the boxes in **Design View**.
>
>

12. Close **Print Preview**, then close the report, saving any changes.

13. Close the **Attendees** database.

7.26 Report Labels

Special sheets of sticky mailing labels are available to buy for use with printers. Usually A4 in size, each sheet features lots of small, rectangular address labels that can be peeled off and stuck on envelopes and delivery boxes. There are lots of label sizes available.

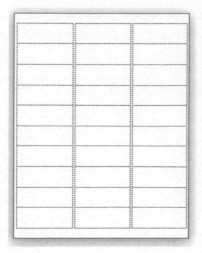

Activity:

1. Open the **Lost And Found** database. The **Addresses** table contains the contact details of park visitors who have lost private property at *Pirate's Cove*. To make sure items are returned to their owners, *Zahra* would like to print address labels for each record.

2. With the **Addresses** table selected in the **Navigation** pane, display the **Create** tab and click **Labels** in the **Reports** group. The **Label Wizard** dialog box appears.

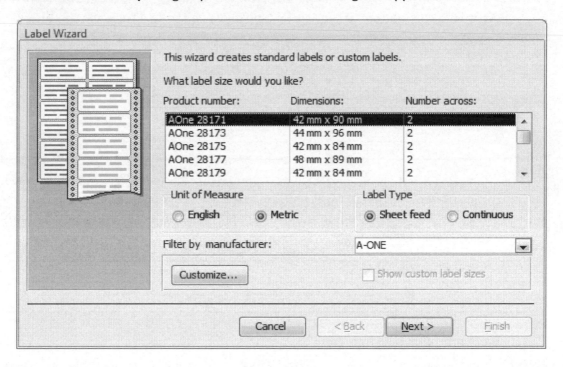

3. *Zahra* uses A4 sheets of labels with each label approximately 42mm high and 90mm wide. There are two labels on each row. Examine the options available on this screen, and then select the first type of label in the list.

4. Click **Next**. The default **Font** formatting settings are fine, so click **Next** again.

5. Add all available fields as shown on the following page. Leave a space between **Title**, **First Name** and **Surname**, and start each address field on a new line (by pressing <**Enter**>).

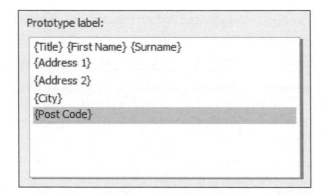

6. Click **Next**. Move **Surname** from **Available fields** into the **Sort by** box. Labels will now be sorted by surname.

7. Click **Next** and then click **Finish**. The labels are created, ready to be printed.

8. Close the **Lost And Found** database.

7.27 Importing Data

Data can be imported into an *Access* database from a variety of external sources. As with Excel, however, it is usually far simpler to only import data contained in plain text files.

Text files must contain information **delimited** (separated) by single characters such as tabs, spaces, or much more commonly, commas.

Activity:

1. Create a new database in this section's data files folder called **contractors**. *Zahra* has a list of people's wages who have worked at the *Pirate's Cove* recently and would like to import it. The list is currently stored in a simple **Comma Separated Values** (.csv) file.

2. Select the **External Data** tab and examine the types of file that can be imported from the **Import & Link** group.

3. Click the **Text File** button. The **Get External Data - Text File** dialog box appears.

4. Read the text on this screen, and then click the **Browse** button to find a file to import.

5. Locate the data files folder for this section. Then, select the file **Wages** and click **Open**.

6. Make sure **Import the source data into a new table...** is selected and then click **OK**. The **Import Text Wizard** is displayed. Notice that *Access* has recognised that the file contains data delimited (separated) by commas. A preview of the file's contents is shown.

7. With **Delimited** selected at the top of the dialog box, click **Next**.

8. Make sure **Comma** is selected as the delimiter and check **First Row Contains Field Names**. Click **Next**.

9. *Access* will attempt to automatically find the **Data Type** for each field based on the values imported. Click each column in the preview and notice that **Text** has been selected for the first two columns and **Currency** for the last two, which is correct. Click **Next**.

> **Note:**   Most complex database tables feature a **primary key**, which is simply the name given to fields that contain unique values for each individual record in a table. Although very useful and important, they are not required for simple tables.

10. Select **No primary key** and then click **Next**. In **Import to Table**, change the text to **Contractor Wages** and click **Finish**. When prompted to save the import steps, just click **Close**.

11. The new **Contractor Wages** table appears in the list. Open the table to view the data and check that everything has imported correctly.

12. Close the **contractors** database, saving any changes, and then close Access.

7.28 Database Design Tips

If a database is well designed, it will be easy to use and allow you and others to enter and extract information quickly and accurately. So, when creating your own databases, it is always useful to consider the following points of good practice:

* Always take care when designing the structure of tables in your database. Think carefully about which fields are needed as they can be difficult to change later.

* When choosing fields, try to break information down into the smallest useful parts. For example, a person's name could be broken down into title, first and last name. This allows you to manipulate the data with more precision.

* Consider the information that you want to get <u>out</u> of a database. This will help you to identify any fields, tables, queries and reports needed.

* Choose the right data types to ensure that only information in the correct format is entered into a table (this a very simple form of **data validation**).

* If you are creating a database to replace or improve an existing paper-based system, gather together all forms and use these as the basis for your table design (for example, each box that needs to be filled in on a form should be a separate field in a table).

* Ask colleagues or potential users for their opinions when developing a database. What types of information would they want to store and extract from the system?

* Give all of your fields, tables, queries and reports meaningful names that provide an indication of what they contain. If other people access your database it will then be much easier to navigate and use.

* Test tables, reports and queries to make sure that the data they store, select and present is correct, accurate and "fit for purpose".

On occasion, it may be useful to **code** information in a table. For example, in a staff database, codes may be used to refer to departments: *CS* for *Customer Services*, *TS* for *Technical Support*, *HO* for *Head Office*, and so on. Coding information can reduce the space used by a database and allow quicker data entry with fewer errors. Of course, you should always create meaningful codes whenever you use them.

> **Note:** Coding information may also be of use in other applications such as *Excel*. For coding to work, however, everyone must know the codes and what they mean.

> **Note:** Always respect and value information – especially if that information belongs to someone else – and treat it with the care it deserves. Keep your databases safe and secure and never disclose private or sensitive information to anyone who does not have permission to use it.

7.29 Data Capture Forms

It is not always practical for people to enter information directly into a database. For example, colleagues or customers may complete paper-based forms and then send them to you. In this case, the information must be **input** into the database. However, as it is important for all records to be consistent and store the same kinds of information, data capture forms should be used.

For example, visitors to the *Pirate's Cove* who misplace personal possessions are required to complete a *Lost Item Report*. To make sure all of the required information is obtained, *Zahra* created a **data capture form** in *Word* that can be printed out when needed. This is shown below and can also be found in the data files folder for this section (**Lost Item Report**).

> **Note:** Notice that the boxes on the form map directly to the fields in the database.

> **Note:** These days, many paper-based forms can be read by special optical character readers to save you having to input information manually. These will automatically place data into the correct fields in a database

7.30 Next Steps

Well done! You have now completed all of the exercises in this section. If you feel you are ready to test your knowledge and understanding of the topics covered, move on to the following **Develop Your Skills** activities. If there are any features of *Microsoft Access* that you are unsure about, you should revisit the appropriate exercises and try them again before moving on.

If you are interested in exploring some of *Microsoft Access's* more powerful features, why don't you use the Internet to find out a little more about the following advanced topics.

Feature	Description
Forms	Forms are another object in an *Access* database. They can be thought of as an interface to your database and are often used to control data entry or to present information to users in a very specific way. They are generally used to show and edit one record at a time and are extremely useful when creating a database for other people to use.
Validation	In addition to **Data Type** restrictions, simple validation rules can check values entered into a field for accuracy. For example, validation rules can check that a telephone number is a certain length or that a postcode uses the correct pattern of letters and numbers.
Primary Keys	It is an advantage to have one field in a table that uniquely identifies each record. That way, any record can be referred to individually and duplicate data will be prevented. For example, in a table of motor vehicles, registration number would be a good choice for primary key as the values it contains will always be unique for each record.
Advanced Queries	In addition to the simple queries described in this section, you can also create more advanced queries which summarise data or perform useful actions such as creating, editing and deleting records.
Calculated Fields	Similar to *Excel*, queries and reports can include calculated fields which contain formulas. These fields are calculated whenever needed, but do not exist as separate fields in any table. For example, if a table contains a **Price** field and a **Discount** field, it is not necessary to have a **Discounted Price** field. This value can (and should) be calculated wherever it is needed.
Macros	Macros are a powerful feature of most practical databases. They are commands which can be triggered by buttons on forms (e.g. press a button to close a form and open a different one) or by events (e.g. when a table is updated, run a report).

Develop Your Skills...

At the end of every section you get the chance to complete two activities. These will help you to develop your skills and prepare for your exam. Don't forget to use the planning and review checklists at the back of the book to help organise and review your work.

> **Note:** Answers to these activities are provided in this section's **Sample Solutions** folder.

Develop Your Skills: Event Booking Database

In this activity you will be asked to create a simple database for *Zahra*. You will need to use all of the ICT skills that you have learned in this section to plan, develop and present an appropriate solution.

Activity 1

Next month we're planning to host a number of special evening events for visitors attending the *Pirate's Cove* pool. As space will be strictly limited at each event, we will need to create a database to record visitor bookings – can you help?

Start by creating a database called **evening events** in the data file folder for this section, and then add a table called **Bookings**. The table will need an *event code*, an *event name*, a *location*, a start *date*, a start *time,* and an event *duration* (in minutes). Set up the appropriate fields, data types and properties.

The first event we have planned is for a show called **Pirates Have Talent**. The event has a code *E001* and is a *90 minute* show in the *Large Pool* at *8pm* on the *first* day of next month. Enter the record and make sure all the data is fully displayed in the table.

Oh, I forgot to mention that we will be charging *admission* for each event. Add another field to the table and include the charge *£8.50* for the first show.

Enter a new event, *E002*, called **Celebrity Walk the Plank**. The event costs *£9* and is a *2* hour show based in the *Large Pool* at *6pm* on the *third* day of next month. Enter the record and make sure that all the data is fully displayed.

Finally, print the table and then close the database.

Develop Your Skills: Age Analysis

In this activity you will be asked to create a detailed database report for *Zahra*. You will need to use all of the advanced ICT skills that you have learned in this section to create a suitable solution. It may help you to break the problem down into smaller parts first.

Activity 2

You have just received the following note from *Zahra*:

> I need to find out how many Junior and Senior ticket holders have attended an activity at Pirate's Cove. Can you find out this information for me please? Thanks, Zahra.

Using the **Bookings** database, create a query based on the **Reservations** table that selects all records where **Ticket Type** is either **Junior** or **Senior**. Run the query, note the number of records selected (31), and then save the query as **Tickets**.

> I forgot to mention, from the records found, can you also tell me how many attended an activity on or before August 1st 2011, and what that activity's code was? Thanks again, Zahra.

Edit the **Tickets** query so that only records where the **Visit Date** field is less than or equal to **01/08/2011** are selected. Add the **Activity** field to the query and then run it (25 records).

> One last thing – for the records you have found, can you include the names of each visitor and then sort the list alphabetically by surname? Can you then create a report based on this data? Z.

Edit the **Tickets** query so that the **Title**, **First Name** and **Last Name** fields are included in the query, and sort the **Last Name** field in ascending order. Run and save the query, and then create a simple tabular report based on it. Change the report's title to **Concessions** and the page orientation to landscape. Save the report as **Concessions** and print it.

Internet & E-Mail

8 | Internet & E-Mail

8

Hi, my name's John...

I work in the *IT Centre* at *Big Planet Theme Park's* head office – a building that only staff members are allowed to enter. It's my job to make sure all of the ICT systems in the park work properly by fixing problems and keeping everything up to date with the latest hardware and software upgrades.

A lot of my time is spent providing ICT support directly to park staff via e-mail, which is a really quick and easy way to communicate with people. However, even though I'm a computer expert, I'm still often faced with problems I don't know how to fix. Fortunately, the answers can usually be found on the Internet... if you know where to look, of course.

It is worth remembering that using e-mail and the Internet in education or at work is slightly different to using it at home. As you will find out in this section, to protect you and your place of study or employment, there are usually strict rules on what you can and can't do online.

What you will learn:

In this chapter you will use an Internet browser and the *Microsoft* e-mail program *Outlook* to help *John* complete a number of everyday tasks at *Big Planet Theme Park*.

Knowledge, skills and understanding:

* ✱ Use an Internet browser to successfully search for and download information

* ✱ Learn to evaluate the relevance of the information that you find online

* ✱ Avoid common pitfalls and be aware of copyright and other legal issues

* ✱ Use e-mail and the Internet to communicate with others

* ✱ Work accurately, safely and securely

Data files

 The files needed to complete the activities in this section are provided in the **Section 8** data folder (see note on page **vii** to download these files). Files that you create or receive by e-mail can also be saved to the same folder.

8.1 Internet Basics

The **Internet**, or net for short, is a global network of linked ICT devices that allow people from all over the world to communicate and share information. Many different types of devices are able to connect to the Internet, from desktop and laptop computers to mobile phones and printers. By connecting to the Internet, both you and your equipment are able to interact with and benefit from the many features and services that it offers.

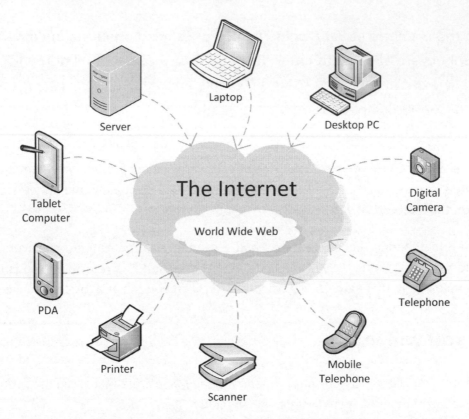

Most people use the Internet to access the **World Wide Web**. This is the name given to a vast collection of interconnected files called **web pages**. At its most basic, each web page contains information in the form of text and images. However, most web pages today also contain a variety of other multimedia features including video, music and interactive programs.

> **Note:** The World Wide Web is not the same thing as the Internet – in fact, "the web" is just one of the many services that runs on the Internet.

To move between web pages on the Internet you use **hyperlinks**. With a single click of the mouse (or tap of the finger), a hyperlink allows you to quickly and easily move to another web page anywhere on the World Wide Web. As each page links to other pages, which in turn link to many more, you can see where the concept of a "web" of information comes from.

> **Note:** Web pages are stored on computers called **servers**. These are very similar to your own home, school or college computer, but they are always connected to the Internet and are accessible to everyone.

© CiA Training Ltd 2012

When combined, two or more related web pages form a **website**. This is a fairly loose term which refers to any collection of web pages that belong together (in the same way that the individual pages of a printed magazine belong together). Most web pages in a website also share the same basic design features and are usually located on the same server.

8.2 Connecting to the Internet

As you learned in Section 1, there are many ways of connecting compatible ICT devices to the Internet. The easiest technique is to use cables to link computing hardware and peripherals directly to a router/modem (which in turn connects to the Internet). However, it is becoming more and more practical for modern mobile devices to use wireless technologies instead.

> **Note:**   Most individuals and organisations use an **Internet Service Provider** (**ISP**) to gain access to the Internet. As well as handling network connections, service providers also rent any necessary hardware such as routers/modems.

Short-range Wi-Fi connections are ideal for people "on the move" who need to access Internet resources on their laptops, tablet computers or mobile phones. Connecting is usually a simple case of finding a public network and logging on – it really is that easy! In fact, it is so convenient that you can now commonly find **Wi-Fi access points** (or **hotspots**) in many public places, from school and work to coffee shops, airports, hotels, and even trains and planes.

> **Note:**   Wi-Fi access is provided by wireless routers/modems that broadcast their name (known as an **SSID**, or Service Set Identifier) for users within range to find. The closer the device, the better the signal strength and faster your connection.

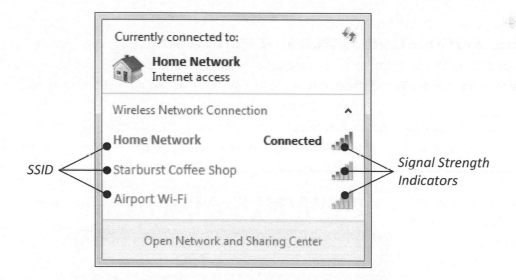

> **Note:**   When out and about, you may need to pay a small charge to connect to and use a public Wi-Fi access point. As you learned in Section 2 (Exercise 2.25), you should always choose firewall settings appropriate to your location and connection type.

To make sure only authorised people can access a network, Wi-Fi access points are often protected by a **security key**. This is simply a password used by the owner of the wireless router/modem to control who logs on to their network and, in turn, the Internet. Whenever you try to connect to a password-protected Wi-Fi network, your device will usually prompt you to enter a security key.

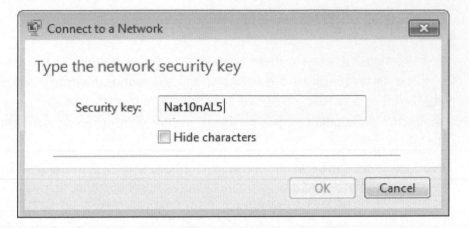

> **Note:** If you use a wireless router/modem at home, be sure to use your own strong and secure password (or security key) to prevent unauthorised access.

Devices such as mobile phones also have the ability to connect directly to the Internet. Although coverage is often limited to cities and towns, popular **3G** and **4G** data connections are provided by the mobile phone's service provider and offer access anywhere, anytime.

> **Note:** Be careful when using your mobile phone to access the Internet. Charges can sometimes be very high, especially if you use your device in another country.

8.3 Connection Types and Bandwidth

Information on the World Wide Web is not just available as simple text and images. Many types of applications, services and multimedia video and audio can also be accessed online. However, the amount of data that you can download is limited by your Internet connection's **bandwidth**. This is basically the speed of your Internet access and describes the amount of data that can be transferred over a network at any one time.

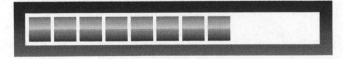

> **Note:** Think of your Internet connection as a pipe through which data flows like water. The larger the pipe – or bandwidth – the more information that can pass through it.

Low bandwidth can result in slow downloads and may restrict how you use the Internet. For example, you may not be able to watch videos online or download large files. The table below describes some of the most popular connection types in increasing order of bandwidth.

Connection	Description and Bandwidth
Dial-up	This is an older form of Internet connection which uses a modem connected to a standard telephone line. Although very slow, it is often the only cost effective connection type for people who live in remote rural areas.
Satellite	One of the most expensive types of Internet connection, satellites are also useful for people living in remote areas. Although still fairly slow by modern standards, satellite connections are usually much faster than dial-up.
3G and 4G	A popular form of wireless Internet access, 3G and 4G connections provide a direct link between an ICT device and a mobile phone operator's network. Connection speeds are highly variable and depend greatly on mobile phone signal strength. 4G is a newer, faster replacement for 3G.
DSL/Cable	Popular at home and in small business, DSL (Digital Subscriber Line) and cable connections are wired links to the Internet (using either special telephone lines or fibre optic cables). Because of the high bandwidth, they are usually known as **broadband** connections. Most wireless Wi-Fi routers/modems use DSL or cable connections to access the Internet.
Leased Lines	Popular in big business, these are dedicated wired connections to the Internet with extremely high bandwidth. They are often *very* expensive!

As an example, an MP3 song that is 5Mb in size would take approximately 10 to 15 minutes to download using a dial-up connection. Using a fast home broadband connection, however, this is reduced to less than one minute, and on a leased line only a few seconds.

> **Note:** Given the ever-increasing bandwidth requirements of the modern Internet, a fast and reliable broadband service is often the best choice for home and small business users who want to download lots of files and watch videos online.

8.4 Surfing the Web

The World Wide Web contains an enormous amount of information covering almost every subject you can think of. If that wasn't enough, vital services such as banking, shopping, health care, news and even education can now all be accessed online.

In fact, as the Internet has no international boundaries, you can interact with websites *anywhere* in the world, from local councils and businesses to multinational companies and organisations. To access this vast worldwide "web" of information, you must use a special type of software known as a **web browser**.

Activity:

1. *John* has created a website which he uses to help train new staff members at *Big Planet Theme Park*. It contains a lot of interesting information including files to download and links to other useful websites.

2. Start the *Internet Explorer* application found on your computer's **Start Menu**.

> **Note:**   *John* recommends that you use the popular *Internet Explorer* web browser. If you choose to use a different application, some of the features mentioned in this section may appear and function slightly differently to that described.

3. Click once in the **Address Bar** at the top of the browser window and enter the following website address: **www.bigplanetsupport.co.uk**

Address Bar

> **Note:**   Always make sure you enter a web address *precisely*. One character out of place and you may be taken to another website.

4. Press <**Enter**>. The *Big Planet Support* website's home page is downloaded and displayed.

Navigation links

> **Note:**   The first web page that you see when you visit a website is called the **home page**. It is the front door to a site and usually contains links to all other accessible areas.

5. Locate the **Navigation** hyperlinks on the left of the home page. These "links" will appear on every web page on the *Big Planet Support* website.

Note: To help you find your way around, it is standard practice for websites to include navigation hyperlinks at the top or left side of all pages on a website.

6. Move your mouse pointer over **Hyperlinks**. The pointer changes to a hand, 🖑, indicating this is a link to another web page.

7. Click <u>once</u> to display the **Hyperlinks** page (you should not double-click links), and then read the information about the types of hyperlink that exist.

8. Click the browser's **Back** button, ⬅, to return to the previous page.

Note: The **Back** button can be used to return to any web page viewed earlier in a session.

9. Notice that the browser's **Forward** button, ➡, is now available. Click this once to revisit the **Hyperlinks** page again.

Note: If you move back to a previously viewed web page, the **Forward** button can be used to move forward again (unless another link is clicked). If there are no more pages to move back or forward to, these buttons will become ghosted (inactive).

10. Next, click **Image Gallery** link from the **Navigation** hyperlinks on the left of the page, and then follow the **Cartoons** hyperlink.

Note: Notice that the **Cartoons** hyperlink also appears as a subentry under the **Image Gallery** hyperlink. This is a common website navigation technique.

11. Use the **Back** button to return to the *Big Planet Support* website's home page.

12. Leave the *Big Planet Support* website open for the next exercise.

8.5 Tabbed Browsing

Normally, when you click a hyperlink, the web page it connects to is downloaded and displayed (replacing the web page that was previously open). However, it is possible to have more than one page open at the same time, each contained within its own **Tab**.

> **Note:**   Tabs are a useful way to explore links without needing to navigate away from a web page. They can really help improve your productivity when browsing.

Activity:

1.   With the *Big Planet Support* website open, right-click once on the **Image Gallery** hyperlink. A pop-up shortcut menu appears.

> **Note:**   Notice that you can open the link in a new *window*, which will appear as a separate item on the *Windows* **Taskbar**. There is not much difference between opening new tabs and opening new windows. However, you will often find it easier to open new tabs as this keeps all of the websites you are browsing in one place.

2.   For this exercise, select **Open in new tab**.

> **Note:**   If you chose to use a web browser other than *Internet Explorer*, specific menu options such as **Open in new tab** may appear slightly differently to that described.

3.   The **Image Gallery** web page is opened in a new tab which appears at the top of the browser window.

4.   If the new tab is not automatically selected, click it once now to activate it.

Close Tab

5.   Click the **Computers** hyperlink shown on the **Image Gallery** page. Then, select any of the image previews (known as "thumbnails") to open a larger version of that picture.

> **Note:**   Each tab maintains its own list of recently viewed web pages that can be accessed using the **Forward** and **Back** buttons.

6.   Click the **Back** button once to return to the previous page (**Computers**).

7.   Notice that the active tab has a **Close Tab** button. Click this once to close the new tab and return to the first tab (which still shows the site's home page).

8.   Next, follow the **Useful Links** hyperlink. A page containing a number of hyperlinks to other websites is downloaded and displayed in the current tab.

> **Note:**   The creator of a web page can design a link to always open in a new tab/window.

9. Click any hyperlink that interests you from the **News and Current Affairs** group.

10. Notice that, this time, the linked web page is opened automatically in a new **Tab** (which may appear in its own window). The links were set up by *John* to do this when clicked.

> **Note:**   Each web page that you visit is recorded in your browser's **History**. This list of recently viewed items is stored for 20 days (by default) and can be used to revisit web pages again at a later date. If you would like to delete this log of your online activity you can do so at any time from within your browser's settings.

11. Feel free to explore the content of the selected website.

> **Note:**   To reload a page and download the most up-to-date information, click the browser's **Refresh** button, ↻ (also sometimes known as the **Reload** button).

12. When you are finished, close the new tab (or window, if the new tab appeared in one).

13. You can explore some of the other hyperlinks on the **Useful Links** page, but remember to close each tab when you are finished.

> **Note:**   Within your browser settings you can also set up a favourite website as your default **Home** page. This will always be displayed when you start the browser and can be returned to again at any time using the **Home** button, 🏠.

14. Leave the *Big Planet Support* website open for the next exercise.

8.6 Copying Text and Pictures

Text and pictures can easily be copied from the World Wide Web and used in other *Windows* applications. However, unless you have the permission of the owner or creator of these items, international **copyright** restrictions prohibit you from using them in your own work.

> **Note:**   It is <u>very important</u> that you do not use or distribute any material obtained from the Internet unless you are totally sure that copyright restrictions do not apply.

Activity:

1. The *Big Planet Support* website should still be open. As *John* created this website, he has given you permission to copy content from it during this exercise.

2. Click the **Information** hyperlink, and then follow the link to **Internet**.

3. Select the main body of text on this page (i.e. from "**This page contains information about the Internet…**" to "**…explore the World Wide Web for yourself.**").

> **Note:**   There are two ways of copying selected text from a web page: use either **<Ctrl C>** or right click and choose **Copy** from the shortcut menu that appears.

4.   Press <**Ctrl C**> on your keyboard. The selected text is copied to the **Clipboard**.

5.   Start *Microsoft Word* (and a new blank document).

6.   With the cursor flashing at the beginning of the empty document, click the **Paste** button on the **Ribbon**. The copied text from the web page is pasted into the new *Word* document.

> **Note:**   Notice that the formatting of the text is preserved. **Paste Special** (available via the **Paste** button's drop-down arrow) can be used if **Unformatted Text** is required.

7.   Without closing *Word*, use the **Taskbar** to return to your web browser application. Visit the **Image Gallery** page and then follow the link to **Places**. Click any picture that you like to view a larger version.

8.   Next, right click the picture to display a shortcut menu.

> **Note:**   **Save picture as** (or similar, depending on your chosen browser) can also be used to save a picture directly to your computer's **Picture** library.

9.   Select **Copy** (or similar, depending on your chosen browser) to copy the picture. Then, return to *Word* and paste the picture at the end of the document.

> **Note:**   This technique can be used to copy and paste text and pictures into most other *Microsoft Office* applications.

10.   Save the document as **information** in the folder for this section, and then close *Word*.

11.   Click the hyperlink labelled **Home** to return to the *Big Planet Support* home page.

> **Note:**   Nearly all web pages feature a link back to a website's main home page. Hint: if you can't find this, try clicking the site's logo at the top of the page.

12.   Leave the *Big Planet Support* home page open for the next exercise.

8.7   Search Engines and Keywords

The Internet can be used to find information on almost any subject you can think of. However, finding the exact information you want from the billions and billions of websites on the World Wide Web is not always easy. To help, you can use a **search engine**.

As you probably already know, a search engine is a website that you can use to search for **keywords** on other web pages. Although a search engine may look simple, behind the scenes it is connected to a very large and complex database. When you perform a search, the search engine *very quickly* selects every web page in the database that contains your keywords. These pages are then presented to you as a list of hyperlinks.

> **Note:**   The web pages that a search engine finds are often referred to as **hits**.

There are many useful search engines available on the web, some of which are more specialised than others. Today, the best and most popular *general* search engines include:

Google	**www.google.co.uk**
Bing	**www.bing.com**
Yahoo	**www.yahoo.co.uk**
Ask	**www.ask.com**

In this exercise you will use the *Google* search engine. This is probably the best search engine available and *John* highly recommends it for general everyday use. Of course, the search techniques that you learn in this exercise will apply equally well to any other search engine that you choose to use in the future.

Activity:

1. Your web browser should still be open. Enter **www.google.co.uk** into the **Address Bar** and press **<Enter>**. The **Google** search engine appears.

Search box

> **Note:**   All search engines have a search box where you can enter keywords, and a button to start the search. However, as websites change frequently, the page you see may not exactly match the screens shown in this section.

2. *John* is working on a research project and needs to find the names of competing *theme parks* in the *UK*. In the **Search** box, enter the keyword **park** and press **<Enter>**.

> **Note:** *Google* may automatically start searching as you enter keywords. It may also provide a number of search suggestions as you type. If the search text you are entering appears you can select it to save time.

3. *Google* finds every site in its database which contains the required keyword **park**. Make a note of the number of results found (which will be shown at the top of the page).

> park
>
> About 2,990,000,000 results (0.10 seconds)

> **Note:** Due to the ever-changing nature of the Web, you will probably find a different number of results than that shown above.

4. All of the web pages found are placed in order of relevance (the first ten or so are the *most* relevant and are shown first). Scan the results and notice that a number of pages have been found which have nothing to do with theme parks.

> **Note:** As well as providing hyperlinks to web pages where your keywords are found, *Google* also shows a small extract of the text on those pages.

5. Let's try to make the search more specific. At the top of the page, change the current keyword text to **theme park** and press **<Enter>**.

6. Fewer results are found. Scan the small extracts for each "hit" and notice that the web pages are now much more relevant.

> **Note:** The best way to find accurate and relevant information on the web is to use the most suitable keywords in your searches.

7. To narrow the search even further, change the keyword search text to **UK theme park**.

8. Press **<Enter>**. Fewer, more relevant results are found.

9. Have you noticed that the search keywords can appear in any order in the results? To search for the specific phrase **UK theme park** only (with all of the words in that *exact* order) place quotation marks around the keywords in the search box at the top of the page and press **<Enter>**.

> "UK theme park"
>
> About 41,600 results (0.15 seconds)

> **Note:** The quotation mark symbol can usually be inserted by pressing **<Shift 2>**.

10. The number of results will be further reduced and only web pages that feature the exact phrase "UK theme park" somewhere in the text will appear.

11. Recall that *John* was searching for the names of other competing theme parks in the UK. Examine the results found and then visit the web page that seems most relevant.

> **Note:** If you find it difficult to read the text on a web page you can adjust the **Zoom** level in your browser's settings.

12. If the selected web page does not contain the information *John* requires, click the **Back** button and try another. If the first set of *Google* search results is not relevant, you can view more by clicking the **Next** link (or similar) at the bottom of the page.

> **Note:** The first page you visit on a website may not contain all of the information you need, but other pages on that website might. You may need to explore.

13. Did you find a list of UK theme parks? If you did, well done! When you are finished, use the **Back** button to return to *Google's* home page.

14. For his research project, *John* also wants you to find out about the history of the *Ferris wheel*. In particular, he wants to know when the first one was created and who built it. Use *Google* now to find this information before moving on.

15. How did you do? Although there are many ways to search for this information, *John* used the keyword search **ferris wheel created by** to find out that George W. Ferris created the first Ferris wheel in 1893.

> **Note:** There are many possible keyword searches that will produce the same results.

16. Next, *John* recalls a famous quote he would like to include in his research project: "*Here age relives fond memories of the past, and here youth may savor the challenge and promise of the future*". So that *John* can use this quote, use *Google* now you find out who said it.

17. *John* used the search **"Here age relives fond memories of the past" quote** to find out that that it was *Walt Disney* who said this.

18. Well done. Return to the *Google* home page and leave it open for the next exercise.

8.8 Advanced Search Techniques

To help you perform more precise searches online, the - (minus) operator can be used to *exclude* keywords and find fewer results. The asterisk wildcard * can also be used to search for *partial phrases* where you are unsure of one or more words.

> **Note:** In searches, wildcards will find matches with anything and everything (and can produce a lot of hits). They are most effective when used with phrases in quotes.

Activity:

1. The *Google* search engine should still be open. As part of his research project, *John* would like to find the names of a few popular *international theme parks*. In the **Search** box, enter **theme parks** and press **<Enter>**.

2. *Google* again finds every site in its database which contains the required keywords. Make a note of the number of results and observe that many of the results *include* UK parks.

3. To refine the search and *exclude* UK parks, change the keyword text to **theme parks -UK**.

> theme parks -UK

> **Note:** Do not insert a space between the minus operator and the excluded keyword.

4. Press **<Enter>**. Fewer, more relevant results are found. Visit some of the sites shown and find the names of one or two international theme parks. When you are finished, return to *Google*.

5. Next, *John* wants to find out about the first ever *steel roller coaster*. He wants to know when it was built and what is was called, but isn't at all interested in *wooden* roller coasters. Use *Google* to find this information now.

6. Did you find the relevant information? *John* used the keyword search **first steel -wooden roller coaster** to find out that the first tubular steel roller coaster, the *Matterhorn*, was opened in 1959.

7. *John* would now like to include a few interesting facts about rollercoasters in his project, such as the *fastest*, *steepest* and *longest* in the world. Return to *Google* and, in the **Search** box, enter **"the world's * roller coaster"** (including quotes) and press **<Enter>**.

> "the world's * roller coaster"

8. *Google* finds web pages with the exact phrase **"the world's * roller coaster"**, but with *one or more* words in place of the wildcard asterisk symbol, *****.

9. Try to find information on the world's fastest, highest, steepest, longest and oldest roller coasters. When you are finished, return to *Google*.

> **Note:** You can use more than one asterisk wildcard in your search queries.

10. To show you can use the asterisk wildcard, *John* would like you to perform searches and find the missing words (shown with a ❓) for each the following famous proverbs:

    a) A ❓ in the hand is worth two in the bush

    b) A ❓ is worth a thousand words

    c) A ❓ is as good as a rest

    d) A ❓ in time saves ❓

    e) A ❓ saved is a ❓ earned

    f) Remember, remember, the ❓ of ❓

> **Note:** Many search engines also allow you to restrict your keyword searches to images, videos, documents, news sites, books, shopping sites, and so on. Advanced search options also allow you to search for items published within a specific time frame.

11. Finally, use *Google* to search for information about the *waltzer* and explore the many advanced search features available on the site (usually available towards the top or left of the page). For example, try restricting your search to news, images, videos and shopping sites, or specifying a publication date in the past year, month, week or day.

12. When you are finished exploring *Google's* advanced search features, leave your web browser open and continue on to the next exercise.

8.9 Search Tips

When you use a search engine such as *Google* to find information, remember these following useful tips:

* Keep your search simple and only use keywords that are important and relevant (search engines will generally ignore common words like **and**, **an**, **of**, **where**, **when**, **is**, etc).

* The more precise your keywords, the more likely you are to find useful results. For example, **theme park** will produce more specific results than just **park**.

* Be descriptive and enter keywords as you think they will appear on a web page. For example, **park admission prices** will produce better results than **park entry costs**.

* If initial results are too broad, you can refine your search by adding more keywords.

* Remember that you can use quotation marks to find specific phrases.

* Use the minus operator to exclude results that contain keywords you do not want, or the asterisk wildcard to complete partial phrases.

* It doesn't matter if you use upper or lower case text.

* Don't bother to include general punctuation marks as these are usually ignored.

✱   Be prepared to follow more than one search result to find the information you need. It
      really does pay to be patient and explore a selection of results.

> **Note:**   These search techniques will work with all general search engines, not just *Google*.

Don't believe everything you read on the Internet! Unlike professionally published material such
as books and newspapers, there is no quality control online – the contents of a website do not
need to be reviewed, approved or checked for accuracy. As such, you need to stop and consider
how trustworthy information is <u>before</u> you use it. This is not always easy to do, but the useful tips
provided in Section 1 will help.

8.10 Favourite Websites

As you browse the web you will probably visit web pages that you would like to return to later. If
so, use your browser's **Favorites** (or **Bookmarks**) feature to record a link to the site.

Activity:

1.   Enter the following address into the **Address Bar**: **www.bigplanetsupport.co.uk**. Press
      <Enter> and the *Big Planet Support* website's home page is downloaded and displayed.

2.   To bookmark this site and make it easier to visit next time (without needing to enter the

      site's address), click the **Favorite** button on the browser's toolbar, ⭐.

> **Note:**   If you chose to use a web browser other than *Internet Explorer*, the **Favorite**
>   button may be labelled as **Bookmarks** or similar. The process for adding bookmarks
>   will also be slightly different to that described here (but the end result is the same).

3.   The **Favorites** task pane appears. To add the current site as a **Favorite**, click the **Add to**

      favourites button, [Add to favorites ▼], to display the **Add a Favorite** dialog box.

4.   Change the **Name** of the **Favorite** to **Big Planet Support** and click **Add**. The address of the
      web page is now saved in your **Favorites**.

5. Let's add another. On the *Big Planet Support* website, navigate to the **Useful Links** page and click the first link under **News and Current Affairs** to open that site.

6. Click the **Favorite** button on the browser's toolbar and then the **Add to favourites** button again. This time, rename the **Favorite** as **News**.

> **Note:**   You can organise your **Favorites** into folders to make them easier to find later.

7. Click the **New folder** button, New folder , to create a new folder in your **Favorites**. Enter the title **Useful Links**.

> **Note:**   Using the **Create in** drop-down box, you can create folders inside of other folders.

8. With the root **Favorites** folder selected in the **Create in** drop-down box, click **Create**. A new subfolder is created in your **Favorites** folder (which is automatically selected in the **Add a Favorite** dialog box). Click **Add** to add the web page to your **Favorites**.

9. Close the new tab to return to the *Big Planet Support* site (or window, if the new tab appeared in one).

10. Next, click the **Favorite** button on the browser's toolbar. Make sure the **Favorites** tab is selected to view your **Favorites** folder.

> **Note:**   Notice that you can also access your browser's **History** from here. This is a list of hyperlinks to your most recently viewed pages.

11. Examine the contents of the **Favorites** folder and notice that the **Big Planet Support** entry and the **Useful Links** folder both appear.

12. Click **Useful Links** to expand the folder and view its contents. Then, click the **News** item that you created earlier. The **Favorites** task pane closes and you are taken to the web address for that **Favorite**.

13. Use the **Favorites** task pane to return to the *Big Planet Support* site.

> **Note:**   **Favorites** can be dragged and dropped into folders. To delete a **Favorite**, simply right click it and select **Delete** from the shortcut menu that appears.

14. Open the **Favorites** task pane again. Then, drag and drop **Big Planet Support** into the **Useful Links** folder. This is a useful technique for organising your **Favorites**.

15. Next, right click the **Useful Links** folder and select **Delete**. At the prompt, select **Yes**. The folder *and all of its contents* are deleted.

16. Leave the *Big Planet Support* website open for the next exercise.

8.11   Downloading Files

As well as simple text and images, the Internet can be used to download various multimedia files. These range from music and video to games and software applications. Useful files such as spreadsheets, presentations, publications and databases can also be downloaded that you can open and use in *Microsoft Office*.

Activity:

1. The *Big Planet Support* website should still be open. Visit the **Downloads** page using the **Navigation** hyperlinks and read the text displayed.

2. There are a number of files that you can download. Right-click on the hyperlink **Apollo.wav** (an audio file) to display a shortcut menu.

3. From the list of options that appear, select **Save target as**.

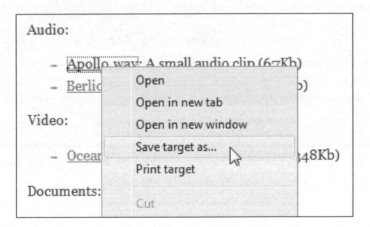

> **Note:**   If you chose to use a web browser other than *Internet Explorer*, this option may appear slightly differently (e.g. **Save link as** or **Save file as**).

> **Note:**   If you left-click a file download link, your browser will attempt to download and open it automatically. However, as files downloaded in this way are only saved temporarily on your computer, this method is not recommended.

4. The **Save As** dialog box appears. Locate the data files folder for this section and then click **Save**. The file is downloaded from the Internet and saved on your computer.

5. Using the same technique, download the files **Ocean.avi** (a video file), **Testimonial.doc** (a *Word* document) and **Turnover.xls** (an *Excel* spreadsheet) to the data files folder.

> **Note:**   File downloads from the Internet can be a potential source of viruses that can damage your computer. However, the files available on the *Big Planet Support* website are quite safe to use.

6. Open your **Documents** folder and navigate to the data files for this section. The four downloaded files appear. Double-click **apollo** to play the music file in your computer's default music player. When the music finishes playing, close the media player.

7. Next, double-click the video file **ocean**. The file is played in your computer's default video player. When it finishes playing, close the media player.

8. Then, double-click the document **Testimonial**. When opened, this document appears in *Microsoft Word*.

> **Note:**   *Microsoft Office* applications know when a file has been downloaded from the Internet. To protect your computer from any viruses they may contain, they are opened in **Protected View** which only lets you read the content. To edit the file, click the **Enable Editing** button.

9. Close *Word* and then double-click the **Turnover** file. It opens in *Microsoft Excel*.

10. Close *Excel* and your **Documents** library, leaving only your web browser open.

8.12 Using Online Forms

Online forms are used across the Internet wherever information needs to be entered by users. Using simple interface components such as text fields, buttons and checkboxes, online forms can be used to communicate with other people, log-in to websites, complete applications, and order goods and services. In fact, the possible uses of online forms are endless.

Activity:

1. The *Big Planet Support* website should still be open. Visit the **Online Forms** page using the **Navigation** hyperlinks and read the text displayed. *John* has created a number of example online forms that you can use.

2. Select the **Booking Form** link to open the **Online Library Services** form. Examine the text boxes (or fields) on this page, and then enter the following information:

> User Name: **John Olivier**
> Account Number: **913486739**
> Book Title: **OCR Cambridge Nationals in ICT**
> Author's Name: **CiA Training Ltd**

> **Note:** You can use <Tab> and <Shift Tab> to move between form fields.

3. Enter a starting date of next Monday (in the form **DD/MM/YY**), and choose to be notified by e-mail when the book becomes available.

4. When you have completed the boxes form, click the **Submit** button at the bottom of the page. A confirmation page appears indicating that your information has been received.

> **Note:** When you *submit* a form, all of the information you have entered is sent to a server to be processed.

5. Close the booking form tab (or window, if it opened in one), returning to the *Big Planet Support* site's **Online Forms** page. Finally, try opening and completing some of the other forms shown on this page. Feel free to make up information to enter into the text boxes.

6. When you are finished, close your web browser and any open tabs.

8.13 Communicating Online

There are many ways to interact with other people online. As the Internet has no international boundaries, you can talk freely to friends, family, colleagues and organisations throughout the world – instantly and with little or no cost. In fact, modern ICT has completely changed the way we communicate with each other and how we do business, giving us access to a worldwide network of advice, debate, feedback, opinion, conversation, support and knowledge. The following table briefly describes the most popular technologies available today.

Technology	Description
Chat Rooms	Chat rooms are online spaces that allow people with similar interests to come together and talk about topics which interest them. A keyboard is used to type text into a shared window which everyone connected to the chat room sees.
Instant Messages	With instant messaging tools you always know when your contacts are online, and you can easily start a text or video based conversation in "real-time". These tools are very useful for communicating with colleagues instantly and can be used to request help and support.
E-mail	Short for electronic mail, this basic ICT system for sending short messages and files to other people online is still the most dominant form of online communication – especially in business. You will learn more about e-mail later in this section.
VoIP	*Voice over Internet Protocol* (VoIP) software such as *Skype* can turn your PC into a video phone, allowing you to talk to friends, family, colleagues and customers anywhere in the world.

Conferencing	Using the same kind of technology as VoIP, video conferencing tools allow two or more people to attend an online meeting together. It is very popular in business and saves people from needing to travel large distances to meet up.
Forums	Businesses and people with similar interests can share their views and post messages on specifically dedicated websites called forums or bulletin boards. These can also be used for requesting help and support from others who are often experts in their fields.
Blogs	A blog (which is short for web-log) is simply an online diary in which you can "post" anything that is on your mind. They are very easy to set up and readers are often able to comment on individual posts.
The Cloud	The "cloud" is the name given to a range of online storage areas and Internet-based tools and services. Popular collaboration technologies such as *Office 365* and *GoogleDocs* operate in the cloud, allowing people to access, create, share and edit files from anywhere in the world using only their web-browser.
Social Networking	Social networking sites such as *Facebook* and *Twitter* allow people to communicate with friends and family online by sharing photos, videos, links and comments. You can also chat with friends in real time anywhere in the world. However, networking is not seen as an appropriate use of your time at work and could get you into trouble.

> **Note:** Don't forget that you can use *Microsoft Office's* tracking features to share and co-create documents with others. These can be exchanged using e-mail or can be stored in a shared location in the cloud or on a local intranet.

Along with simple mobile phone calls and SMS text messages, the technologies mentioned above help people interact and work together "on the move". They also make it much easier for people to work from home (known as **teleworking**), which reduces office and travel costs and gives employees more flexibility in their job. However, although working from home sounds great, it often leads to time-wasting, poor teamwork, and negative feelings of isolation and loneliness.

8.14 Netiquette

When you are working online it is very easy to forget your basic manners and say things that you would never say in a face-to-face conversation. So, before you interact with others online or via e-mail, try to familiarise yourself with the rules of **netiquette** – "network etiquette":

* Behave online as you would in real life and respect other people and their opinions.

* Be clear and keep your contributions brief, accurate and relevant.

* Be tolerant of others and never send angry messages (known as **flames**).

* Use appropriate language (especially when representing a business).

* Don't use UPPERCASE words – this is the same as shouting.

* Make sure your contributions are spelled correctly and make sense.

* Avoid forwarding irrelevant junk e-mail, jokes and chain messages.

* Always respect copyright and data protection laws.

* Don't post anything that could get you into trouble or embarrass you in the future!

> **Note:** Always remember that your views and opinions are as valid as anyone else's, and your contributions or requests for help and advice online are very welcome.

Unfortunately, no matter how well-mannered you are online, you will eventually read comments or interact with others who are not so considerate. Inappropriate behaviour and offensive material is a constant problem on the Internet and you will do well to simply ignore it. However, if any behaviour or content is particularly offensive or worrying (for example, if you feel you are being bullied or that another person is at risk) you <u>must</u> report it to a person in authority.

> **Note:** Whether at work or in education, you have a responsibility to act professionally and make a good impression when communicating with others.

8.15 Staying Safe

The Internet is an amazing resource and people find new uses for it every day. However, all of this potential and freedom does have a price – your privacy and safety. Fortunately, you can avoid many of the risks involved in using ICT with a little common sense:

* Firstly, always be careful when downloading files of any sort from the Internet. Unless you *completely* trust the source of the file, it may contain damaging viruses and other malware that can harm ICT devices or allow criminals to steal information from it.

* If you do download a file, scan it <u>first</u> using the antivirus software before you open or run it (if you are using a computer outside of the home, locate the antivirus software that is installed and learn how to scan files with it).

* To prevent other people from accessing your computer and stealing the data it contains, always make sure your **Windows Firewall** is running. Furthermore, if you receive any security alerts from *Windows*, attend to them immediately.

* If you ever submit private information online (for example, when purchasing items on shopping websites), make sure the padlock symbol, 🔒, appears in your browser's **Address Bar**. This helps guarantee that nobody else can see what you are doing and stops criminals getting hold of personal details.

✳ When at work or in education, remember that personal use of the Internet is usually not allowed. If you ignore this simple rule you may get into a lot of trouble.

✳ Always keep your ICT devices up-to-date by regularly downloading the latest antivirus and software security updates.

✳ Always ignore invitations to win prizes and download free software and files – these will often contain viruses and other malware. Also keep an eye out for fake websites and only purchase items from legitimate and well known sources.

✳ Do not always trust that people are who they say they are. This may seem obvious, but people can very easily exaggerate or lie about their identities to mislead you. <u>Never</u> give personal contact details to – or arrange to meet offline – people you don't know.

✳ Avoid illegally downloading copyright music, videos and pirated programs. As well as getting you into a lot of trouble, these files can often contain viruses and other malware.

✳ When browsing the web, sites can place small text files called **cookies** on your ICT device. These usually store useful information such as log-in details or shopping cart contents, but can also be used to track your surfing habits and build marketing profiles.

Remember that it is your responsibility to protect your own safety and that of others who you work or study with. If you allow a virus to gain access to and damage your own computer, it can also spread and cause harm to other systems that you share a network with – so be careful!

> **Note:** Keep in mind that your connection to the Internet can easily break down (often as a result of hardware failure). If you store files in the cloud or depend on the Internet to work, this can have serious consequences.

> **Note:** Hackers often use illegal **Denial of Service** attacks to bombard web services with traffic (simulating lots of people trying to access the service all at once). This overloads the site and prevents genuine users from gaining access.

8.16 E-mail Basics

By far the most popular use of the Internet today is sending and receiving electronic mail (**e-mail**). E-mail is an extremely important communication tool that allows people to send messages to other ICT users anywhere in the world instantly. Think about how much more quickly business documents can be sent using e-mail rather than by traditional surface or airmail.

The following exercises will introduce you to *Microsoft Outlook*, a popular **Personal Information Management (PIM)** tool that allows you to send, receive and organise e-mail messages. *Outlook* can also be used to attach files to messages, maintain an address book of contacts, and create useful calendars and to-do lists.

> **Note:**   There are many online services that you can use to send and receive your personal e-mail. However, in most professional situations, an e-mail program such as *Outlook* is used.

Before you can fully use *Outlook* or any other e-mail system, you will first need your own **e-mail address**. In the same way that a phone number uniquely identifies you on a telephone network, your e-mail address uniquely identifies you on the Internet.

E-mail addresses all follow the same general format, as the following example shows:

john@bigplanetsupport.co.uk

The **@** symbol is pronounced "at" and is used to separate a person's username from the name of their organisation or Internet Service Provider (ISP).

> **Note:**   If you do not know your <u>own</u> e-mail address, contact the person who runs your computer network. If you are a home user, contact your Internet Service Provider.

8.17 Using Microsoft Outlook

Outlook stores all of your e-mail messages in a number of different folders. This folder structure is known as your **mailbox**.

Activity:

1.   Start *Microsoft Outlook*.

> **Note:**   If you are prompted to connect to the Internet or select an *Outlook* personal profile, do that now.

> **Note:**   If the **Internet Connection Wizard** or **Add New Account** dialog box appears when you start *Outlook*, your computer is not yet ready to use e-mail. It is recommended that you find somebody who can help you set up an account.

2.   Examine the *Outlook* window. In particular, locate the familiar **File** tab, **Ribbon**, **Status Bar**, **Quick Access Toolbar** and **Zoom** controls.

> **Note:**   The various panes can be resized or hidden by dragging their boundary bars.

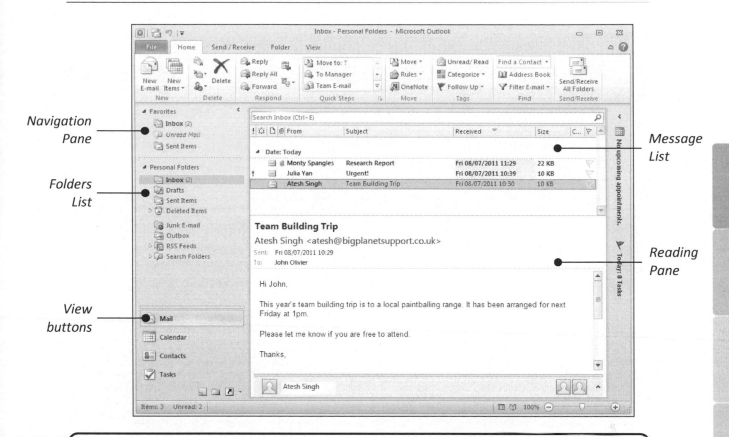

> **Note:** Your screen may not look exactly like that shown above as there are many display options available.

3. Locate the **Navigation Pane** on the left of the window. If your **Inbox** folder is not currently selected in the **Folders List**, select it now (make sure the **Mail** view button is selected, as shown above).

> **Note:** If your screen does not match *John's*, display the **View** tab and click the **Change View** drop-down button in the **Current View** group. Select **Compact**. Then, in the **Layout** group, make sure **Navigation Pane** is set to **Normal**, **Reading Pane** is set to **Bottom**, and **To-Do Bar** is set to **Minimized**.

4. All messages that you receive are placed in your **Inbox** folder. These will appear in the **Message List**. Any message selected in the **Message List** can be read in the **Reading Pane**.

5. You will explore other mailbox folders and features in later exercises. For now, leave *Outlook* open for the next exercise.

8.18 Creating a Message

New e-mail messages can be created easily in *Outlook*. All you need is the e-mail address of the recipient (the person you are sending the message to). Always be careful when you enter an address, however, as one letter out of place will result in the message being returned "undelivered" or – even worse – going to the wrong person.

Activity:

1. With *Outlook* open and your **Inbox** selected, display the **Home** tab and click the **New E-Mail** button in the **New** group to start a new e-mail message. An **Untitled Message** window appears.

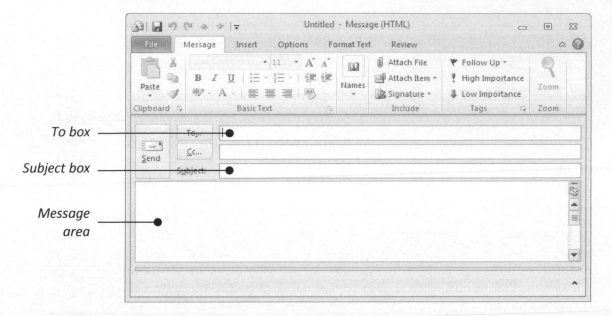

To box — To...

Subject box — Subject:

Message area

Note: To give you more space to work in, you should **Maximize** the message window.

---

2. Notice that the cursor is currently flashing in the **To** box (if it is not, click inside the **To** box now). The **To** box is where you enter the e-mail address of the person who will receive the message. For this exercise, type in your own e-mail address.

Note: Entering your own e-mail address in the **To** box will cause any message you send to be immediately returned to you. This allows you to observe the results of sending messages. Sending a message to another person follows exactly the same steps.

---

3. Click once in the **Subject** box. The text you enter here is used to briefly describe the content of your e-mail message; it allows the person who receives your message to see at a glance what it is about.

4. Enter the following subject text: **Cambridge Nationals**.

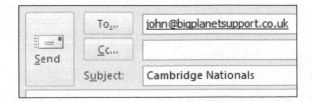

Note: It is good practice to always enter a short but relevant subject for every new message that you create.

---

5.   Click once in the **Message Area** (which is where you write your e-mail message). Notice that the title of the e-mail, shown on the **Title Bar**, now changes to **Cambridge Nationals**.

6.   Type the following message as follows (including the obvious spelling mistakes):

I am sendin this e-mail messige as part of my studies for Cambridge Nationals. I hope it meets with your apruval.

> **Note:**   Notice that the spelling mistakes are underlined in red as you type. These will be corrected in the next exercise.

7.   Press <**Enter**> twice and type your name. Leave the message open for the next exercise.

8.19 Sending a Message

Before you send any e-mail message, you should first use *Outlook's* spell checking feature to check for errors. Once an e-mail has been sent, it is practically impossible to get it back again!

Activity:

1.   The **Cambridge Nationals** e-mail created in the previous exercise should still be open. Display the **Review** tab and click the **Spelling and Grammar** button.

2.   The **Spelling and Grammar** dialog box appears. If an error is found, you can choose to **Ignore** it or **Change** the selected word to one of the **Suggestions** given.

3.   Correct any errors found. When a message appears informing you that **The spelling check is complete**, click **OK** to close it. The message is now ready to be sent.

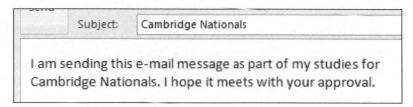

4.   Click the **Send** button (found to the left of the **To** box).

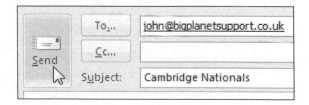

5.   The message window is closed automatically and the e-mail is sent to your **Outbox**.

> **Note:**   E-mail messages that you send are first moved to your **Outbox** folder. If you are connected to the Internet they will be sent immediately from there. If you are not, messages will remain in your **Outbox** until you do connect.

6.   Select the **Outbox** folder in the **Folders List**. Any messages waiting to be sent are shown.

7.   If your **Outbox** is empty then your message has already been sent. If it is not empty, then click the **Send/Receive All Folders** button on the **Quick Access Toolbar**.

> **Note:**   The **Send/Receive All Folders** button forces *Outlook* to send any waiting messages. A progress dialog box (or message on the **Status Bar**) may appear for a moment as the message is sent. If you are prompted to connect to the Internet, please do so.

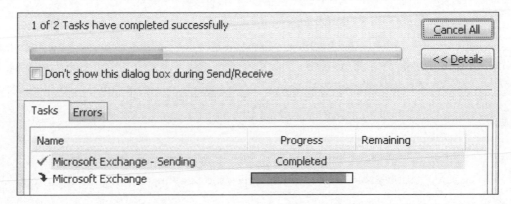

8.   Your message has now been sent. Select the **Sent Items** folder in the **Folders List**. A copy of the **Cambridge Nationals** message is saved here.

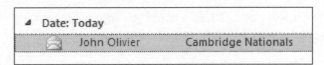

9.   Return to your **Inbox** folder and leave it open for the next exercise.

8.20 Receiving a Message

When you receive an e-mail it is stored in your **Inbox** folder. New and unread messages are shown in the **Message List** in bold type with an unopened envelope icon, ✉. Once you read the message its icon changes to an open envelope, ✉.

> **Note:**   When you are not using *Outlook*, messages are stored for you until they are collected. You do not need to keep the program running all of the time.

Activity:

1.   After a short time you will receive the message that you sent to your own address in the previous exercise. If it has not appeared in your **Inbox** yet, use the **Send/Receive All Folders** button to check for new messages.

> **Note:**   It sometimes takes a little while for messages to be sent and returned to you.

2.   Notice the closed envelope icon and bold text for this message on the **Message List**. This indicates that the received message has not yet been read.

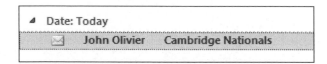

> **Note:**   E-mail messages are stored on a mail server where they will remain until you download them. *Outlook* will regularly check for new messages automatically, but clicking the **Send/Receive All Folders** button forces it to check immediately.

3.   The name on the message indicates who the e-mail was sent from, its subject, and the date and time it was received. Click the message once on the **Message List**, if it is not already selected, to preview its contents in the **Reading Pane**.

4.   Double click the e-mail on the **Message List** to open it in a new window. Notice the features available on the **Ribbon**.

5.   Close the e-mail by clicking the **Close** button, ⚌, found towards the top right corner of the message window.

6.   Notice the **Cambridge Nationals** e-mail on the **Message List**. The closed envelope icon will have changed to an open envelope and the bold formatting will be removed. This indicates that the message has now been read.

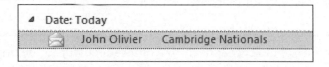

> **Note:**   Sometimes you will open an e-mail but not have time to read it. Being able to mark items as **Unread** so that you can return to read them later is a very useful feature.

7.   To mark the **Cambridge Nationals** e-mail as **Unread** again, make sure the **Home** tab is displayed and click the **Unread/Read** button in the **Tags** group. The open envelope icon changes back to a closed envelope and the text to bold.

8.   Leave your **Inbox** open for the next exercise.

8.21 Replying to Messages

When you receive an e-mail message, it is very easy to create and send a reply. A message window will appear where your reply text can be entered.

Activity:

1. With the **Cambridge Nationals** e-mail selected in your **Inbox** folder, click the **Reply** button in the **Respond** group. A message window, addressed to the sender of the original message (you), will appear.

Reply

> **Note:** The body text of the original message is displayed below your reply. This provides a history of a conversation and allows you to refer back to earlier messages.

2. Notice that the **Subject** begins with **RE:** indicating a reply to a previous message.

3. Enter the following text in the **Message Area** (above the original message):

   Thank you for your message. Good luck.

> **Note:** Notice that your reply appears in a different colour to the original message text.

4. Send the e-mail. After a moment you will receive the e-mail reply (which was again addressed to yourself). Remember to use the **Send/Receive All Folders** button if necessary to check for new messages.

5. Select the reply in the **Message List** to examine it.

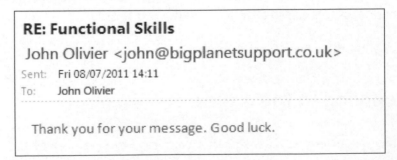

6. Leave your **Inbox** open for the next exercise.

> **Note:** When connected to a business network, *Outlook* can send automatic responses to incoming messages (which is really useful when you are on holiday or out of the office for a long time). This feature is called the **Out of Office Assistant** and works even when *Outlook* is not running. If available, it can be set up using the options available under **Info** on the **File** tab.

8.22 Forwarding Messages

A message that you receive can also be forwarded to another person. In business, always consider the *Data Protection Act* and be careful to only forward messages to authorised people.

Activity:

1. The reply that you sent in the previous exercise should currently be selected in your **Inbox**. To forward this message, click the **Forward** button. Notice that the **Subject** now begins with **FW:** indicating a forwarded message.

2. Enter your <u>own</u> e-mail address in the **To** box again so that you can observe the results of this exercise. In the **Message Area**, enter the following text:

   Here is a copy of a message I thought might interest you.

3. Send the e-mail.

4. After a moment, you will receive the forwarded e-mail (which was again addressed to yourself). Remember to use the **Send/Receive All Folders** button if necessary to check for new messages.

5. Select the forwarded message in the **Message List** to open and examine it, and then leave your **Inbox** open for the next exercise.

8.23 Creating Contacts

Over time you will find that many of the e-mail messages that you create will be sent to the same group of people (your "contacts"). Often these will be friends, family or work colleagues. To avoid having to remember their e-mail addresses and contact details, you can store them in *Outlook's* **Contacts** (also known as the **Address Book**).

Activity:

1. From the *Outlook* **Navigation Pane**, click the **Contacts** view button.

2. The **Contacts** view appears. If you have never used this view before the list will probably be empty.

3. To create a new **Contact**, click the **New Contact** button in the **New** group on the **Home** tab.

4. An **Untitled Contact** window appears. Enter your own personal details into the text boxes (you do not need to complete every box). Make sure you enter your real e-mail address correctly, however, as this will be used in later exercises.

> **Note:** If any further dialog boxes appear (e.g. prompts to check full name or conversion of telephone numbers), click **Cancel** to continue.

5. After all of the information has been entered, click the **Save & Close** button in the **Actions** group. A personalised contact has now been created for you.

6. The new contact will appear as a "virtual" **Business Card** (make sure **Business Cards** is selected on the **Ribbon** in the **Current View** group).

7. *John* often sends information to *Fiona* at reception. Click the **New Contact** button again and enter her contact details:

Full Name:	**Fiona Jones**
Company:	**Big Planet Theme Park**
Job Title:	**Reception Manager**
E-mail:	**fiona@bigplanetsupport.co.uk**
Business Phone:	**0770 0900 823**

> **Note:** Always make sure you enter details accurately, especially e-mail addresses and phone numbers. Personal details such as date of birth, nickname, spouse's name or anniversary can also be included by selecting **Details** in the **Show** group.

8. **Save & Close** the new contact. The contact's business card is created.

9. *John* also likes to keep in touch with his friend *Hassan* at the park entrance. Add him as a new contact:

Full Name:	**Hassan Khan**
Company:	**Big Planet Theme Park**
Job Title:	**Retail Assistant**
E-mail:	**hassan@bigplanetsupport.co.uk**
Business Phone:	**0770 0900 472**

> **Note:** As you will learn later, when you create a new e-mail message (or forward a message to another person), you can use your list of **Contacts** to quickly look up and select e-mail addresses.

10.   Leave the **Contacts** view open for the next exercise.

8.24 Creating Contact Groups

As well as individual contacts, it is possible to create **Contact Groups** (also known as address or distribution lists). A message sent to the group will be sent to every contact in it.

Activity:

1.   To create a new **Contact Group**, click the **New Contact Group** button in the **New** group on the **Home** tab. An **Untitled Contact Group** window appears.

2.   The cursor will currently be flashing in the **Name** box. Enter **Colleagues** as the name of this group and press <**Enter**>.

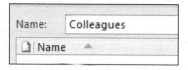

3.   To add contacts to the new group, click the **Add Members** button in the **Members** group. From the submenu that appears, select **From Outlook Contacts**.

> **Note:** It is possible to have more than one list of contacts. If your list of contacts does not appear, other lists can be selected in the **Address Book** drop-down box.

4.   Select **Fiona Jones** from your list of contacts and click the **Members** button. The contact is added to the **Members** box.

5.   Using the same technique, add **Hassan Khan**. Then, add your <u>own</u> contact record.

6.   Click **OK**. The selected contacts now appear in the **Contact Group**. Click **Save & Close**.

> **Note:** You will get the chance to send an e-mail to the contact group later in this section.

7. Click the **Mail** view button on the **Navigation Pane** to return to your mailbox, and then leave your **Inbox** folder open for the next exercise.

8.25 Carbon Copies

If you would like other people to receive a copy of a message, their e-mail addresses can be entered in the **Cc** box (which stands for **Carbon copy**). Typically, recipients of carbon copies are not regarded as participants in a conversation but as observers. For example, if you send an important e-mail to a customer, you could also send a carbon copy to your manager for information purposes.

> **Note:** The e-mail addresses of people in the **To** and **Cc** boxes are visible to *all* recipients of a message. To prevent recipients seeing an address, simply enter it in the **Bcc** (**Blind carbon copy**) box instead.

Activity:

1. *John* wants to send a message to *Fiona* about a new computer for her department that has arrived at the entrance gates. Use the **New E-Mail** button to start a new message.

2. Locate the **To** button. This can be used to select one or more e-mail addresses of people in your **Contacts** list.

3. Click the **To** button to display your list of contacts.

> **Note:** Again, it is possible to have more than one list of contacts. If your list of contacts does not appear, other lists can be selected in the **Address Book** drop-down box.

4. Select the entry for **Fiona Jones** and then click the **To** button, `To ->`. Her e-mail address is copied to the **To** box.

5. Click **OK**. Fiona's e-mail address now also appears in the e-mail's **To** box.

6. *John* would like to send a copy of this message to *Hassan* at the park's entrance. Click the **Cc** button (under the **To** button) to open your list of contacts again.

7. Select *Hassan's* contact record and click the **Cc** button, `Cc ->`. His e-mail address is copied to the **Cc** box. Click **OK**.

> **Note:**   The **Bcc** box is not visible by default. However, it can be activated by toggling the **Bcc** button in the **Show Fields** group of the **Options** tab.

8. Display the **Options** tab and toggle the **Bcc** button in the **Show Fields** group. The **Bcc** box appears below the **Cc** box. Click the **Bcc** button to display your list of contacts.

9. Select your own contact record and click the **Bcc** button, Bcc ->. Your e-mail address is copied to the **Bcc** box. Click **OK**.

10. Enter the e-mail message subject: **Your new computer**.

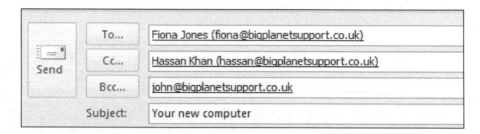

11. Then, enter the following message in the **Message Area**:

    Hi Fiona,

    The new computer that you requested for reception is now ready to collect from the entrance gates. Could you please pick it up before 5pm today?

    Thanks, John.

12. Click **Send** to send the message. This will send the message to *Fiona*, a carbon copy to *Hassan*, and a blind carbon copy back to you.

> **Note:**   *Fiona* and *Hassan's* e-mail addresses are <u>real</u> addresses that can be used to practice sending messages to. The first message you send may receive an automatic reply, but all others will go unanswered and will be deleted.

13. After a moment you will receive your copy of the message back in your **Inbox** (use the **Send/Receive All Folders** button if necessary to check for new messages).

14. Examine the new message and notice that *Fiona's* address appears in the **To** field and *Hassan's* in the **Cc** field. However, the **Bcc** field does not appear.

> To: Fiona Jones (fiona@bigplanetsupport.co.uk)
> Cc   Hassan Khan (hassan@bigplanetsupport.co.uk)

> **Note:**   To send a message to a distribution list, simply select the **Group Contact** from your **Address Book**. **Group Contacts** can be placed in the **To**, **Cc** or **Bcc** boxes.

15. Leave your **Inbox** open for the next exercise.

8.26 Attaching Files

It is possible to attach files stored on your computer to an e-mail message in *Outlook*. The attached files are then sent along with the message and can be saved or opened by the person who receives it. This makes it easy to send documents, spreadsheets, presentations, publications or pictures anywhere in the world.

In this exercise you will attach a simple *Word* document to an e-mail message. When the message reaches its destination, a paperclip icon, ⬚, will appear which lets the recipient know there is an attachment.

Activity:

1.   Start a new message and address it to yourself so that you can observe the results of this exercise.

2.   Enter the subject as **Upgrade Schedule** and, in the **Message Area**, enter the following text:

Please find attached this year's computer upgrade schedule.

3.   Click the **Attach File** button in the **Include** group on the **Ribbon**.

4.   The **Insert File** dialog box appears. Navigate to the location where the data files for this section are stored, and then click **Schedule** once to select it.

5.   Click the **Insert** button and the *Word* document is attached to the e-mail. The attachment appears in a new **Attached** box under the **Subject**.

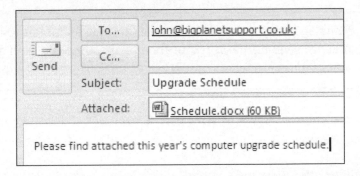

Note: You can add more than one attachment to a message. Depending on your default settings, attachments may appear as icons in the **Message Area**.

Note: If you are sending multiple files, it is often a good idea to **zip** them up together. This gathers all files into one compressed package, reducing the overall size and making the message much quicker to send.

6.   Send the message and leave *Outlook* open for the next exercise.

8.27 Receiving Attachments

When you receive an e-mail containing an attachment, it will appear in the **Message List** marked with a paperclip icon, . The attachment may then be opened and/or saved to your computer.

Activity:

1. After a moment you will receive the **Upgrade Schedule** message back in your **Inbox** (use the **Send/Receive All Folders** button if necessary to check for new messages). Notice that the message features a paperclip icon in the **Message List**.

2. Select the message to view its contents in the **Reading Pane**. The attached file appears on a bar at the top of the message.

3. Click the **Schedule** item once to preview the contents of the file. If a warning appears, click the **Preview file** button.

> **Note:** E-mail attachments are one of the biggest sources of computer viruses. Never open an e-mail attachment unless you know and fully trust the person who sent it to you. Even then, you should save the attachment to your computer first and scan it with your antivirus software before opening it.

4. To save the attached file to your computer (outside of your *Outlook* mailbox), click **Save All Attachments** on the **Ribbon** in the **Actions** group. The **Save All Attachments** dialog box appears.

5. With the **Schedule** file selected in the **Attachments** box (which it should be by default), click **OK**. The **Save Attachment** dialog box appears.

6. Rename the file as **upgrades** by replacing the text in the **File name** box.

7. Locate the data files folder for this section and then click **Save** to save the attached file.

> **Note:** You can now find the file in **Windows Explorer** and check it for viruses.

8. Leave *Outlook* open for the next exercise.

8.28 Signatures

An e-mail **signature** is a personalised block of text – usually containing your name and contact details – that is automatically added to the end of your messages. Once created, you will not need to enter this information every time you create or respond to an e-mail.

Activity:

1. To create a new e-mail signature, display the **File** tab and select **Options**. When the **Outlook Options** dialog box appears, select **Mail** (which appears on the left side of the window). A number of e-mail settings appear on the right.

2. Under **Compose messages**, locate and click the **Signatures** button. The **Signatures and Stationery** dialog box now appears.

3. Click the **New** button to start a new signature. When prompted to enter a name, enter **My Signature** and click **OK**.

4. In the **Edit signature** box, enter your name. Then, using click and drag, select all of your name text.

5. From the font drop-down box, select **Freestyle Script** (or if that font is not available, select any other that resembles handwriting).

6. From the font size drop-down list, select **20**.

7. Click **OK**, then **OK** again to close the **Outlook Options** window.

8. Start a new message. Notice that your new signature has appeared in the **Message Area**.

9. Click to **To** button and address the message to the **Colleagues** group. Enter the subject as **Maintenance** and, above the signature, enter the following text:

    Hi everyone,

    Just to let you know that the Big Planet Theme Park servers will be down for maintenance tonight between 9pm and 10pm.

    Thanks,

10. Click the **Signature** drop-down button in the **Include** group. Notice that **My Signature** appears.

Note: You can create more than one signature; each appears in the **Signature** drop-down.

---

11. To delete your signature, select **Signatures** to display the **Signatures and Stationery** dialog box. With **My Signature** selected in the **Select signature to edit box**, click **Delete**.

12. Click **Yes** to confirm the deletion and then **OK**. Although your signature has been deleted, it still appears in all messages where it was inserted.

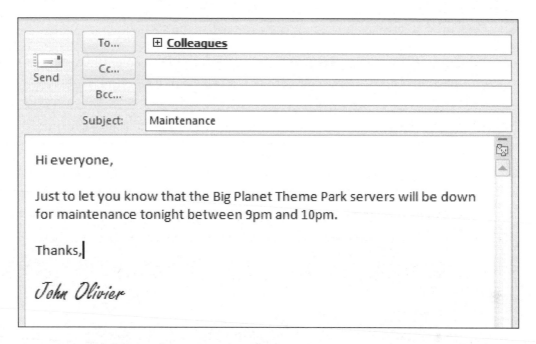

> **Note:** As the e-mail was addressed to the **Colleagues** contact group, everyone in that group will receive the message (including yourself).

13. Send the message and leave *Outlook* open for the next exercise.

8.29 Sorting Messages

To help you find messages quickly, you can sort the contents of a folder into order by sender name, date, subject, and so on. You can also quickly search through messages for keywords.

Activity:

1. With your **Inbox** selected, notice that information in the **Message List** is grouped into columns. At the top of the screen, these columns are labelled **From**, **Subject**, **Received**, **Size**, and so on.

Search ⎯⎯⎯⎯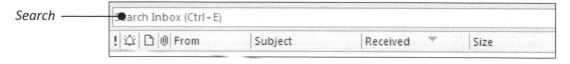

2. By default, e-mail messages in your **Inbox** are shown in the order that they were received, with the newest at the top. This order of sorting is indicated by the small arrow, ▼, on the **Received** column header.

3. Click the **Received** column header once. The arrow turns upside down, indicating that the sort has been reversed. E-mails are now shown in reverse order with the oldest first.

4. Click the **Subject** column header. All e-mail messages are now sorted in alphabetical order by subject.

5. Click the **Subject** column header again to reverse the sort.

6. Explore the other sorts available by selecting each of the column headers on view. When you are finished, click **Received** once to restore the original sort (newest first).

> **Note:** You can also quickly search for messages that contain specific keywords.

7. Click once in the **Search** box and enter the keywords **Cambridge Nationals**. As you type, the current folder's **Message List** is *filtered* to display only those messages that match your search criteria (the keywords can appear in any part of the e-mail message).

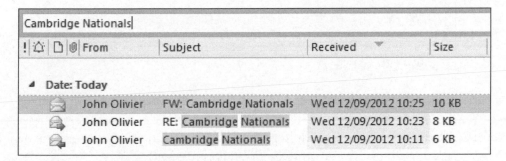

> **Note:** Notice the advanced search options available on the **Search** tab on the **Ribbon**.

8. Replace the search text with the keyword **upgrade** and notice the effect. Feel free to experiment with other search keywords and options.

9. To close the search and remove the filter, click the **Close Search** button on the **Search Tools - Search** tab on the **Ribbon**. All messages in the folder reappear.

> **Note:** It is often useful to **flag** important e-mail messages so that you can "follow them up" later. For this reason, *Outlook* allows you to add a small coloured flag to the item in the **Message List**, . When you have taken action on or responded to the message, you can then mark it as complete, ✓.

10. Leave *Outlook* open for the next exercise.

8.30 Organising Messages

To help organise your mailbox folders, it can sometimes be a good idea to create a system ICT subfolders in which to store specific types of e-mail (e.g. **personal**, **important**, **enquiries**, **orders**, **newsletters**, etc). Messages can then be moved between folders as required.

Activity:

1. As *John* receives a lot of e-mail messages about *Cambridge Nationals* training, he would like to store them in their own folder (to make them easier to find later).

2. Display the **Folder** tab on the **Ribbon** and click the **New Folder** button in the **New** group.

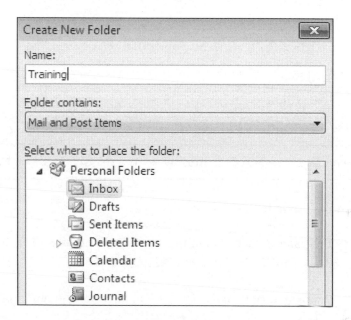

3. The **Create New Folder** dialog box appears. Notice that the **Inbox** folder is currently selected in the folder list (if it is not, select it now).

4. Enter the name for the new folder as **Training**.

5. Click **OK**. The new folder appears directly beneath the **Inbox** folder in the **Folders List**.

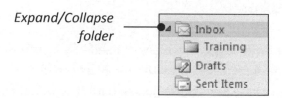

Expand/Collapse folder

> **Note:** If the **Training** folder is hidden, show it by clicking the **Expand/Collapse** toggle button, ◢, found to the left of the **Inbox** folder.

> **Note:** Subfolders can be created within *any* of the folders in the **Folders List**, and messages can be moved freely from folder to folder.

6. Within your main **Inbox** folder, select the message **Cambridge Nationals** that you sent to yourself earlier. You are going to move this message to the new **Training** folder.

7. With the **Home** tab displayed, click the **Move** button within the **Move** group.

8. From the submenu that appears, select the **Training** folder.

9. The selected message is moved. Open the **Training** folder from the **Folders List**. The message appears in the **Message List**.

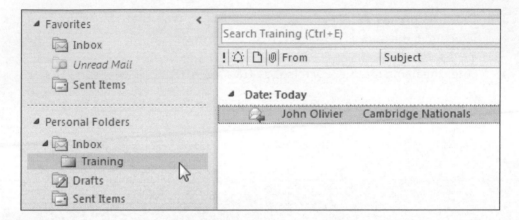

> **Note:** You can also drag and drop messages from the **Message List** to any folder.

10. Return to the **Inbox** folder.

11. Then, use drag and drop to move the two e-mail messages **RE: Cambridge Nationals** and **FW: Cambridge Nationals** to the new **Training** folder.

12. Return to the main **Inbox** folder and leave it open for the next exercise.

8.31 Deleting Messages

To help you to save space, when a message is no longer needed you can delete it from your mailbox – simply select the unwanted message in the **Message List** and click the **Delete** button. A deleted message will be sent to the **Deleted Items** folder until it is permanently removed (or restored again if you change your mind later and want it back).

Activity:

1. With your **Inbox** folder open, select the **Upgrade Schedule** e-mail message on the **Message List**.

2. To delete this message, click the **Delete** button on the **Home** tab of the **Ribbon**. The message is moved immediately to the **Deleted Items** folder.

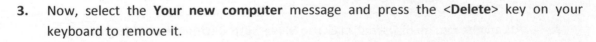

3. Now, select the **Your new computer** message and press the <**Delete**> key on your keyboard to remove it.

4. Next, right-click the **Maintenance** message and select **Delete** to remove it.

5. In the **Folders List**, right-click the **Training** subfolder and select **Delete Folder**. Click **Yes** at the prompt to confirm the deletion and remove the folder.

6. Open the **Deleted Items** folder. Notice that all of the deleted items are shown here. You could now restore any item by simply moving it to another folder.

> **Note:**   All deleted *Outlook* items, including tasks and contacts, will also appear here.

7. To permanently remove all deleted items from the **Deleted Items** folder, display the **Folder** tab and click the **Empty Folder** button. A prompt will appear asking you to confirm the deletion. Click **Yes** (or **No** if you'd rather keep the contents of this folder).

> **Note:**   Only empty *Outlook* folders when you are absolutely <u>sure</u> you will never need their contents again.

8. Leave *Outlook* open and continue on to the next exercise.

8.32 E-mail Tips

E-mail is one of the most popular forms of online communication available and is frequently used at home, in education and at work. To help you get the most out of this technology, consider the following useful tips:

*   Keep e-mail to the point and do not forget to add a meaningful subject.

*   Do not send e-mails that are likely to offend the person receiving them (including discriminatory or inflammatory information or material).

*   Avoid sending large e-mail attachments as these can cause problems for the recipient. As a guideline, anything more than 5Mb is probably too large.

*   Use appropriate language and always spell check your messages (try to avoid overuse of fancy fonts and colours).

*   Do not send illegal information or material (i.e. material that is protected by copyright or the *Data Protection Act*).

*   Consider carefully who you copy in to e-mails. Respect others people's confidentiality and avoid inappropriate disclosure of information.

*   Do not be distracted by irrelevant messages (especially jokes and junk mail), and <u>do not</u> use work e-mail for personal activities.

*   Prioritise messages and respond to urgent requests first.

> **Note:**   Learn to deal with "e-mail overload". Research shows that people receive around 40 messages per day on average – it doesn't take long for your mailbox to fill up.

8.33 Phishing and Spam

Phishing (also known as **identity theft**) is the process of attempting to gain private information such as user names, passwords and credit card details by pretending to be a trustworthy business or organisation. If you ever receive an official-looking e-mail asking for this type of information, delete it. This includes requests to reset login information or verify an account.

> **Note:**   Businesses will never ask for personal details to be confirmed by e-mail.

Although less of a security risk, junk mail can also be a nuisance and can take up a lot of your time. Also known as **spam**, these messages are often used by companies to advertise products. If they become a problem, anti-spam software can be used to filter out these unwanted messages before they even reach your inbox.

8.34 Creating Appointments

Outlook features a handy **Calendar** tool. This can be used to plan your daily activities and schedule appointments and meetings with others. Reminders can also be set up to inform you of upcoming calendar events.

Activity:

1.   From the *Outlook* **Navigation Pane**, click the **Calendar** view button.

2.   The **Calendar** view appears. Today's date is shown with each hour of the day displayed in rows. Examine the layout of this screen.

> **Note:** Notice the buttons in the **Arrange** group on the **Ribbon**. These allow you to view your **Calendar** by day, week or month.

3. Try selecting all of the views in the **Arrange** group on the **Ribbon**. Observe the effect of each selection. When you are finished, return to **Day** view.

Date Selection
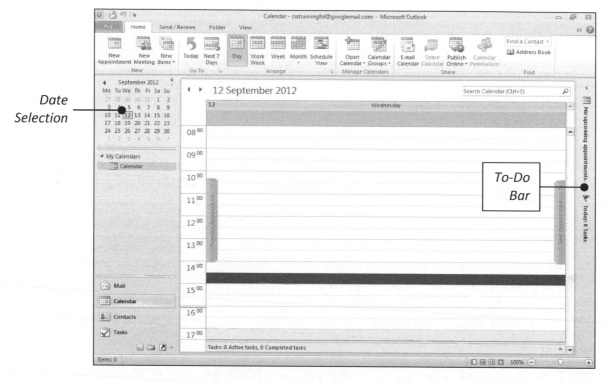
To-Do Bar

4. *John* has an *10am* appointment tomorrow at a local ICT hardware store (he is planning to buy a new printer for *Fiona*). So that he doesn't forget, he wants to enter it into his **Calendar**. Using the **Date Selection** panel, select <u>tomorrow's date</u>.

5. Click the **New Appointment** button to open an **Untitled Appointment** window. Examine the options available on this screen.

6. Enter the **Subject** as **Visit PC Planet** and the **Location** as **31 High Street**. The **Start time** is **10.00** and the **End time** is **11.00**.

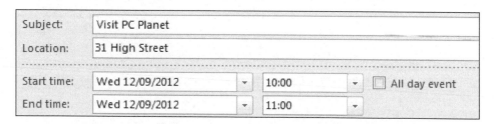

> **Note:** Notice the **All day event** checkbox. This is useful for **Calendar** entries that run all day, such as holidays or time spent "out of the office".

7. Click the **Reminder** drop-down button, [🔔 15 minutes ▼], and change the default time to **30 minutes**. A reminder will now appear in *Outlook* half an hour before the event.

8. Click **Save & Close** to create the new appointment and set the reminder. It appears as a new entry in the **Calendar**.

Note: If *Outlook* is running tomorrow, an appointment reminder will appear at 09.30. Also note that upcoming events, meetings and tasks appear on the **To-Do Bar**.

9. Next, *John* wants to set up a meeting with *Fiona* to discuss her new printer. Click the **New Meeting** button to open an **Untitled Meeting** window. Examine the options available.

Note: Contacts in your **Address Book** can be asked to attend meetings that you organise. They can be invited as a **Required** (must come) or an **Optional** attendee.

10. Click the **To** button. First, select **Fiona Jones** and click the **Required** button, .

11. As *Hassan* will receive the new printer when it is delivered, *John* decides to invite him too. Select **Hassan Khan** and click the **Optional** button. Click **OK**.

12. Enter the **Subject** as **Printer Meeting** and the **Location** as **Main Meeting Room**. Arrange for the meeting to occur from **14:30** to **15:30** (1 hour).

13. In the large text box in the lower half of the dialog box, enter the following invitation text:

Hi Fiona and Hassan,

I've arranged a meeting tomorrow to discuss Fiona's new printer. I look forward to seeing you there.

John

Note: Meeting invitations are sent by e-mail. Recipients can accept or decline the request, state they are tentative (unsure), or propose a new time. Their replies will be sent back to you by e-mail and their decision shown in your calendar.

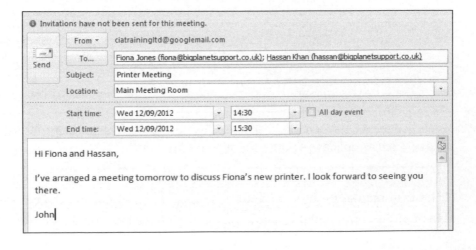

14. Notice that a default **Reminder** of **15 minutes** has been set in the **Options** group.

15. Click **Send** to send out invitations. The appointment, indicating who has organised it, is shown on the calendar.

14 00	
15 00	**Printer Meeting** Main Meeting Room John Olivier

> **Note:**   If *Outlook* is running tomorrow, a meeting reminder will appear at 14:15.

> **Note:**   To delete a meeting where invitations have been sent, you must cancel it using the **Cancel Meeting** button in the **Actions** group. This sends meeting cancellation messages to all attendees.

16. From the *Outlook* **Navigation Pane**, click the **Mail** view button. Then, select the **Sent Items** folder in the **Folders List**.

17. Notice the **Printer Meeting** message in the **Message List**. Select this to examine the e-mail invitation that was sent to *Fiona* and *Hassan*.

18. Leave *Outlook* open and continue on to the next exercise.

8.35 Organising Tasks

Outlook's useful **Tasks** feature can be used to create "to-do" lists with reminders. These allow you to keep track of outstanding and completed tasks and help to keep you organised.

Activity:

1. From the *Outlook* **Navigation Pane**, click the **Tasks** view button.

2. The **Tasks** view appears with **To-Do List** automatically selected in the **Navigation Pane**. Examine the layout of this screen.

3. *John's* life is very hectic and, to keep himself organised, he likes to create "to-do" lists in *Outlook*. Click the **New Task** button to open an **Untitled Task** window.

4. Enter the **Subject** as **Upgrade Office Computers**.

5. Notice that an optional **Start date** and **Due date** can be set. Leave the **Start date** as today but change the **Due date** to tomorrow. Notice the indicator at the top of the dialog box now shows that the task is **Due tomorrow**.

6. Drop down the **Status** button and examine the options available. Leave the selection as **Not Started** to indicate that the task is still outstanding.

7. Next, drop down the **Priority** button and examine the options available. Change the selection to **High** to indicate that the task has high priority.

> **Note:**   The **% Complete** box can be used to keep track of task progress.

8. To set a reminder so that *John* doesn't forget this important task, place a check in the **Reminder** box. By default, a reminder is set for **08:00** on the **Due date**, which is fine.

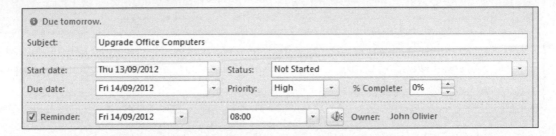

> **Note:**   If needed, useful task notes can be entered in the lower text box.

9. Click **Save & Close** to create the new task and set the reminder.

Quick Task

Task List

Task View

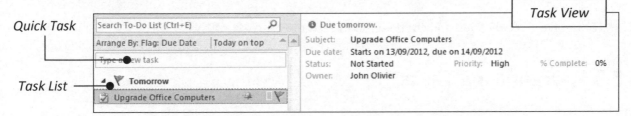

> **Note:**   If *Outlook* is running tomorrow, a task reminder will appear at 08:00.

10. Select the new task in the **Task List** and its details are shown in the **Task View**.

11. Let's add another task. Click once in the **Quick Task** box and enter the subject **Order Printer Ink**. Press **<Enter>** and a new task is created with default settings. Select the task to view these settings in the **Task View**.

12. Double-click the task to edit its settings. Change the **Start date** and **Due date** to tomorrow and change the **Priority** to **Low**. Set a reminder for **08:00** tomorrow morning, and then **Save and Close** the task to update it.

13. *John* mentions that he has the following outstanding jobs to do. Add these as new tasks:

Next Tuesday, update the office's firewall software (normal priority, reminder at 10am on the due date).

Next Wednesday, arrange a presentation on data security (needs to be completed by next Thursday with a reminder that morning at 10am).

> **Next Friday, run a full backup of the office server (high priority, needs to be completed on Friday with a reminder that morning at 8am).**

> **Note:** The **To-Do List** only shows outstanding tasks that have not yet been completed.

14. *John* has just ordered printer ink for the office. Select the task **Order Printer Ink** and click **Mark Complete** in the **Manage Task** group.

15. The task is marked as complete and disappears from the **To-Do List**. However, it is still present in **Tasks** view. Click **Tasks** in the **Navigation Pane** to view *all* tasks (both completed and outstanding). Notice the completed task appears with strikethrough text and a small tick, ✔.

16. Select the completed task **Order Printer Ink**. Then, click **Delete** on the **Ribbon** to remove it. Use the same technique to delete all outstanding tasks created in this exercise.

17. Close *Outlook*.

8.36 Next Steps

Well done! You have now completed all of the exercises in this section. If you feel you are ready to test your knowledge and understanding of the topics covered, move on to the following **Develop Your Skills** activities. If there are any *Internet* and *E-mail* features covered in this section that you are unsure about, revisit the appropriate exercises and try them again before moving on.

If you are interested in exploring some of the more powerful features of your web browser or *Microsoft Outlook*, use the Internet to find out more about the following advanced topics.

Feature	Description
History	Expand on the notes in 8.5 and learn to manage and delete your browsing **History** (including temporary internet files and cookies).
Home Page	Set up one or more websites as your browser's default **Home** page(s).
Drafts	Unfinished messages can be saved so that they can be completed and sent at a later date. E-mails saved in this way are known as a **Draft** messages and are saved in your **Drafts** folder.
Rules	**Rules** can be created in *Outlook* to automatically perform actions when certain messages are received. For example, messages containing specific keywords can be automatically moved to a different folder or can generate an automatic reply.
Message Priority	It is possible to change an e-mail message's priority to either **High Importance** or **Low Importance**. This does not mean the message is sent any more quickly or slowly, only that a flag is placed on the message that alerts the recipient to its importance.

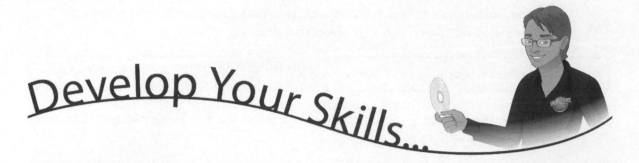

At the end of every section you get the chance to complete two activities. These will help you to develop your skills and prepare for your exam. Don't forget to use the planning and review checklists at the back of the book to help organise and review your work.

> **Note:** Answers to these activities are provided in this section's **Sample Solutions** folder.

Develop Your Skills: Pirate's Cove Quiz

In this activity you will be asked to perform some simple online research for *John*. You will need to use all of the ICT skills that you have learned in this section to plan, develop and present an appropriate solution.

Activity 1

Zahra at *Pirate's Cove* has created a brand new quiz for an event she is running next week. However, she has lost all of the answers and now needs our help to find them again. This sounds like a perfect job to test your new Internet search skills! Information you will need is available in the following files:

* **Quiz Sheet**   A *Microsoft Word* document containing *Zahra's* quiz (without the answers, of course).

Start by opening the file **Quiz Sheet**. Notice that a space is available for you to enter each of the five missing answers. Use your favourite web browser and a search engine of your choice to find those answers and complete *Zahra's* document.

Notice the image of a pirate ship in the **Quiz Answers** document. You have reason to think *Zahra* has downloaded this from an Internet site. Why is this a problem?

Notes:

Develop Your Skills: Using E-mail at Work

In this activity you will be asked to compose and send an e-mail to *John's* friend. You will need to use all of the advanced ICT skills that you have learned in this section to create a suitable solution. To get started, it may help you to break the problem down into smaller parts first.

Activity 2

I've just received the following e-mail from my friend *Pete* who works at *Reception*:

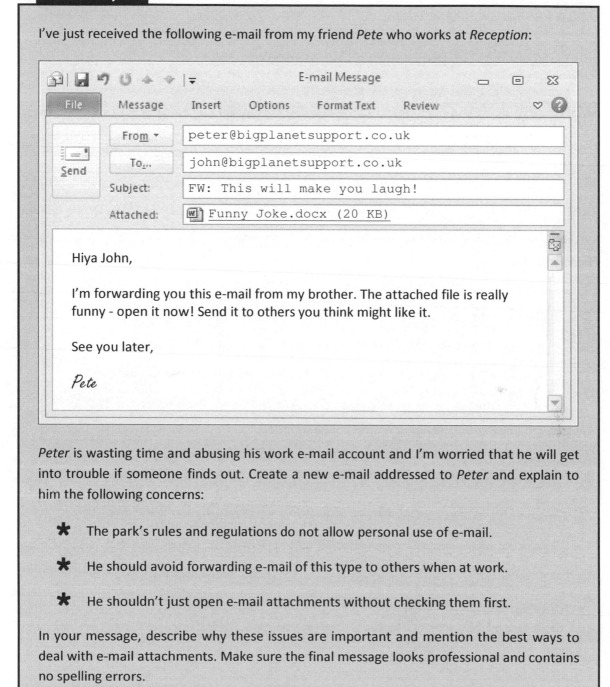

Peter is wasting time and abusing his work e-mail account and I'm worried that he will get into trouble if someone finds out. Create a new e-mail addressed to *Peter* and explain to him the following concerns:

* The park's rules and regulations do not allow personal use of e-mail.

* He should avoid forwarding e-mail of this type to others when at work.

* He shouldn't just open e-mail attachments without checking them first.

In your message, describe why these issues are important and mention the best ways to deal with e-mail attachments. Make sure the final message looks professional and contains no spelling errors.

When you are finished, send the message (*Peter's* e-mail address is a <u>real</u> address that can be used to practice sending messages to).

Planning Checklist

Before creating a solution to a problem it is always a good idea to spend a moment reviewing the task's requirements and planning how you will go about solving it. Consider what the solution you are creating will look like, who it is for, and what kinds of information it will contain?

Issues to Consider

Using ICT

1.	What are the exact ICT requirements of the task?	✓
2.	What are the stages of development and how will I approach the problem?	✓
3.	Does the task need to be broken down into smaller subtasks? What are they?	✓
4.	Do I need to prioritise one subtask before another?	✓
5.	Which software application(s) do I intend to use?	✓
6.	Who will use the solution? Will it work for them or is there a better way?	✓
7.	Do I have enough time to finish the task? If not, what should I do?	✓

Finding and Selecting Information

8.	Is all of the information that I need to solve the problem available?	✓
9.	If more information is needed, where and how will I find it?	✓
10.	Is the information that I have accurate and fit for purpose?	✓
11.	What pieces of information will I use? Only the relevant parts are needed.	✓
12.	What is the best way to store and manage the information on my computer?	✓

Developing, presenting and communicating information

13.	Are there any new skills that I need to learn to complete the task?	✓
14.	What skills and techniques will I use to create my solution?	✓
15.	What is the best way to organise and combine the information I have found?	✓
16.	Will the planned solution be suitable for the intended audience?	✓
17.	Do I have the necessary hardware and software to complete this task?	✓
18.	Are there any house styles and design guidelines that I need to follow?	✓
19.	What safety and security issues do I need to take into account?	✓
20.	Are there any laws or regulations that may affect the task or my solution?	✓
21.	Are there any ICT problems that I can expect to encounter?	✓
22.	If I encounter any problems, how will I resolve them? Who can I ask for help?	✓
23.	How will I deliver the solution (e.g. by e-mail or printed document)?	✓

Review Checklist

When you have created your solution, you should review the effectiveness of the choices you've made. Does the solution meet the requirements of the task, does it solve the problem correctly, and are there any improvements that can be made?

Items to Evaluate

Using ICT

1.	Was my initial understanding of the task's ICT requirements correct?	✓
2.	Did my solution actually solve the problem? If not, how can I improve it?	✓
3.	Did my approach allow me to tackle the problem in the best possible way?	✓
4.	Did I underestimate the time/resources needed to create the solution?	✓
5.	Would another software application have done the job better?	✓

Finding and Selecting Information

6.	Was I able to find all of the information that I needed for the task?	✓
7.	Was all of the information that I used relevant and appropriate?	✓
8.	Was the information that I used accurate and fit for purpose?	✓
9.	Was the information that I created or edited clear, accurate and correct?	✓
10.	Was the format that I used to present the information suitable?	✓
11.	Was my approach to data storage sufficient and could it be improved?	✓

Developing, presenting and communicating information

12.	Were there any additional skills that would have helped complete the task?	✓
13.	Were there any alternative ICT techniques that I could have used?	✓
14.	Do I need to learn or revise any skills for the future?	✓
15.	Was the person I created the solution for happy with the end result?	✓
16.	Was the solution that I created suitably professional?	✓
17.	Did I correctly resolve any safety or security issues that I encountered?	✓
18.	Did I correctly resolve any ICT problems that I encountered?	✓
19.	Am I certain that I followed all relevant laws and regulations during the task?	✓
20.	If applicable, have I tested the solution to make sure it works in all cases?	✓
21.	Was the chosen delivery method suitable or would an alternative be better?	✓
22.	For items 1 to 21, have I considered what I would do differently next time?	✓

Other Products

CiA Training is a leading publishing company which has consistently delivered the highest quality products since 1985. Our experienced in-house publishing team has developed a wide range of flexible and easy to use self-teach resources for individual learners and corporate clients all over the world. Supporting many popular qualifications including *ECDL*, *CLAIT*, *ITQ* and *Functional Skills*, our products are an invaluable asset to tutors and training managers seeking support for their programme delivery.

At the time of publication we currently offer materials for:

*   Cambridge Nationals in ICT

*   Functional Skills

*   ITQ Level 1, Level 2 and Level 3

*   New CLAIT, CLAIT Plus and CLAIT Advanced

*   ECDL and ECDL Advanced

*   CiA Revision Series

*   Start IT

*   Skill for Life in ICT

*   e-Citizen

*   Open Learning Guides

*   CourseNotes

*   Trainers Packs with iCourse Professional

*   And many, many more...

> **Note:**   *CiA Training* learning resources are available in individual printed book format or as a site licence in editable *Microsoft Word* format.

We hope you have enjoyed using this book and would love to hear your opinions about our materials. To let us know how we are doing and to get up-to-the-minute information on our current range of products, please visit us online at:

www.ciatraining.co.uk

Index